ALSO BY CHARLES PETERS

How Washington Really Works

Tilting at Windmills

CO-EDITED BY CHARLES PETERS

Inside the System
first edition with Timothy Adams,
second edition with John Rothchild,
third edition with James Fallows,
fourth edition with Nicholas Lemann,
fifth edition with Jonathan Alter

A New Road for Tomorrow
with Phil Keisling

The System
with James Fallows

Blowing the Whistle
with Taylor Branch

The Culture of Bureaucracy
with Michael Nelson

FIVE DAYS IN PHILADELPHIA

THE AMAZING

"WE WANT WILKIE!"

CONVENTION OF 1940

AND HOW IT FREED FDR

TO SAVE THE WESTERN WORLD

FIVE DAYS IN PHILADELPHIA

CHARLES PETERS

PUBLICAFFAIRS

NEW YORK

Copyright © 2005 by Charles Peters.
Published in the United States by PublicAffairs™, a member of the Perseus Books Group.
All rights reserved.
Printed in the United States of America.
No part of this book may be reproduced in any manner whatsoever without written per-
mission except in the case of brief quotations embodied in critical articles and reviews.
For information, address PublicAffairs, 250 West 57th Street, Suite 1321, New York NY
10107. PublicAffairs books are available at special discounts for bulk purchases in the U.S.
by corporations, institutions, and other organizations. For more information, please contact the Special Markets Department at the Perseus Books Group, 11 Cambridge Center,
Cambridge MA 02142, call (617) 252-5298, or email special.markets@perseusbooks.com.

BOOK DESIGN AND COMPOSITION BY JENNY DOSSIN. TEXT SET IN VILLAGE.

Library of Congress Cataloging-in-Publication Data
Peters, Charles, 1926–
    Five days in Philadelphia : Wendell Willkie, Franklin Roosevelt, and the 1940 conven-
tion that saved the Western World / Charles Peters.
       p. cm.
ISBN-13 978-1-58648-112-4
ISBN 1-58648-112-6
    1. Presidents—United States—Election—1940. 2. Republican National Convention (1940 :
Philadelphia, Pa.) 3. Willkie, Wendell L. (Wendell Lewis), 1892–1944. 4. Roosevelt, Franklin
D. (Franklin Delano), 1882–1945. 5. United States—Politics and government—1933–1945.
6. World War, 1939–1945—United States. 7. Political candidates—United States—Biography.
8. Presidents—United States—Biography. I. Title.
    E811.P47 2005
    324.2734'09'044—dc22   2005041946

FIRST EDITION

10 9 8 7 6 5 4 3 2 1

TO BETH

CONTENTS

PART ONE

DANGER LOOMS

CHAPTER ONE

★

"WORLD OF TOMORROW"

Almost everyone has seen the old newsreel pictures of Winston Churchill standing on the balcony of Buckingham Palace, acknowledging the cheers of the vast crowd that had assembled to celebrate V-E Day. It is a heartwarming scene, because a great man is receiving his just reward. Churchill, more than any other individual, was responsible for Britain's survival. And not so incidentally—by giving America precious time to prepare for war and by being a valiant ally once we were involved, he may have saved the United States from defeat by Germany and Japan. At the very least he saved it from an infinitely more arduous path to victory.

Watching these pictures over the years—they are a standard feature of World War II documentaries—I have sometimes thought of others who deserve to be on the balcony. Franklin Roosevelt, who died less than a month before, is the most obvious choice. But a less well-known figure occurs to me. Wendell Willkie is only mentioned once in the most recent Churchill biography, the one written by Roy Jenkins, and his name is now nearly forgotten. Yet in Britain's survival, and the ultimate Allied victory, Willkie's role was crucial.

Nineteen forty was an election year in the United States. In general, politicians avoid actions that risk alienating a large proportion of the voting population. In an election year, this risk aversion is at

its height. As 1940 began, the great majority of the country was isolationist, determined to keep out of the war in Europe. So it was almost unimaginable that Roosevelt would dare take the risks he took
that year to aid Britain and to prepare this country for entry into
World War II. Before Wendell Willkie entered the race, all the Republican candidates for the presidency were running as isolationists.
The possibility explored in Philip Roth's *The Plot Against America*, that
someone like Charles Lindbergh could have been elected, was not at
all remote. Indeed, the Republican who came the closest to defeating
Wendell Willkie at that year's convention was Robert Taft, a man
whose views, except for his lack of anti-Semitism, were almost identical to Lindbergh's. If Taft had been nominated he would have vigorously opposed the efforts FDR made to aid Britain and to enact a
military draft in this country. This isn't a matter of speculation; it's
on the record in innumerable speeches that Taft made and, more significantly, in actual votes in the Senate against such measures as
Lend-Lease and the Selective Service bill.

Taft did not win because Wendell Willkie, a business executive
who had never run for office but who possessed a magnetic personality and a determination to see Hitler stopped, emerged from
nowhere—garnering literally zero percent in the polls just three
months before the 1940 GOP convention—to inspire thousands of
volunteers whose enthusiasm overwhelmed the political bosses and
allowed him to seize the nomination. This is the story of how
Willkie accomplished that improbable feat and of the impact his victory had on this country and the world.

It is also the story of what Franklin Roosevelt was up against in
1940 and 1941 as he sought to save Britain, prepare this country for
its part in World War II, and run for an unprecedented third term
at a time when his political strength had been sapped by his failed
attempts to pack the Supreme Court with his allies and to purge the
Senate of his foes. Only by understanding the difficulties FDR faced
can one appreciate the significance of Wendell Willkie and of his triumph over partisanship. Willkie gave Roosevelt essential support on
issues like the draft and Lend-Lease even as he was running a spir-

ited campaign to deny FDR a third term, actually winning several million more votes than any previous Republican presidential candidate and later serving as the leader of the opposition party. Simply put, Roosevelt could not have done it without Willkie.

And what these two leaders accomplished could not have happened without the American people—a majority of whom managed to rise a notch or two above the usual limits of human nature. Something about the time seemed to heighten their generosity, idealism, and public spirit. Their generosity supported sending ships and guns and planes to England when our own military cupboard was nearly bare. Their idealism fueled the outpouring of unpaid volunteers whose dedication propelled Willkie to the Republican nomination. And their public spiritedness led a generation of Americans to subject themselves to a draft that would not exempt the privileged and that would end up costing many of them several years of their lives—in the case of more than 400,000, life itself. Even many of the people who were wrong—the isolationists—had an admirable motive. They wanted to save our young men from another bloodbath like the First World War. If we can understand how and why people rose to their best then, maybe we can make it happen again.

I can shed some light on the time because I lived through it. I had just turned thirteen as 1939 became 1940 and this story begins. I lived in Charleston, West Virginia, with my father, who was a lawyer, and my mother, who, like most women of the era, was a housewife. We were barely bit players in a drama that starred Wendell Willkie and Franklin Roosevelt, but there are facts about our lives that help explain what the country was like back then.

My parents came from the farm, as did most Americans born before 1920. Their families had been hard hit by the decline in farm prices that began a decade before the Great Depression engulfed the entire nation in 1929. The economic distress in agriculture accelerated the migration from farm to city that had started earlier. At various times during my childhood, a total of six relatives lived with us as they looked for work in Charleston.

Their rural roots explained much about Americans during that era, especially their identification with the down-and-out and their unpretentious Norman Rockwell self-image. Every Saturday night, my father listened to the *Grand Ole Opry* on the radio. He still thought of Will Rogers, who was the personification of that Norman Rockwell image, as his favorite movie actor even though Rogers had been killed in an airplane crash in 1935.

No figure is more important to an understanding of the times than Will Rogers. The cowboy comedian was a unique figure in American history. He grew up in what was then Indian territory. "My father was one-eighth Cherokee Indian and my mother was a quarter-blood. My ancestors didn't come over on the Mayflower—they met the boat."

The rope tricks Rogers mastered in his youth led him to vaudeville, then to the Ziegfeld Follies, where he interspersed his act with remarks like "I'm not a member of any organized political party—I'm a Democrat." And "You can't say civilization doesn't advance—in every war they will kill you in a new way." His combination of humor and wisdom made him a star, not only on the stage, but in the movies and on the radio as well. He even had a regular column in the *New York Times* and other papers. Yet he remained without pretension, always identifying himself as "an old country boy." His weathered skin, his shy grin with a lock of hair falling over the right side of his forehead, and, most of all, his common sense made him the most beloved figure of his time. The writer Damon Runyon said Rogers was "The closest approach to what we call the True American." Rogers's biographer, Richard Ketchum, added "What people saw in him was what they wanted to be themselves."

I didn't share my father's enthusiasm for country music, but I loved the big bands—Benny Goodman, Tommy Dorsey, Glenn Miller, Artie Shaw, and Duke Ellington. To me the big bands were cooler or hipper (of course these expressions were not then in use) than the country music my father liked. Although similar feelings in regard to one's parents are a classic rite of passage for adolescents, I mention them here because they were otherwise so rare in those days. Fewer people felt the need to show they were smarter or had better taste than the next fellow. Teenagers did not obsess about SATs because there were no SATs. Their parents did not know or care to know which was the right wine to serve or who was in or out in the world of art and literature. Almost everyone went to public school. And nobody agonized about getting their children into the right kindergarten. Our favorite sports were professional baseball and high school and college football and basketball. They were played in arenas not a single one of which had the enclosed, climate-controlled luxury boxes that separate today's privileged from the average fan.

The time, to be sure, fell short of the egalitarian ideal. There was racial segregation, legal in the South, de facto in the North. Not only blacks, but women, Jews, and Catholics faced discrimination at work and school. Except in a few large cities, homosexuals had to hide in the closet. Social snobbery also existed, but—and this is important— it was widely ridiculed, especially among men for whom avoiding pretension was the eleventh commandment. Incomes differed but the gap between the average union worker and the top executive was less than it is today. And instead of getting a tax cut in wartime, these Americans would agree to higher and higher taxes in the next few years, culminating in a top tax rate of 90 percent. Franklin Roosevelt would even suggest a limit of $25,000 on net income to prevent war profiteering. It is not easy to imagine such a proposal being made today.

Television was still in its infancy; radio was the medium that brought me the music of the big bands. It was a unifying force in the life of the country. Even large cities had, instead of several hundred television channels, only four network and a handful of independent stations. I was a fan of the shows that featured comedians like Jack Benny, Bob Hope, Fred Allen, and the ventriloquist Edgar Bergen and his dummy Charlie McCarthy. These were the shows we all talked about at school the next day.

Every evening after dinner, my mother, my father, and I, and whichever relatives happened to be living with us at the time, listened to *Amos 'n Andy* at 7:00 PM. This was a ritual shared by practically everyone we knew. I think it had a benign affect on race relations and—along with the popularity of Bill Robinson, and Hattie McDaniel of the movies, Olympic star Jesse Owens, and boxing champion Joe Louis—helped pave the way for Roosevelt's Fair Employment Practices Commission in the '40s and the Great Civil Rights triumphs of the '50s and '60s. *Amos 'n Andy* has since been described as a show that ridiculed blacks. This is dead wrong; Amos was respected, always portrayed as responsible, honest, hard working, and forever trying to talk Andy out of the implausible get-rich-quick schemes into which the Kingfish had conned him.

There was a dark side to relations between the races. Not only was segregation widespread, colored men—"colored" was the term used by people who wanted to treat, or at least appear to treat, African Americans respectfully—were still being lynched by white people who called them niggers. Just a few years later, when I was a student chief of police during students' day in Charleston, the real chief showed me a closet full of bloody garments and confided, man-to-man, "This is how we take care of niggers."

The movies were our other major form of entertainment and another unifying force. Sixty percent of Americans went at least once a week. Our family usually went on Friday nights and I often managed to squeeze in one or two others during the week. The Andy Hardy series was the family favorite. Andy, played by Mickey Rooney, had a spirit of mischief that I liked, while Judge Hardy and his wife were the ideal parents that appealed to my mother and father. Andy's good-humored irreverence for stuffiness was characteristic of the time. Indeed the same spirit—think of the Marx brothers and their favorite foil, the sanctimonious society lady played by Margaret Dumont—helped fuel the explosion of comedy that occurred during the 1930s. Yet Andy retained a respect for authority as personified by his father, the judge. Indeed movies almost always depicted judges as wise and just. Franklin Roosevelt's scheme to pack the Supreme Court with justices sympathetic to the New Deal may well have failed because it seemed to disrespect the judiciary.

Nineteen thirty-nine had been the movies' best year so far with *The Wizard of Oz*, *Gunga Din*, *Wuthering Heights*, *Stagecoach*, *Goodbye, Mr. Chips*, and *Ninotchka* being only a few of the memorable films. December brought the crowning event, the premiere in Atlanta of *Gone With the Wind*, attended by stars Clark Gable, Vivian Leigh, Olivia de Haviland, Leslie Howard, and Hattie McDaniel. Nothing better illustrated the importance of movies in the life of the country during those years than the thousands of people who crowded the streets outside Loews Grand Theater to cheer the actors. It was unquestionably the movie of the year. But my favorite was *Mr. Smith Goes to Washington*. It told the story of Jefferson Smith, played by James Stewart, an idealistic non-politician who was made a senator by the bosses who thought they could control him but found out that they could not.

Mr. Smith Goes to Washington was my favorite because, even as a kid, I had an unusually intense interest in politics. My parents were both active workers in the Democratic party, and ardent supporters of Franklin Roosevelt. Current events were a major topic at our dinner table from which we always adjourned at 6:45 to listen to NBC's Lowell Thomas present the news. The author of *Lawrence of Arabia* was a natural storyteller with a gift for making the news dramatic. But he was sponsored by Blue Sunoco, an oil company owned by the very conservative Republican Joe Pew, and so he rarely had a kind word for FDR. Our consolation was a five-minute newscast at 8:55 PM on CBS that featured a real liberal, Elmer Davis. Davis was a rarity. There weren't a lot of pro-FDR voices in the media back then, which was largely dominated by publishers whose politics were very much to the right. Other notable exceptions were Drew Pearson, who, along with Robert S. Allen, wrote a widely read syndicated column called the "Washington Merry-Go-Round," and the immensely popular gossip columnist, Walter Winchell, who interspersed the chatter about celebrities in his column in the *New York Daily Mirror* and on his fifteen-minute Sunday night radio show with paeans of praise to Roosevelt that struck me as perfectly objective.

Notice that the news came in five- or fifteen-minute segments. If a half hour was ever devoted to the news, it would only come after 10:30 PM or during the day on Sunday. The time devoted to the news increased only slightly as the situation in Europe worsened. H. V.

Kaltenborn's fifteen-minute commentary moved from once a week in 1939 to three per week in 1940. Minutes were found for brief reports from the war capitals, with William L. Shirer in Berlin and Edward R. Murrow and Eric Severeid in London. Even on December 7, 1941, only one network devoted a full hour to a news show.

For the kind of pictures television brings us today, we had only the movie newsreels, which ran between five and ten minutes and were changed twice a week—*Fox Movietone News* was an example—and the picture magazines, *Life* and *Look*, which had come along in the second half of the 1930s. *Life*, which published photographic reports of news and cultural events, took the country by storm when it first appeared in 1936. The power it quickly attained can only be compared to that of today's television networks if they were all combined. George Gallup, the pollster, said that "A two-page spread in *Life* was worth a front-page story in every newspaper in America." *Look*, though it had much less muscle, was still very popular.

We faithfully subscribed to *Life*, the *Saturday Evening Post* (with its Norman Rockwell covers), and *Time*. The first two could be found in almost every middle-class household, and *Time*—both it and *Life* were owned by Henry Luce—was the most popular of the publications devoted primarily to politics and current events.

Our main source of information, however, was the newspapers—the morning *Gazette* and the evening *Daily Mail* (the *Gazette* was Democratic and the *Mail* was Republican). My father and I read practically every word in both, including such items—called "Personals" in those days—as "Miss Ida Smith is visiting her cousin in Kansas City." Back then, friends and neighbors could be celebrities just like the movie stars.

The big news was the war in Europe. In the middle of the night of August 31/September 1, 1939, Franklin Roosevelt had been awakened by a phone call from William Bullitt, his ambassador to France. "[Ambassador to Poland] Tony Biddle has just gotten through from Warsaw, Mr. President. Several German divisions are deep in Polish territory, and fighting is heavy. He said there were reports of bombers over the city. Then he was cut off."

Bullitt called again at 6:30 to say that the French would go to war with Germany. A few minutes later, Ambassador Joseph Kennedy called from London to say that England would do the same.

I was intensely anti-Nazi. At Sunday school I engaged in a weekly debate with a pro-Hitler classmate. Mild anti-Semitism was quite common in Charleston—even my parents had a trace of it—but Hitler's hatred of Jews seemed crazy to most of us. And most of us were against wars of aggression, including Japan's in China, Mussolini's in Ethiopia, and Germany's in Poland, and were glad that England and France had finally decided to fight Hitler.

But the conflict that really gripped us that winter was the fight that Finland was putting up against the Soviet Union. Finland had been invaded in late November, and in January actually seemed to be beating the Russians. Not only were we rooting for this David against a Goliath—so morally corrupt that it aligned itself with Nazi Germany in dividing up Poland—but Finland held a special place in our esteem because it was the only country that hadn't missed a payment on its World War I debt to the United States.

The inspirational effect of the Finnish struggle was also felt in England, and by no one more than Winston Churchill: "Only Finland—superb, nay sublime in the jaws of peril, shows what free men can do." Churchill felt so strongly that he advocated sending British military assistance to Finland. Even after the war, when the inadvisability of giving Britain's precious military equipment to a lost cause was painfully obvious, Churchill confessed, "I supported every proposal to aid Finland."

As for the larger war, most Americans' sympathies were with the Allies. But, an overwhelming majority—the polls indicated more than 80 percent—was determined that this country keep out of war. Indeed, our help did not appear to be needed. On the western front, the situation was so calm that it was called the Sitzkrieg or the Phony War. The French Army, widely regarded as the best in the world, stood behind an elaborate system of fortifications known as the Maginot Line, which was supposed to be impregnable.

That supposed impregnability contributed to a smug isolationism that prevailed among Americans. When former president Herbert Hoover was asked after a speech, in January 1940, what should be the policy of the United States if Hitler would seriously threaten the existence of France and England, he replied, "It was too impossible an event to warrant comment."

Still, the war was beginning to make itself felt in popular culture. On Broadway, during the 1939–1940 season there was the anti-Nazi *Margin for Error* by Clare Boothe Luce, who was the wife of the publisher of *Time* and *Life*, and the anti-Soviet, pro-Finland *There Shall Be No Night*, by Robert Sherwood (who was to become a speechwriter for FDR). Hollywood spoofed Hitler in Charlie Chaplin's *The Great Dictator* and Soviet communism in Greta Garbo's *Ninotchka*. Ernest Hemingway was completing his novel *For Whom the Bell Tolls* about the Spanish Civil War, the curtain raiser for World War II.

Next to the war, the news was mostly about two closely related subjects, the economy and the 1940 election. Millions were still unemployed, but things were getting better. All our rural relatives who had come to Charleston looking for work had found it. The parade of desperate men who had come to our kitchen door begging for a meal dwindled to a trickle and then stopped. Wages had risen to a point that my mother no longer felt that she could afford a full-time maid, so she hired a high school girl who would arrive at 3:30, after her classes, and work until 7:30 or 8:00. The first half of 1940, wages in West Virginia rose 25 percent above the same period in 1939 according to the state chamber of commerce. During the same period nationally more than one million jobs had been added in just the industrial sector of the economy.

Higher wages meant more purchasing power, because prices stayed stable and low. Bread was still ten cents a loaf, milk fifteen cents a quart, eggs twenty cents a dozen. A new Ford, Chevrolet, or Plymouth could be had for around $650. The least expensive model of the elegant Packard was just $995.

The Union Central Life Insurance Company was running ads saying its $200 a month annuity would permit you to "retire and forget your worries, and spend happier days in traveling, sports, or just

loafing if you want to." For many years, that $200 a month repre-
sented my ideal of a splendid income.

More jobs, higher wages, and low inflation were creating hope in
the land. The good times had arrived, or they were just around the
corner.

The lyric of one of George Gershwin's last songs, "Love Walked
In," which appeared in the movie *The Big Broadcast of 1938*, in describing the effect of love also described what was happening in the lives
of a great many Americans. It "drove the shadows away" so they
"forgot the gloom of the past" and it "brought a world completely
new." Other songs of 1939 and 1940 were similarly hopeful, including
"Over the Rainbow" (the land that I dream of) "Wishing" (will make
it so), and "When You Wish Upon a Star" (your dreams come true).

The New York World's Fair of 1939–40 expressed the same optimism in its theme of the "World of Tomorrow" and its most popular
display was GM's Futurama, which envisioned a world of superhigh-
ways and two-month vacations. And, of course, no one radiated that
confidence more than the great optimist himself, Franklin Roosevelt.

Roosevelt's optimism could have been grounded in part at least in
his triumph over polio. Polio was known then as infantile paralysis
and the prognosis for its victims was usually grim. Roosevelt had
managed to rise from his bed to take an active part in public life and
be elected president of the United States. If he could overcome this
severe handicap, other obstacles in his path and that of his country
must have seemed less formidable to him. Another source of Roosevelt's faith in the future—and of his ability to communicate with
his fellow citizens—was the Christianity he shared with a great majority of them.

"I've always felt that Franklin's religion had something to do with
his confidence in himself," observed his wife Eleanor. "It was a very
simple religion," she added. He "never seemed to have any intellectual difficulties about what he believed." This was certainly true of
the Peters family and of most of the Christians we knew. We did not
dwell on doubts that may have fleetingly passed through our minds
as we considered Noah and the Ark, Jonah and the whale, and

Moses at the Red Sea. We believed in the Ten Commandments and most of all in the Golden Rule. Roosevelt saw the New Deal as applied Christianity. When he spoke to the nation on Christmas Eve, he quoted the Sermon on the Mount. Later that evening he read *A Christmas Carol* to his family, gathered by a White House fireside.

In his speech, Roosevelt asked his countrymen to "Pray that we be given the strength to live for others" and tied the story of Scrooge to what was then happening in America.

"Old Scrooge found that Christmas wasn't humbug. He took to himself the spirit of neighborliness. But today neighborliness no longer can be confined to one's little neighborhood. Life is become too complex for that. In our country neighborliness has gradually spread its boundaries from town to county to state and now, at last, to the whole nation.

"For instance who would have thought that a week from tomorrow—January 1, 1940—tens of thousands of elderly men and women in every state, in every county, in every city in the nation, would begin to receive checks for old age retirement insurance."

Although right-wing Christians were already a fact of life even then—the Reverend Gerald L. K. Smith and Father Charles Coughlin, who called FDR's program the "Jew Deal," the most extreme among them—the gospel according to FDR prevailed for most of us.

One good thing about Prohibition, which had ended in 1933, is that it tended to make Christianity less self-righteous. A story about my father may illustrate. Until I was six years old, his churchgoing was foregone every other Sunday so we could drive up a country road into the nearby hills to visit his bootlegger. Who would suspect a fellow citizen out on a Sunday morning? Besides, law-enforcement officials could be counted on to be taking a well-deserved day of rest. That similar considerations occurred to a good number of people was evidenced by the traffic on that country road. The "Great Experiment," which was another name for Prohibition in those days, had not worked. Tens of millions of Christians were violating not only man's law, but what a great many of their preachers had told them was God's law. Memory of the experience seemed to breed—

for a while at least—humility, tolerance, and a merciful attitude towards other sinners.

As Roosevelt celebrated that Christmas of 1939, he was still loved by millions who hoped he would run for a third term, but there was no question that his popularity had declined from its height at his great victory in 1936. His effort to add justices to the Supreme Court had been defeated in 1937. And in 1938 voters had rejected most of his attempts to defeat conservative senators.

Other Democratic presidential possibilities were being discussed, and all were more conservative than Roosevelt. As the country emerged from the Depression, its normal tendency toward conservatism was asserting itself. In 1939, Henry Wallace, the Secretary of Agriculture, had written Roosevelt that "on a straight division of the electorate on the basis of the broadly liberal and the generally conservative, the definite majority is conservative."

Roosevelt's possible opponents included his vice president, red-faced, gray-haired John Nance Garner; the distinguished-looking secretary of state, Cordell Hull; and big, hearty James A. Farley, the postmaster general who was also chairman of the Democratic National Committee and had managed Roosevelt's landslide in 1936. Farley enjoyed the affection of party regulars but New Dealers suspected his devotion to the cause and thought he lacked gravitas. Garner and the president disliked each other—FDR was said to delight in CIO president John L. Lewis's characterization of Garner as a "labor-baiting, poker-playing, whiskey-drinking, evil old man." Of the potential candidates, Hull enjoyed the widest regard but he was sixty-nine—when the life expectancy of the American man was fifty-nine years. Hull also had a slight lisp—"Jesus Christ" came out "Jesus Cwist"—that did not bode well for campaign speeches.

There was a fourth possible candidate, Paul V. McNutt, who might be called the candidate from Central Casting. Gray-haired but still vigorous and handsome, he was the federal security administrator and former high commissioner of the Philippines. But the almost universal opinion of political observers was that he was even more of a lightweight than Farley, who at least was regarded as a heavy hitter in the world of politics. McNutt was also suspected of being on the take.

Roosevelt had other problems. For one, he was hated by the rich. Country club locker room jokes about Eleanor and Franklin were usually unfunny, always vicious, and as ubiquitous as tennis rackets and golf bags. "Let's go to the Trans-Lux (a New York movie theater, featuring newsreels) and hiss Roosevelt," a fur-clad matron says to her obviously affluent friend in a classic Peter Arno cartoon. And the rich weren't his only opponents. Roosevelt may have liked John L. Lewis's opinion of Garner, but he definitely did not like Lewis's opinion of him. Lewis was so violently opposed to a third term that he said he would resign his presidency of the CIO if FDR won.

Another problem for FDR was the sentiment of young people, who had been among his most ardent supporters in 1936. Now many of the most idealistic youths were anti-war. Many were also a part of the far left, and the far left had followed the Communist Party in opposing the war once the Soviet-Nazi pact was made in August 1939. So from that time until the Nazi invasion of Russia in 1941, the Communist Party worldwide and the far left in America were united in opposing aid to Britain and the Allies. They saw Roosevelt, in the words of James McGregor Burns, "as a weak Kerensky-type pawn, or worse a power mad militarist bent on plunging the country into an imperialist war." They booed and hissed when FDR spoke to members of the American Youth Congress in February 1940.

The American Youth Congress had passed a resolution opposing American aid to Finland on the ground that it was "an attempt to force America into the Imperialist forum." In their antiwar stance, if not in their pro-Soviet position, these young people were not that different from the overwhelming majority of Americans who, like the great national hero Charles A. Lindbergh, were isolationists as 1940 began.

A Roper poll stated the various positions people had on the war. Those who said "take no sides and stay out of the war entirely but offer to sell supplies to anyone on a cash and carry basis" amounted to 37.5%. The next largest group, "have nothing to do with any warring countries—don't even trade with them on a cash and carry basis," were 29.9 percent. On the other hand, those who favored entering the war immediately on the side of England, France, and Poland were just 2.5%. Those who favored getting into the war in the event Britain and France seemed to be in real danger of losing comprised only 14.7%. The remainder was isolationist in varying degrees.

Responding to the overwhelming strength of the isolationists, Congress had passed a series of neutrality acts in the 1930s banning the shipment of arms and munitions to all belligerents. Roosevelt had attempted to shift prevailing opinion. In 1935, he tried to get the original Neutrality Act amended so that its prohibitions would apply to aggressor nations but not to their victims. He failed then as he did again in 1937, when he delivered a major speech in Chicago calling for a quarantine of aggressor nations. The speech was greeted by either indifference or hostility, and Roosevelt retreated. "It's a terrible thing," he told his aide Sam Rosenman, "to look over your shoulder when you are trying to lead and find no one there."

In the fall of 1939, Roosevelt did manage to get the Neutrality Act amended so that arms could be sold on a "cash and carry" basis, but only managed to do so by never mentioning the fact that only Britain and France could actually take advantage of the provisions because Germany could not get anything through the British blockade.

It is thus easy to understand why all the leading Republican candidates in 1940 were isolationists. They included Thomas E. Dewey, Robert Taft, and Arthur Vandenberg.

Tom Dewey was only thirty-seven when he announced he was going to run for president. "He threw his diaper into the ring," remarked FDR's caustic secretary of the interior Harold Ickes. Dewey had been born in Michigan, but moved to New York, where he became district attorney in 1937, having previously served as a special prosecutor under Mayor Fiorello LaGuardia. Then Dewey, having received an immense amount of publicity as a crusading crime fighter, ran for governor in 1938. He lost a very close race to the highly respected incumbent, Governor Herbert Lehman, who had been expected to win by a wide margin. This put Dewey on the front pages as a contender for the Republican nomination for president. By January of 1939 he had 27 percent of the Republicans choosing him as their presidential candidate, and by March 50 percent.

Dewey's strategy was to demonstrate vote-getting ability by winning primaries. His lead in the polls reached 60 percent by early 1940. Other than attacking Roosevelt and the New Deal, he hoped to preserve his popularity by being vague about his stance on major issues. When advised by the National Committeeman from Missouri not to be "prematurely specific" about his positions, Dewey called the advice "particularly swell."

Nevertheless, Dewey was a forceful speaker, trained by radio's Lowell Thomas, who inspired an enthusiastic reaction from the large crowds attracted by his celebrity. In January, he drew an audience of 12,000 to Boston's Mechanics Hall and got the endorsement of former Massachusetts governor Alvin Fuller. Then came a 2,500-mile tour through midwestern states. The turnouts, even in tiny towns, impressed even the most skeptical observers. At 1:00 AM in Miles City, Montana (definitely not a large metropolis nor a place where people stay up late), he was greeted by a crowd of 500. In Lincoln, Nebraska, he attracted the largest political crowd in the city's history. In March, he drew 16,000 to the Chicago Stadium and then an incredible 20,000 turned out for a barbecue in Washington, Indiana. In April, Dewey defeated Senator Arthur Vandenberg in two primaries, each time getting more than 60 percent of the vote. The first victory in Wisconsin prompted the *New York Herald Tribune*'s Jack Beall to write on April 4 that "it would be exceedingly hard to head off Mr. Dewey from the Republican nomination."

The second Dewey triumph occurred in Nebraska on April 9. But April 9 was also the date Dewey's fortunes took a turn for the worse, for that was the day Hitler invaded Norway and Denmark—followed soon by Belgium, Holland, and France—and foreign affairs became the major issue of the election. To the extent he couldn't fudge—as he usually tried to do since the major newspapers in his home state, the *New York Times* and the *New York Herald Tribune*, were internationalist—Dewey campaigned as an isolationist following the counsel of his chief foreign policy advisor, John Foster Dulles, whose law firm, Sullivan & Cromwell, represented German companies and who believed Hitler was a "passing phenomenon."

Other of Dewey's shortcomings had begun to emerge, least of these but still distracting the gap between his middle teeth, which Lowell Thomas called the Grand Canyon. More unsettling was his tendency to be what is today called a "control freak." Once he ordered a fellow Republican candidate in Illinois to stop waving from the train window: "[L]et us handle things our way and we'll get along better." Pressing the flesh as he worked the campaign crowd was, in his words, "absolute torture." And even one of his most loyal aides, Ruth McCormick Simms, said that "he was cold, cold as a February iceberg."

Dewey still maintained a substantial, if diminishing, lead in the polls, right up to the opening of the Republican Convention. He continued to follow Dulles's counsel and refused to speak out clearly against Hitler.

The candidate closest to Dewey in the 1939 polls was Arthur Vandenberg. The fifty-five-year-old Michigan senator was perhaps the most respected of the Republican leaders in the Senate. Although Vandenberg became known as an internationalist in the second half of the 1940s, he was at this time a firm isolationist, insisting that the United States should not be an international policeman, and that the best defense against war was a limitation on arms. Until Dewey came close to defeating Lehman in 1938, Vandenberg had seemed the most likely Republican nominee and even in early 1940 a poll of newspaper editors showed him to be the candidate they were betting on.

Vandenberg was viewed as a statesman of the Senate, wise in its ways, and always open to reason from his colleagues. But, like many other great figures from Capitol Hill—most notably Lyndon Johnson in 1960—he mistook his colleagues' regard for a mass movement. Vandenberg seemed to hope that if he put his name forward he would, in effect, be drafted. That's only happened twice in the last century, however, when Dwight Eisenhower and Adlai Stevenson were chosen by their representative parties in 1952 without having campaigned.

Vandenberg's disdain for primaries was most memorably expressed when he said, "[W]hy should I kill myself to carry Vermont?" His indifference to campaigning may have been influenced by his mistress, Mitzi Sims, the wife of a British diplomat whose country would not have wanted to see an isolationist like Vandenberg win the nomination. Whatever the reasons, Vandenberg did not campaign in Vermont and he didn't even bother to visit his neighboring state of Wisconsin, where he had entered his name and where Dewey had vigorously contested the primary. The result was that Vandenberg not only lost but was humiliated by Dewey, who won all twenty-four of the state's delegates.

Senator Robert A. Taft was the other serious contender. He had only come to the Senate in 1938, at the age of forty-nine, but was the son of the former president William Howard Taft and had been prominent in Ohio politics, having been placed in nomination as a favorite son in the 1936 Republican Convention.

Taft was brilliant, relentlessly honest, but often stubborn and often wrong—qualities that he shared with many of his party's best and brightest. Indeed, he would come to be known as Mr. Republican.

John F. Kennedy devoted a chapter to him in *Profiles in Courage*. Turner Catledge, of the *New York Times*, even though he was more liberal and internationalist in his views than Taft, still said that of all the 1940 candidates, Taft was "the one I cared for most personally," explaining:

> He was not a warm, congenial man—he could be cold and could be extremely hard and righteous—but there was a tremendous honesty about him that commanded respect, and beneath this rigid exterior he was a shy, pleasant sort of man. Sometimes his stubborn honesty made him seem awkward in the context of the Senate—it was the very opposite of the to "get along go along" philosophy that prevailed in Congress. Bob Taft would not "go along" with anything he was not convinced was right.

As more and more Americans became concerned about Hitler's conquest in Europe, Taft stubbornly clung to his isolationist faith. On May 18, he went to Topeka, Kansas, to make a speech. Alf Landon, the state's former governor, who had been the Republican presidential candidate in 1936, and other local friends told him of the increasing sympathy for the allied cause. After all, Holland had just fallen and allied forces in Belgium were in great peril. In his speech, however, Taft urged the audience not to be concerned with foreign battles: "It is the New Deal which may leave us weak and unprepared for attacks." Two days later in St. Louis, he said "[T]here is a good deal more danger of the infiltration of totalitarian ideas from the New Deal circles in Washington than there ever will be from activities of the communists or the Nazis."

Taft was invited to dinner at the home of the dedicated internationalists and *Herald Tribune* owners Helen and Ogden Reid, where the other guests shared their hosts' views on foreign policy. Guests included the columnist Dorothy Thompson, the head of the House of Morgan Thomas Lamont, the British ambassador Lord Lothian, and Wendell Willkie, a utility executive who had recently emerged as a possible candidate for the Republican presidential nomination. Taft and his wife both sought to avoid a confrontation with influential people whose help, assuming Taft got the nomination, he would need to win the presidency. But when Willkie said that he would vote for Roosevelt over a Republican who was not for helping Britain and France, Taft, in the words of his wife Martha, "exploded," declaring: "I had not intended on taking any part in this discussion, but I feel I cannot sit here and let my silence be interpreted as agreement."

Then, in Martha's words, "[T]he fat was in the fire. Everybody began screaming at once with Dorothy Thompson screaming more than anybody else. Bob got in the most violent argument with her. I thought I was going to have to throw pepper on them!"

But Taft's strength was that most of the time his feelings were practically identical to those of most Republicans. The question now, however, was would most of the time include the week of the 1940 Republican Convention?

CHAPTER TWO

★

"A STUNNING COMBINATION OF INTELLECT
AND HOMELY WARMTH"

Who was this man who could make Taft explode? Wendell
Willkie was the only outright internationalist among the Republican
candidates. His strong opposition to Hitler and his spirited advocacy
of aid to the Allies combined with the reputation Willkie had earned
as a thoughtful critic of the New Deal to attract the interest of some
powerful and not-so-powerful people. Among the not-so-powerful
was my father. This may be because of similarities in his life story
and Willkie's.

Both were rooted in rural America, my father having grown up
on a farm in West Virginia and Willkie in a small town in Indiana.
Both had graduated from law school just before World War I, both
had enlisted in the army, and both had risen to the rank of captain
while serving in France. Instead of going home to practice law, both
had sought their fortunes in moderate sized cities, Akron, Ohio, in
Willkie's case. Both had been trial lawyers; both had been active participants in Democratic politics. But there the similarity ended.
Willkie went on to the big city—New York—to serve as counsel for
Commonwealth and Southern, a large utility holding company, and
became its president in 1933.

Though Willkie stayed in the Democratic party—he attended its
national convention in 1932 as he had in 1924—he became increas-

ingly critical of FDR's policy on electric power and, as he spoke out publicly, began to gain national recognition. In 1937 *Fortune* hailed him as having "presidential stature."

Willkie's *Town Meeting of the Air* appearance on NBC's Blue Network on January 6, 1938, was his first exposure on national radio. The show, moderated by George V. Denny Jr., had a faithful following among people seriously interested in public affairs. The other guest that night was Robert Jackson, FDR's attorney general and a man considered by many—including, it was said, Roosevelt himself—to be the president's likely successor. The topic—"How can government and business work together"—was right up Willkie's alley. Coming across as a businessman with a heart, he hit a home run—Jackson seemed dull in comparison. The result was that Jackson's prospects plummeted while Willkie's rose dramatically.

In 1939, a series of mentions in the media steadily heightened interest in Willkie as a possible candidate. In February, an article in the *Saturday Evening Post* praised him as "attractive, articulate, and courageous." Also in February, Arthur Krock, the leading political columnist of the *New York Times* wrote:

> Willkie is a long shot candidate, he'll go down as the darkest horse of the stable for 1940. 1940 will be a little early to bring out a utilities man, but if anyone like that can be put over, I'd watch Willkie. He still has his hair cut country style.

Will Rogers endured in hearts and minds other than my father's. Willkie was not unmindful of the resemblance and its positive aspects. A lock of hair fell Rogers-style over the right side of his forehead. He confided to one reporter, "In my business it's an advantage to look like an Indiana farmer." Whether he meant the business of business or the business of politics he was right.

The writer Booth Tarkington, another native of Indiana, described Willkie as "a man wholly natural in manner . . . a good, sturdy, able, plain Hoosier . . . a man as American as the courthouse yard in the square of an Indiana county seat."

On March 3, the New York *Herald Tribune* published a letter by G. Vernor Rogers saying that Willkie should be the Republican candidate in 1940. The letter drew attention because many thought that Rogers was speaking for Helen and Ogden Reid, the paper's owners, to whom he was related. The *Trib* was then generally considered to be the voice of the Republican establishment.

On May 22, columnist David Lawrence, who was also publisher of *US News*, wrote, "[I]n Wendell Willkie the Republicans would have an independent candidate with business ability that nine out of 10 Republicans really want but do not venture to ask for."

Also in May, Willkie himself appeared in the *Atlantic Monthly* as the author of an article entitled "Raise Up, America." In June, he wrote another article for the *Saturday Evening Post*.

Then, in July, came the big one: A laudatory cover story in *Time* that said, "[H]e is the only business man in the United States who has been even mentioned as a presidential candidate for 1940."

All this attention was being stirred up by a handsome forty-eight-year-old, 6'1", 210-pound burly bear of a man. "He was a big, shambling, rumpled, overweight, carelessly dressed man, and he radiated a stunning combination of intellect and homely warmth," wrote Marcia Davenport, one of his New York friends. "He speaks a twangy Indiana burr in a rumbling bass voice, grating down hard on the vocal cords as many mid-western Americans do. He has a delightful, instantly responsive chuckle."

Veteran columnist Drew Pearson wrote, "[F]or sheer force of personality and character I believe Willkie makes the greatest impact of any man I've ever talked to. He rings true."

Drew Pearson would not have admired Willkie if Willkie hadn't shared Pearson's liberalism to a very large degree. Although Willkie did have a conservative pro-business side, a fight against the Ku Klux Klan had been one of the highlights of his life in Akron. Later, in New York, Willkie wrote an article in the *New Republic* defending the free speech rights of Nazis and Communists.

Not only had Willkie taken part in the Democratic conventions of 1924 and '32, but as late as October 26, 1938, while speaking at a dinner, he referred to the Democratic Party, noting, "of which, incidentally, I am a member." In December of that same year, Willkie had lunch with James Farley, who reported to FDR that Willkie professed great admiration for the president and his program. He said that Willkie disagreed with FDR "only on the [electric] power question."

In his listing in *Who's Who in America,* the contents of which are not only supplied by the listee but are annually reviewed by him or her, Willkie was identified as a Democrat as late as the 1938–1939 edition. (This fact turned up not during research on Willkie, but when going through Robert Taft's papers in the Library of Congress. Taft had kept Willkie's 1936–1937 and 1934–1935 *Who's Who* listings, as well as the 1938–1939 one, with the word "Democrat" circled in each.) All in all, the evidence suggests that Willkie did not change his registration to Republican until late 1939 or early 1940. The first public notice of the change came in the January 16, 1940, issue of the *New York Sun.*

Willkie had been born in 1892 in Elwood, a small Indiana town of around 10,000 people. His father, Herman, was a lawyer, as was his mother, Henrietta, the first woman admitted to the state's bar. Willkie was the fourth of six children. His siblings were all bright, with his sister Julia, who was later to become a research chemist, considered to be the brightest. Intensely competitive, the children were encouraged by their parents to engage in nightly debates at the dinner table. Herman Willkie owned the largest private library in Elwood. Willkie would later recall "a constant atmosphere of reading and discussion." Since the children had to match wits with two lawyers, they learned to think fast and to avoid leaving holes in their arguments that their parents could pounce on.

Both Herman and Henrietta Willkie were formidable personalities. Their parents had fled Germany, having been on the losing side in the unsuccessful 1848 revolution against the militaristic and autocratic government. Henrietta's mother and father, Lewis and Julia Trisch, had settled first in Indiana, then moved to Kansas, but they were abolitionist, and when Kansas was opened to slavery in 1854 they returned to Indiana, where Julia became an itinerant Presbyterian lay preacher known as "Mother Trisch" who had the gumption to ride all over rural Indiana holding revival meetings.

Julia's daughter Henrietta had inherited her toughness, and it was Henrietta who was the disciplinarian in the Willkie family. Her children respected her, but it seemed that the children's affection was largely focused on their father.

Herman Willkie was a passionate liberal. In his law practice, Herman often took the side of workers and their unions, for Elwood was the site of two chemical plants and a tin mill. He campaigned for the populist Democrat William Jennings Bryan, who was once an overnight guest at the Willkie home. Wendell grew up with first Bryan and then Woodrow Wilson and the Wisconsin progressive Robert LaFallotte as his political heroes.

Although the Willkie family's circumstances were relatively comfortable—they lived in a three-story green-frame home with a stained-glass window and a large fireplace—Wendell Willkie learned how hard the lot of labor could be by working one summer in the heat of the local tin mill, where rubber shoes would melt on the floor.

In school, he was an Andy Hardy, with some form of mischief never very far from his mind. Once Willkie purloined the physiology class's skeleton, hanging it from a tree outside. Having been identified as one of the culprits who climbed Elwood's tallest gas tank to paint his class numerals in six-foot-high letters and who then painted graffiti on the school sidewalks, he was suspended. His parents dispatched him to Culver military academy, where a summer of hazing made him miserable enough to return gratefully to Elwood High School. There, a redheaded Irish teacher, Phillip Carlton Bing, from the University of Chicago, finally got Willkie fired up about his studies. In his senior year Willkie made all As.

Bing also brought Wendell together with another of his best students, Gwyneth Harry, a beautiful black-haired daughter of Welsh immigrants. Willkie quickly fell in love with her and their romance was to continue not only through the rest of high school but through all of his college years. One of his earliest expressions of devotion to Gwyneth was resigning as president of his high school fraternity because a sorority had blackballed Gwyneth due to her immigrant background.

Gwyneth's rejection by the sorority seemed to fortify her desire for upward mobility. She began to insist that her ancestry was British, not Welsh. She urged Willkie to join her in the Episcopal Church instead of continuing in his family's Methodism. She encouraged him to work hard in high school, to stop swearing, and to behave in a more cultivated and gentlemanly fashion.

Willkie tried hard to please Gwyneth. He not only did well in his studies, he ceased swearing and performed endless volunteer work at the church. Still, he remained a nonconformist in significant respects.

Although Gwyneth joined a sorority when she went to Butler University, Willkie did not abandon his stand against fraternities when he followed his brothers and sisters to the Bloomington campus of the Indiana University (the campus newspaper reported "Another Willkie arrives") and quickly became known as a student rebel. He chewed tobacco, read Karl Marx, and petitioned the faculty to add a course on socialism to the curriculum. Willkie fought fraternity dominance of student politics by managing the successful campaign of his non-fraternity Elwood friend, Paul Harmon, to become president of the sophomore class. He also worked hard to democratize elections to the student union. Participating in the students' mock Democratic Convention in 1912 as chairman of the Pennsylvania delegation, he supported Woodrow Wilson.

Gwyneth, finding that the sororities and fraternities dominated social life at Butler, later wrote, "[T]he fact that [Willkie] did not belong to a fraternity caused me some embarrassment." She kept urging Willkie to join, and finally, as he was entering his senior year, she delivered an ultimatum: "become a fraternity man or lose me." His roommate, Maurice Bluhm, reported that Willkie told him that "[I]f I don't join a fraternity, I lose my girl and if I do I lose my soul." Willkie chose the girl.

After college, Willkie taught high school history and—despite his

own ineptitude at sports—coached basketball and track in Coffeyville, Kansas. He was immensely popular with the students and
with the female teachers (separation having cooled his relationship
with Gwyneth). The student yearbook mentioned romances with
three different women on the faculty, noting that "[A] telephone between his room and that of one teacher would save time."

But, after a year at Coffeyville, Willkie decided he needed to make
money and went to Puerto Rico to work for his brother. There he
saw terrible poverty and brutal employers. He never forgot seeing
one boss strike a worker with a machete. A few months in Puerto
Rico was enough, so the fall of 1915 saw him back at Indiana University, this time as a law student.

Back then, law school could be finished in one year, and that is
what Willkie did. He not only excelled in his studies, but he won
both the moot court competition and the prize for the best essay by
a student, and was also named class orator by his fellow students.
The oration was a memorable denunciation of Indiana's failure to
regulate banks and businesses with some severe criticism of the law
school thrown in. It took the faculty several days to recover and actually present Willkie with the diploma he had earned.

Willkie then went home to Elwood to practice law. In his first
court appearance his father was his opponent. There was one problem with young Willkie's case: He had no witnesses. Still, he put up
a spirited fight, and in his closing argument Herman Willkie observed, "I believe my son will be a very good lawyer. He can make
so much out of so little."

Needless to say, Willkie lost the case, but Elwood knew it had a
future legal star on its hands. The star, however, did not have much
time to rise. April 1917 brought America's entry into World War I,
and Willkie immediately enlisted.

Part of Willkie's military training was conducted at Fort Benjamin
Harrison near Indianapolis and at Camp Zachary Taylor outside
Louisville, Kentucky, which was just across the Ohio River from Indi-
ana. When Willkie got leave, he went home to see his new girlfriend,
Edith Wilk. She was a $12-a-month assistant librarian in Rushville

(pronounced "roosh-e-ville"), a small town a few miles from Elwood. The head librarian, Mary Steeth, had introduced her friend Wendell to Edith. At 5'2" and 110 pounds, Edith was a foot shorter and 100 pounds lighter than the burly Willkie. Like Gwyneth she was more socially advanced than Willkie. She loved to dance, but Willkie's awkwardness in sports extended to the dance floor. "I realized," she said, "that he lacked all sense of time, tune, or rhythm." But she added, "it didn't matter." They fell in love and were married while Willkie was still in the army. In 1940, she told reporters that her husband "never let me down," adding words that a candidate's wife would probably not utter today, "I wouldn't marry a man who wasn't boss."

Soon after his marriage, Willkie was sent to England and then to France, arriving too late to become involved in the fighting. His main activity seems to have been using his legal skills to defend fellow soldiers who went AWOL to enjoy the pleasures of Paris.

He returned to Elwood in February 1919, and briefly considered running for the U.S. House of Representatives. The Democratic nomination was his for the asking. But the incumbent, Albert Vestal, was popular and the district was traditionally Republican. Willkie sought the advice of the prominent Indianapolis attorney Frank Dailey, who told him: "Sure you'll win with a war record, but it's normally a Republican district . . . you'll come home in a couple of years and be just another political lawyer in an Indiana county seat."

Dailey had another idea. He would write Willkie a letter of introduction to Harvey Firestone. The Firestone Tire and Rubber Company was booming, as was its home, Akron, Ohio, riding the coattails of the automobile industry's spectacular growth. Willkie thought his prospects were better here than in a small town like Elwood, so when Firestone offered him a job at $175 a month he accepted. Willkie arrived in Akron in May, leaving Edith behind in Indiana. She was pregnant and wanted to remain at home until their first child, a son they named Philip, was born in December.

Willkie immediately immersed himself in a wide range of community activities, establishing an American Legion post—the Legion was by far the most popular of the World War I veterans' organizations—becoming active in politics, and speaking to lunch clubs like Rotary and Kiwanis. Within little more than a year, he had made enough of an impression to be asked to introduce the Democratic presidential nominee, James Cox, when Cox made a campaign stop in Akron. Shortly thereafter, Willkie accepted an offer to join a major Akron law firm, Mather and Nesbitt. Its impressive roster of blue-chip clients included several public utilities. Willkie quickly established himself as a skilled trial lawyer, also winning respect for his talent at presenting rate and franchise cases to the Ohio Public Utilities Commission.

Meanwhile he continued to gain political prominence. In 1924, he was chosen a delegate to the Democratic National Convention in New York. Willkie supported Al Smith, who became mired in a historic multi-ballot deadlock with William Gibbs McAdoo. Each state voted on each of 102 roll calls before the delegates compromised on John W. Davis on the 103rd ballot. More important to Willkie, however, was his fight for platform planks condemning the Ku Klux Klan and endorsing the League of Nations. These were causes close to his heart.

It was Willkie's passionate conviction that the United States should not go it alone, that it should work with other nations to maintain peace in the world. The Democratic Party, however, was no longer the party of Woodrow Wilson. Isolationism ruled the land. Willkie's plank went down to defeat. He also failed to get the Ku Klux Klan condemned by name. The South still played a powerful role in the party and a shameful one insofar as toleration of the Klan was concerned. And the Klan's influence did not stop at the Mason-Dixon Line. It was strong in several northern states, including Indiana, where Willkie's father had fought it, and Ohio, where Willkie himself had joined the battle. In 1925 he led the effort to defeat Klan members on the local school board. This time he won.

The same year, Willkie was elected president of the Akron bar association, as he continued to impress the local legal community. Soon he began to attract the notice of the big bosses in New York. One of them was B. C. Cobb, who headed Commonwealth and

Southern, the utility holding company that owned Willkie's client, Ohio Power and Light. Cobb wrote the senior partner of Willkie's firm, "I think he is a comer and we should keep an eye on him." In 1929 Cobb offered to bring Willkie to New York to be counsel for Commonwealth and Southern at a salary of $36,000 a year. Willkie accepted.

Why did Willkie leave Akron? He had been happy there. "I wanted to stay," he later recalled; "I thought I was fixed for life." In Akron he couldn't walk a block without meeting a friend. In New York he looked at the crowds scurrying along Wall Street and said "My God, there isn't a soul here I know." This was the disadvantage of the anonymity New York confers on its new arrivals. But that anonymity had another side that appealed to Willkie—it offered sexual freedom. Aunt Ida wasn't going to spot you leaving a hotel with a woman who didn't look a bit like your wife.

Willkie's marriage was not in good shape. He was spending less and less time at home. He had grown and Edith had not. The wandering eye he had shown in Coffeyville began to emerge again. "He loved girls," wrote one woman friend. "He was very attractive to women . . . he had a great deal of masculine charm. He was a very masculine man." For a male who had been as awkward athletically as Willkie was, this kind of reaction from women had to be especially gratifying.

Ambition, however, was probably the major factor in Willkie's move. It drove him to seek a larger pulpit. So it was that on October 1, 1929, he arrived in New York to launch a career in the public utility business that would take him just a step away from the bulliest pulpit in the land.

Whatever Willkie's initial reservations about New York, he soon fell in love with it. He found an apartment at 84th Street and Fifth Avenue, across the street from the Metropolitan Museum of Art, attended the theater regularly, and became involved in New York Democratic politics. In 1932, he went to the Democratic Convention as an assistant floor manager for Newton D. Baker, who had won Willkie's admiration as they fought together for that plank endorsing the League of Nations at the 1924 convention. This time Baker was opposed by Al Smith, Franklin Roosevelt, and the Speaker of the House, John Nance Garner. Willkie and Roosevelt were of similar enough mind that Roosevelt offered to support Baker if the convention should deadlock. But before that could happen, the influential publisher William Randolph Hearst switched his support from Garner to Roosevelt, giving the latter the two-thirds votes majority then required for the Democratic nomination.

The next year, in January 1933, Willkie was named president of Commonwealth and Southern. He launched a vigorous effort to attract new customers to the power companies it owned. The result was that those companies doubled their sales in the next six years. Meanwhile, Willkie was fighting the New Deal's various efforts to regulate the utility industry. Most of all, he was concerned about the threat posed by the Tennessee Valley Authority's (TVA) use of its own rates as a competitive yardstick that would keep the private utility companies from charging excessively for their electricity. TVA was assaulting what the utility barons regarded as the sacred right of free enterprise to determine its own prices.

At the same time that Willkie was crusading against TVA and New Deal regulators, however, he was becoming known as a critic of industry abuses, particularly those of the holding companies that played a shell game with their assets, moving them from one state to another to stay one step ahead of both regulation and taxation. Willkie's criticism infuriated men like Samuel Insull, who had been one of the industry's more infamously corrupt leaders. Indeed, Willkie's effort on behalf of self-regulation by the holding companies led him to be called "the Jesus Christ of the industry."

This awareness of industry's faults combined with Willkie's firm opposition to government control to win Willkie attention from moderate businessmen and from the press. Articles were written about him and he became a sought-after speaker.

One of the invitations he received was to speak at the *Herald Tribune* Forum. There he met Irita Van Doren, the editor of the *Trib*'s book review.

If women had not been a motive for Willkie's move to New York, they proved to be one of its unintended benefits. He had been romantically involved with several by the time he met Irita. She, however, was special.

Irita was not a great beauty. But she was considered very attractive nonetheless—"[T]he kind of woman I like, good to look at, physically well set up, but intelligent," was the way Harold Ickes described her.

She was also very nice. "Among the kind hearted editors I have known, she was by far the kindest," said Malcolm Cowley. Lest the cynical leap to observe that the universe of kindhearted editors is of modest dimension, Hiram Hayden of the *American Scholar* explained, "[H]er graciousness was innate, not simply bred. It came from some well of sweetness within her." Hayden's tribute was especially impressive because he was an editor competing with her for book reviews instead of being a potential reviewer or author eager to win her favor.

Two years older than Willkie, Irita had been born in Birmingham, Alabama, but in early childhood moved to Tallahassee, Florida. Her father, a mill owner, was murdered by an employee he had fired, leaving his widow and four children in modest circumstances. Irita attended Florida State College for Women, from which she graduated at age seventeen. After getting a master's degree, she went to New York to seek a Ph.D. at Columbia. There she displayed her eye for talent by marrying a promising graduate student named Carl Van Doren in 1912. Although she proceeded to have three daughters and did not get her Ph.D., the title of her dissertation—"How Shakespeare Got the Dead Bodies Off the Stage"—indicated that she might be someone worth watching.

Meanwhile, Carl had become literary editor of *The Nation*. Having followed him there in 1920, Irita succeeded him three years later when he left. Not much more than a year after that, Stuart Sherman asked her to join him at the *Herald Tribune*, where he was book editor. Sherman died in 1926 and Irita replaced him.

Richard Kluger, who knew Irita at the *Herald Tribune*, describes her as: "Equally merry and serious with sparkling dark eyes, a low, gentle

Southern voice, a mass of pretty curls, and a slender figure even after bearing three daughters." Her charm was accompanied by what her friend Elizabeth Barnes described as an understanding of "the uses of power." Starting out at the *Herald Tribune* book review in 1924, Irita had become its editor by 1928. She became a close friend of the paper's owners, Helen and Ogden Reid, and was made a member of its board of directors—not exactly a customary role for a book editor.

She "traveled in liberal intellectual circles," writes Kluger, "and moved easily between academia and the more bohemian life of Greenwich Village." Having divorced Carl in 1935, Irita was living at 123 West 11th Street when she met Willkie during the winter of 1937–38 at the forum. They had in common an interest in Southern history. Irita was the granddaughter of a Confederate general, William Booth, who was one of Willkie's favorite figures from the Civil War.

Soon after they met, she asked Willkie to review a book. Since corporate executives do not rank high on book editors' list of potential critics, it is not a great leap to conclude that Willkie had made an unusually favorable impression on her. Indeed, her daughters said that Irita had found him "terribly attractive." His reply to the assignment suggests that the feelings were mutual. "My dear Mrs. Van Doren. You are certainly a sweet thing to send such an attractive and what I believe will prove interesting book to a 33rd degree member of the Power Trust. Don't tell any of your friends at *The Nation* that you did such an indiscreet act."

In closing he said, "I shall read it over the weekend and when you let me buy you that drink I will tell you about it and other things."

By January 1939, they had grown close enough for him to send this playful telegram from Springfield, Illinois: "Your cousin Tom tells me that Irita was a very smart girl, to which I sharply dissented." Perhaps more significantly that message was sent at 4:17 in the afternoon, and closed saying, "I will call you tonight from Evansville." In that era, a telegram and a long-distance telephone call in one day indicated a relationship that was more than casual. After another *Herald Tribune* lunch Willkie wrote Irita that watching her preside reminded him of Sir Walter Scott's tribute to Jane Austen, underlining Scott's reference to Austen's "exquisite touch." The letter begins "My dear, dear Irita" and ends "You whom I admire inordinately and love excessively." Soon they were spending weekends together at her home in West Cornwall, Connecticut.

Willkie used his girlfriends as a means of self-improvement. Gwyneth and Edith had been more socially polished. Now Irita was his mentor. Not only did she introduce him to New York's literary and intellectual world—including such prominent figures as James Thurber, Dorothy Thompson, Sinclair Lewis, Carl Sandberg, and her brother-in-law the poet, critic, and teacher Mark Van Doren—but Irita also helped him write his magazine articles and speeches. "You would never let me write anything," Willkie once told her, "which would be subject to the slightest criticism by the most fastidious of critics." She was, wrote his friend Joseph Barnes, largely responsible for his "acceptance of himself as a political leader with original and important ideas."

Although he spent increasing amounts of time with Irita, he remained married to Edith. "In these times," recalled Marcia Davenport, "a political candidate could not possibly have anything like a divorce." Irita's daughter recalls that "at the time I felt like she might be getting the short end of the stick, but that wasn't the case. She was wise enough to know that she had everything except the title." There is no record of Edith Willkie's reaction, but it is hard to imagine that she was pleased. Publicly she remained completely loyal. The situation was ameliorated by long visits to New York, by her mother, by her friend Mary Steeth, and by the press's reluctance to report the private misbehavior of public figures, a reluctance that, of course, is long gone.

Although Willkie was now moving among the sophisticated, he maintained a natural unpretentious personal style that reflected his rural roots. His suits always seemed rumpled, as did his hair, which as Krock had observed was still cut country style. He owned farms outside Elwood that were managed by Mary Steeth. As he began to be mentioned as a presidential possibility, the inconsistency between his rustic air and his life in the executive suite and among the literati did not escape notice. Harold Ickes called Willkie "the barefoot boy from Wall Street," and Alice Roosevelt Longworth said that his candidacy "sprang from the grass roots all right, from the grass roots of a thousand country clubs."

Longworth was onto something. Not only did Willkie have that apartment on Fifth Avenue, he had an office on a twenty-first floor overlooking Broad and Wall Streets and was a member of the Century, University, Recess, Lawyer's, and Blind Brook clubs. Probably the most striking thing about the movement that began to form around Willkie was the country club complexion of the people who first rallied to his cause. His original supporters were much less midwestern farmer than eastern establishment. Their schools were Ivy League, especially Princeton and Yale. Their jobs were in major media organizations, Wall Street law firms, and financial institutions. They were the educated and financial elite who were most likely, through travel and business, to have developed ties to Europe, especially to England and France, that made them concerned about what was happening abroad.

Politicians and public officials were not common among them. There were however a few exceptions, and they were important. One was Sam Pryor, the Republican national committeeman from Connecticut. Guess where Willkie met him? At the Greenwich Country Club, of course. Willkie was a speaker at an event organized by Pryor that also featured Raymond Baldwin, the governor of Connecticut, for whom Pryor was said to have had presidential hopes. Willkie's performance was clearly more impressive than Baldwin's, enough so that Pryor said he became an instant convert to his cause. Pryor was a member of the committee on arrangements for the 1940 Republican Convention. His power over the distribution of tickets to the convention and his influence over the committee, which was soon to increase dramatically, were to be crucial to Willkie's cause.

Pryor, like Willkie, was a New York corporate executive. He could not be called just a politician. Businessman-politician might be a better description. These words also applied to Charlton MacVeagh. He had worked at J. P. Morgan and was not unconnected. MacVeagh's grandfather had been counsel for the Pennsylvania Railroad, ambassador to Italy, and attorney general. His great uncle was William Howard Taft's secretary of the treasury. His father was counsel for U.S. Steel. His brother would become ambassador to Greece. His roommate at Harvard was Corliss Lamont, son of Thomas Lamont, the head of the House of Morgan. During their college years, MacVeagh and Lamont were reformers as Willkie had been at the University of Indiana. They succeeded in opening up the system so that students who were not members of exclusive clubs like Porcellian could still play a prominent role in extracurricular activities.

After his stint at J. P. Morgan, MacVeagh had become a player in Alf Landon's campaign in 1936. He spent most of the next year traveling around the country strengthening and expanding the connections he had made with party leaders at the state and local level. MacVeagh may have been the first person to urge Willkie to run for president. He made the suggestion over a sandwich at the lunch counter of Wall Street's Exchange Buffet in 1937. He also wrote a monograph that year describing the ideal Republican candidate: a man who sounded remarkably like Wendell Willkie. It was read by Sam Pryor and others that MacVeagh had gotten to know during the 1936 campaign and during his subsequent travels around the country for the Republican National Committee. His boss then was committee chairman John D. M. Hamilton, who remained the chairman in 1940. As such, Hamilton would preside over the opening of the convention and have a major role in determining who its officers would be.

MacVeagh recruited as Willkie's fundraisers Harold Talbott, who would eventually become Eisenhower's air force secretary, and Frank Altchul, the leading partner at the investment banking firm of Lazard Freres and the former chairman of the Republican National Finance Committee. Pryor, MacVeagh, Talbot, and Altchul gave the Willkie campaign at least a handful of people with political experience. This was critical for a campaign that was to be largely composed of amateurs. About the amateurs, Marcia Davenport observed, "Nobody had the slightest idea how you organize the vote of delegates or how you reach delegates in a political convention."

The amateurs, however, were to display an astonishing aptitude for their new calling. Of them, none was more typical or more important than Oren Root Jr., the grandnephew of the former secretary of state, Elihu Root. A twenty-eight-year-old lawyer at Davis Polk, the firm that represented J. P. Morgan, Root had first been attracted to Willkie when he had heard him speak at Root's alma mater, Princeton, in early 1939. He would become the vital force behind a powerful Willkie volunteer movement.

Of all the media converts to the Willkie cause, one of the earliest and surely the most influential was Henry R. Luce, the publisher of *Time, Life,* and *Fortune. Life*'s immense power has already been noted. *Time*'s circulation was much smaller, but no magazine had more influence over middle-class thinking about public affairs. On economic issues, *Fortune*'s voice was equally powerful with the nation's business elite.

As a power couple, Henry and Clare Boothe Luce were preeminent in New York and, in the nation, second only to Franklin and Eleanor Roosevelt. But Clare was no Eleanor Roosevelt. She was acid-tongued and definitely not shy. Insiders used to argue about which of the vicious gossips in her play *The Women* was a self-portrait. Sexually adventurous with a pronounced bias for prominent men like Joseph P. Kennedy and Bernard Baruch, she also had enough pure talent to have become a well-known Broadway playwright and to have served as editor of *Vanity Fair* by the time she and Henry were married in 1935. Their marriage was never conventional, but they were probably the closest in the late '30s and early '40s. One of the bonds that held them together was their shared detestation of Adolf Hitler. They were in Belgium together when the Germans invaded. As Belgium was disintegrating, they made their way to Paris, from which they sent increasingly urgent cables and directives to *Time Life* in New York, trying to awaken their colleagues to the dangerous situation in Europe.

Henry Luce had been born in China, the son of American missionaries. He had a missionary's zeal for the people and causes he believed in that was not diminished by the sophisticates he encountered at Yale. Willkie appealed to him in two ways. He was a businessman and Luce was a romantic about businessmen, especially those he saw as "responsible." Willkie was also anti-Nazi and Luce hated Hitler. Thus, Willkie became Luce's hero. The puffery from Luce's publications was shameless and endless.

On May 13, 1940, *Life* devoted an unprecedented eleven-page spread to Willkie that concluded, "In the opinion of most of the nation's political cognoscenti Wendell Lewis Willkie is by far the ablest man the Republicans could nominate for President in Philadelphia next month." Or how about this: "A vote for Taft is a vote for the Republican party. A vote for Willkie is a vote for the best man to lead the country in a crisis."

Second only to *Life* in popularity among the picture magazines was *Look*. It was owned by John and Gardner Cowles, and they, too, were totally committed to Willkie. Although their support would prove valuable and Willkie would ultimately win the support of an impressive array of media heavyweights, including the *Saturday Evening Post*, *US News*, and the New York *Herald Tribune*, none spoke with more ardor than the publications owned by Henry Luce.

Indeed, a Luce employee was to become Willkie's top advisor. Russell Davenport, the editor of *Fortune* and needless to say also a Yale man, met Willkie in August of 1939 when they were both members of a *Fortune* Roundtable.

The Roundtable was a gathering the editors of *Fortune* held once a month at a resort near New York to which they invited leading industrialists, bankers, union leaders, sociologists, economists, and other prominent figures. Davenport was so impressed by Willkie that when he came home he walked into the house and told his wife Marcia, a writer for the *New Yorker*:

> "I've met the man who ought to be the next president of the United States."
> "Whose idea is this," Marcia asked. "His or yours?"
> "It's spontaneous" was the reply. "You see him and you know it."

Davenport added that he had invited Mr. and Mrs. Willkie to visit the Davenports' summer home in Westport. Concerned about her guests becoming bored, Marcia Davenport also invited some of the brightest of the many bright people who lived in the vicinity, and planned a variety of entertainments including golf, tennis, bridge, and poker.

She need not have bothered. Willkie wanted to talk about ideas, politics and the economy, and the threat that Hitler would plunge Europe into World War II.

> I took [Edith Willkie] upstairs to their rooms and left her to get set-tled while I went down to see what I might offer Mr. Willkie in the way of relaxation and refreshment. He had attended to that himself. He was out on the porch with Russell, sprawled in a wicker arm-chair, one leg thrown over the arm. He had taken off his jacket and necktie and opened the collar of his shirt. He was drinking a whiskey and soda, and chain-smoking cigarettes in such a way that most of the ash fell on his shirt front and most of the butts missed the ashtray at which he threw them. He was talking hard, emphatic, concentrated talk with his blue eyes fixed on Russell's absorbed face.

"And there he sat," continues Marcia, "except when he was at meals or asleep for the whole length of his visit. Tennis, golf, bridge, poker and social chat had no reality for him. Food and wine were tossed down unnoticed. Wendell's leisure such as it was, went in a roiling boil of ideas thrashed out with other brilliant and challenging minds."

With Davenport on board most of the leading players had assem-bled by the end of 1939, but the curtain did not really rise on the Willkie campaign until late March of 1940. Willkie's name was still not mentioned in the polls. Then came the April issue of *Fortune*, which appeared in the latter half of March and was devoted almost entirely to articles for and about Willkie. Davenport, who was still the editor, wrote an editorial praising Willkie for "preaching just plain common sense" that "most people will agree with."

Willkie's article, "We the People," appealed to liberal Republicans by saying "government, federal or state, must not only be responsible for the destitute and the unemployed but for the elementary guarantees of public health," and, remembering that liberal though they may be, they were still Republicans, he added an attack on the New Deal's red tape and mismanagement. (GOP cartoonists like the *Herald Tribune*'s Ding Darling depicted the New Deal as a bunch of wild-eyed professors who were constantly gumming up the machinery of government. Quite a few liberal Republicans accepted the New Deal's reforms but thought they were incompetently managed.)

"We the People" also had a carefully crafted appeal to potential internationalists. Among conservatives, as with most Americans, the most popular foreign country was Finland because it had paid its war debt. So Willkie attacked isolationists for blocking the sale of weapons to Finland. "We should not," he argued, as he broadened his point to apply to England and France without naming them, "relinquish our right to sell whatever we want to those defending themselves from aggression."

Usually, Willkie's public utterances were more explicitly anti-Nazi and pro-Allied. Typical was a speech he gave in May to his old American Legion post in Akron: "England and France constitute our first line of defense against Hitler. If anybody is going to stop Hitler from further aggression, they are the ones to do it. . . . It must therefore be in our advantage to help them in every way we can, short of declaring war." But in the *Fortune* article he was trying to walk a very fine line. Among his liberal supporters were some who were also isolationist. He also saw some potential internationalists among the conservatives, so he was trying to reach out to all possible groups.

He clearly succeeded. "We the People" was quickly reprinted by the *Reader's Digest,* which had the largest circulation of any magazine in the country. Within two weeks of the article's original appearance in *Fortune,* Willkie received more than 2,000 speaking invitations.

CHAPTER THREE

★

THE HURRICANE OF EVENTS

On April 9th, 1940, Willkie appeared on *Information Please,* **a** quiz show starring Clifton Fadiman, Oscar Levant, Franklin P. Adams, and John Kiernan that was the darling of the nation's educated elite. Willkie was a big hit, answering questions with wit and erudition on subjects ranging from Matthew Arnold to Nicholas Nickelby to the presidential use of the pocket veto.

Much more important for Willkie was something that had occurred that morning. Hitler had invaded Denmark and Norway. It was the beginning of what Franklin Roosevelt called the "hurricane of events" that culminated in the fall of France just two and a half months later, events that meant that, just as Willkie was becoming better known, the importance of his anti-Hitler internationalist ideas were being made dramatically clear.

Copenhagen fell in a day, as did all of Denmark. Norway fought back and the Allies quickly came to her aid, putting British troops ashore near Trondheim, and British and French troops around Narvik in the far north. The Norwegian troops fought bravely, but were ill equipped, as were the Allies, especially the British contingent at Trondheim. Within a few weeks almost all of Norway fell with only a small foothold at Narvik remaining in Allied hands.

The war in Finland was over. Finally overwhelmed by the enormous Red Army, Finland had been forced to make peace, yielding large chunks of territory to the Soviet Union. Now there was no other war news to distract Americans from the Nazi threat. That threat became even more ominous on May 10, when a banner headline on the front page of the *Charleston Gazette* announced—as did almost every other front page in America—"Nazis invade Belgium, Holland."

In England, Neville Chamberlain had resigned and been replaced by Winston Churchill. Earlier, the French government of Edward Daladier had fallen and had been replaced by one headed by Paul Reynaud. Reynaud, like Churchill, was a determined foe of the Nazis, while the reputations of the men they replaced had been forever stained by their signatures to the Munich Pact that had surrendered Czechoslovakia to Hitler.

But even the most dedicated leaders could not stem the swift German advance. Holland was overrun in four days. A supposedly impregnable Belgian fortress, Eben Emmael, fell in just twenty-four hours. More alarming was the news on May 14–15 that German tanks had broken through the French defenses at Sedan and were racing across northern France toward the English Channel. By May 28, they reached their goal, cutting off British and French forces still in Belgium, into which they had imprudently advanced when the Germans first attacked. The peril of the Allied troops was exacerbated by the sudden surrender of the Belgian army on May 28. The trapped British and French forces retreated to a tiny enclave around Dunkirk.

The end of May and the first days of June witnessed the near-miraculous evacuation of 250,000 British soldiers and 75,000 French troops. The Royal Air Force fought off the German planes attempting to strafe the beaches and evacuation ships. The troops were saved, but their equipment had to be left behind.

The beginning of June also saw the Allies abandon the last foothold in Norway and the main French army retreat toward the Seine. On the 10th of June the French government fled Paris for Tours.

Reynaud begged Churchill and Roosevelt for the planes desperately needed to protect French troops from the relentless pounding they were taking from the German air force. In turn, Churchill implored Roosevelt to re-equip the British army that had been rescued from the beaches of Dunkirk. Churchill and Roosevelt faced similar dilemmas. Should Churchill risk his remaining planes on a France that was probably doomed anyway? Should Roosevelt strip American arsenals to help Britain when Britain seemed unlikely to be able to stand alone against Hitler?

Churchill sent a few planes to France but kept twenty-five RAF squadrons in England. This embittered the French, and strengthened the hand of those Frenchmen who wanted to make peace with the Germans. Roosevelt acted with more generosity, although it must be said that he did so with an ocean to protect his country instead of the English Channel. A French aircraft carrier was loaded with forty-four of the latest dive-bombers, which Roosevelt had managed to pry away from the US Navy, and sixty-two additional military planes. Other ships carried 500,000 rifles, 80,000 machine guns, and 500 field artillery guns (plus plenty of ammunition) to England.

The aircraft carrier did not make it in time. It was in the mid-Atlantic when the Battle of France ended. Diverted to Martinique, the ship and its precious cargo spent the rest of the war in port—but the aid to Britain got through. The number of rifles considerably exceeded those lost at Dunkirk and not only enabled the British to re-equip their soldiers but helped them to arm a newly-formed Home Guard.

"All this reads easily now," Churchill wrote after the war, "but at that time it was a sublime act of faith and leadership for the United States to deprive themselves of this very considerable mass of arms for the sake of a country which many deemed already beaten."

No factor was more important than the rapid growth of the Willkie movement in giving Roosevelt the courage to take this monumental risk. Willkie's rise showed that a substantial group of Republicans and many of the party's most powerful media allies would support, rather than oppose, the president's foreign policy in an election year. It also meant that the opposition of the isolationist Republicans might at least temporarily be muted by the possibility that their party's nominee could turn out to be Willkie.

In France, Paul Reynaud had resigned, his fighting spirit a victim of the relentless defeatism of Marshall Henri Petain—the hero of World War I who had lost the will to fight the second but whose influence remained immense—and by the nearly hysterical anti-British counsel of Reynaud's mistress, Countess Helene dePortes. When Reynaud resigned he was replaced by Petain, who in a few days would agree to an armistice with Germany.

England would soon stand alone. Against it was the seemingly invincible German army, supported by the Luftwaffe—fresh from its terrifying devastation of Warsaw and Rotterdam—and a submarine force that seemed capable of cutting off English supplies, all joined (after Mussolini's June 10th declaration of war against the Allies) by the Italian army, air force, and navy. The Italian army had taken control of Libya and, thus, threatened a second front against British forces in Egypt. The Italian navy seemed capable of disputing the Royal Navy's control of the Mediterranean.

I remember listening to Roosevelt speak the day Mussolini attacked France. The occasion was his son Franklin Roosevelt Jr.'s graduation from the University of Virginia Law School, and FDR seized it to declare "[T]he hand that held the dagger has plunged it into the back of his neighbor." I was struck by Roosevelt's courage. My mother and father both said it could seriously hurt him with Italian voters.

Like millions of Americans, I was worried about what was happening in Europe. If England fell, what would happen to us? I began to think about going to military school to prepare myself. FDR told reporters—off the record—that he feared we might be left standing alone. Practically everyone was shocked by the collapse of France and the loss of the European continent. But what was bad news for this country and much of the world was good news for the Willkie candidacy. He was the only Republican candidate who had clearly understood the Nazis' threat. He stood out as a man whose time had come.

As the "hurricane of events" began in Norway and Denmark, the Willkie team sprang into action. In April, Davenport resigned from *Fortune.* He and MacVeagh, having already opened a headquarters in New York's Murray Hill Hotel, enlisted the help of advertising giants

Bruce Barton of Batten, Barton, Durstine, and Osborne and John Orr Young of Young and Rubicam to help sell Willkie. The Edison Electric Institute, the utility trade association, recruited utility company employees around the country as members of Willkie Clubs.

Oren Root was the man behind these clubs. Since hearing Willkie make that speech at Princeton in 1939, Root had become more and more interested in the possibility of a Willkie presidential candidacy. By the spring of 1940, he was convinced that Willkie was the man—and wondered how many others shared his feeling. He decided to test the waters with a mailing to the Princeton class of 1924 and the Yale class of 1925. He chose Princeton because he had a copy of its alumni directory and Yale because his officemate at Davis Polk had Yale's directory. The years were selected because "the groups consisted of men approximately 35 years old—old enough to be seriously concerned about the country and the world and yet young enough not to be set in their thinking."

Using material from Willkie's *Fortune* article Root cobbled together what he called a Declaration, which began "We the undersigned people of the United States believe that Wendell Willkie should be elected President of the United States" and concluded with spaces for thirty signatures and with instructions on how to order more copies of the declaration. The response was instantaneous and enormous. Recipients not only signed up but ordered more copies to send to their friends. By the beginning of May, Root had collected more than 200,000 signatures for his petitions and had organized them into Willkie Clubs throughout the nation. Marcia Davenport called him "the brains and the core of the volunteer movement."

Root's efforts attracted considerable publicity, including articles in the *New York Times* and *Herald Tribune*. The night the first story appeared, Root was having dinner with his mother when he received a phone call from Thomas Lamont.

I assumed one of my friends was pulling my leg since Mr. Lamont was the senior partner of J. P. Morgan and Company and it seemed most unlikely that a man of his importance would telephone me for any reason. However, it was indeed Mr. Lamont and he told me that at that moment he was having dinner at the Economic Club of New York with Wendell Willkie who was president of the club. What had transpired between him and Willkie, apparently, was a discussion of my highly publicized activity and of the best method of stopping me. I learned later that Willkie expressed a reluctance to talk to me since he feared I was probably an incompetent and at worst an adventurer with the danger that I would misuse his call for the sake of further publicity. When it turned out that the law firm for which I worked [Davis Polk] had Mr. Lamont's bank as one of its principle clients, it was agreed that the telephone call could come more safely from him.

Lamont, unable to persuade Root but convinced that he was not a nut, put Willkie on the phone. Willkie, when he realized his own efforts at persuasion had failed, asked Root if he would meet with Russell Davenport.

Why was Willkie determined to stop Root's efforts? The reason, according to Root, was that "Willkie had his own ideas about how to obtain the Republican nomination and my unauthorized publicity was seriously threatening a strategy that had been carefully thought out and had been in process for many months." The principal architect of that policy was Willkie himself; other participants included Russell Davenport and his wife Marcia, Charlton MacVeagh, and Harold Talbott. This group had been meeting at regular intervals, usually in Davenport's apartment in Manhattan, where MacVeagh was constantly on the phone compiling a virtual book on the already selected or potential delegates to be ready in case lightning struck.

But to get lightning to strike, Root explained,

The plan to which they had agreed was to give Willkie as much publicity as possible in fields of public concern unrelated to the nominating process itself, in the hope that the convention would ultimately deadlock on the leading candidates and would turn to Willkie as a dark horse.

The basic essential of this strategy was that it be low key. Above all there was never to be any mention of the true objective, the Republican nomination. The Willkie name and Willkie's philosophy were to be publicized, but not in terms of the political process and certainly not in any way to rouse the resentment of those who in the event of a deadlocked convention would hopefully turn to him.

So, the morning after Root's conversation with Lamont and Willkie, he was called by Davenport, who "asked me to meet him under the clock at the Biltmore. It was a delightful lunch because Russell Davenport was altogether a delightful man. We ate together, we drank wine, and talked for two hours and a half. The upshot was that Davenport was convinced that my efforts should continue."

Root then had a breakfast meeting with Willkie and Davenport at the University Club—that's the one at Fifth Avenue and 54th Street that used to be a staple of New Yorker cartoons. Root came away with a press release in which Willkie said that "he will not approve or disapprove Root's activities." That was all Root needed.

He was approved enough to come under the Willkie team's protection. When one of his law partners complained about Root's political activities and led an effort to force him to resign that was supposed to culminate in a confrontation on a Monday morning, Root called Thomas Lamont, who agreed to see him the preceding Sunday at Lamont's New Jersey home. Root told Lamont about his enemy at the firm and asked if Lamont, the firm's principle client, would make a call on his behalf. The next morning there was no showdown meeting. Instead Root's antagonist strolled into his office saying "[W]ell Oren my boy, how's the great politician feeling today? You are doing a wonderful job. Keep it up."

Root was right about the Davenport-Willkie strategy. Davenport's battle plan revealed itself in a letter he wrote the columnist Raymond Clapper "[Y]ou will point out that Mr. Willkie is not a political reality. Check. But why the hell don't we make him one?" Davenport believed that the media could turn Willkie into a serious candidate. His strategy was followed when, in early April, Willkie charmed the nation's top political reporters at the Gridiron Club Dinner in Washington. Then, on April 25th, he spoke to their bosses, the American Newspaper Publishers Association, at the Waldorf in New York.

Two nights before, at a dinner given by the Davenports, John and Gardner Cowles amended the Davenport strategy. They told Willkie that he couldn't count on the media alone. The media could get him considered, but to win the nomination he had to get out and get to know the delegates. They invited him to come to St. Paul and Des Moines, where they were influential because they owned the leading newspapers in Minnesota and in Iowa.

Willkie's appearance in St. Paul was to prove a turning point in the campaign. He spoke from a prepared text for thirty minutes and thoroughly bored his audience. Then, he threw away his script and spoke spontaneously. "Some damn fool told me I had to read a speech. Now let me tell you what I think." The result was electrifying. Four Minnesota delegates announced on the spot that they would vote for Willkie at the convention. And Harold Stassen, Minnesota's young governor, who was to be the keynote speaker at the convention, said that he now leaned toward Willkie.

Willkie became a complete convert to grassroots campaigning. One trip he took to New England was typical of the effort he made. Arriving at Boston's Old South Station on June 13, he was taken to the Statler's Hotel, where he lunched with thirty-one of the thirty-four delegates to the Republican convention. That night he delivered a speech to more than 8,000 Massachusetts Republicans.

He left for Hartford on Sam Pryor's private plane with twenty-two Massachusetts delegate votes pledged to him on the second ballot, after they had taken care of their obligation to House Minority Leader Joe Martin as the state's first ballot favorite son. (The favorite son designation enabled a state's delegates to honor one of their own on the first ballot while preserving their choice of a major candidate for later on.) After a lunch at a Hartford hotel, during which he demonstrated that he was mastering the art of politics by declaring "[I]f elected president I would like to have Governor Baldwin and

Sam Pryor with me in Washington," he left for Providence with all sixteen Connecticut second ballot votes in his pocket. In Rhode Island, Governor William Vanderbilt took Willkie to his Newport estate and promised him the support of at least six of the eight Rhode Island delegates.

Willkie also campaigned in Nebraska, Kansas, California, Ohio, Missouri, and back home in Indiana. His old friends and neighbors were getting excited about their native son. They even organized a big event at New York's Manhattan Center to demonstrate to the country that they were behind Willkie.

Charles Halleck, a popular congressman from Indiana, agreed to place Willkie's name for nomination in Philadelphia. Halleck was recognized as one of the most promising young Republican congressmen. (He later became Republican leader of the House.) He and Willkie had several things in common. They were both from the same state, both had attended the state university, and both had been members of the same fraternity, Beta Theta Pi. An even greater bond was that they were both part of the anti-Klan faction. This was an important distinction among Indiana Republicans and a usually reliable way of distinguishing the good guys from the bad guys.

But even if Halleck was sympathetic to Willkie's candidacy, he still had to face the fact that his support of his fraternity brother could hurt him politically by alienating the party's conservative isolationists. He sought the advice of Joe Martin, the House minority leader. Martin, who had himself declined the honor when Sam Pryor had asked him to nominate Willkie, told Halleck: "If I were you, Charlie, I'd do it. You're a young fellow looking for a place in the sun. It won't hurt you any. In fact it will give you a lot of prestige. Of course your man isn't going to [win]." Halleck, who had earlier offered to back Martin if Martin should be a candidate, then replied, "Well what I first said about backing you still goes."

"Oh I'm not a candidate," Martin answered. Martin may have held in the back of his mind the possibility of emerging as the choice of a deadlocked convention but his answer opened the way for Halleck to nominate Willkie. So on June 12, before Willkie made a speech at the National Press Club, they met for a drink and Halleck told him. "Wendell, there's a story out that you're running and I'm nominating you and I just want you to know that if you're ready to go I'm ready to go."

During his speech, a speech that was off the record, Willkie halted at one point and said, "Now this is on the record. I'm going to be a candidate for president and I shall be put in nomination by my fellow Hoosier, Charles Halleck of Indiana."

It was not only his fellow Indianans who persuaded Halleck; it was also Charlton MacVeagh whose political counsel Halleck respected. MacVeagh had also persuaded his old boss, John D. M. Hamilton, the Republican National Committee chairman, to support Willkie. Now MacVeagh and Hamilton persuaded Joe Martin, who was to be the convention's permanent chairman, if not to support Willkie, then to at least be favorably enough disposed that he would not make any rulings as chairman that would hurt Willkie's chances.

Then, on May 16th, came the event that sealed the Willkie forces' control of the convention machinery. Ralph Williams, the Taft supporter who chaired the committee of arrangements, which controlled the distribution of tickets to the convention, was presiding over a meeting of the committee at the Bellevue-Stratford Hotel in Philadelphia when he suddenly suffered a stroke. His replacement was Vice Chairman Sam Pryor, the pro-Willkie committeeman from Connecticut.

One reason that the professional politicians were paying attention to Willkie was the growing enthusiasm around the country that his speeches and all of the favorable publicity were creating. On May 8th, he had 3 percent support in polls of Republicans; by June 21, it was 29 percent. During that same period, the leader, Thomas Dewey, fell from 67 to 47 percent. With the grave international situation seeming to require a more seasoned leader, Dewey's youth had begun to hurt.

Willkie's frank talk gave him the aura of the non-politician. He was Mr. Smith bound for Washington. In addition, as he displayed his appeal to independent voters, he began to smell like a winner.

This helped him with people like Roy Howard, the publisher of the Scripps-Howard newspapers, who was much more conservative than Willkie but who was desperate for a candidate who could beat FDR. Willkie also had something else—his rugged good looks made him what David Halberstam called "the rarest thing in those days, a Republican with sex appeal."

Although Root and Davenport were pleased by the large number of recruits to the Willkie clubs, they were worried about the predominantly northeastern elite character of the movement. They decided to find a more down-home American co-sponsor for the clubs. Root was dispatched to Oscaloosa, Iowa—Root says he didn't know whether "Davenport had ever been there or if he simply plucked the name from his poetic imagination"—to launch a truly grassroots movement. He arrived in Oscaloosa at 7:30 AM, and by noon he had recruited a young lawyer, Charles A. Williams Jr., to spearhead the effort. Williams was willing because, like many Americans outside New York, he knew from the newspapers, magazines, and radio about the growing danger posed by Hitler and about an exciting newcomer to politics named Wendell Willkie who understood that danger.

The grassroots movement spread rapidly, as Willkie clubs were organized throughout the country, including in my hometown, Charleston. The local leader was a coal company executive, L. Newton Thomas. As a Cornell graduate, he fit the early Willkie supporter profile but he was joined by many others who did not have Ivy League pedigrees, including a thirteen-year-old girl who lived in the apartment above ours. She worked so devotedly for Willkie that she was invited to sit on the platform when he came to Charleston to speak. Thomas opened his headquarters in Room 1502 of the Kanawha Valley Bank Building and on June 19th ran a full-page ad in the *Daily Mail* urging readers to send telegrams to the West Virginia delegation to the Republican National Convention, and reminding them that the telegram would cost only fifty cents, then saying that it would "prove to be the most important fifty cents you have ever spent" because "Wendell Willkie is the only Republican who can be elected in November."

Columns urging Willkie's nomination had been running in the local papers—written by the liberal Raymond Clapper in the *Gazette* and by the conservative Frank Kent in the *Mail*. The *Mail* reprinted *Look* magazine's endorsement of Willkie and its own editorials leaned increasingly toward the Indianan. Other journalists, however, while acknowledging the growing enthusiasm for Willkie, noted that he was far behind the leader. Damon Runyon, who was already famous as the author of stories about Broadway's *Guys and Dolls*, and who was both a reporter and a columnist for the International News Service, predicted on June 19 that "Mr. Dewey's first ballot strength in Philadelphia would knock the toupees off the Republicans," adding, "we now make it well over our original estimate of 400 delegates. Far enough over that figure that the addition of just a couple of moderately sized delegations would nominate him on the first ballot."

The West Virginia delegation was reported as having seven votes leaning or committed to Dewey, eight for Taft, and one for Willkie. D. Boone Dawson, Charleston mayor and the Republican gubernatorial nominee, issued this statement: "Seventy-five percent of the people of West Virginia want Dewey and the other 25 percent don't want Willkie." This immediately elicited an indignant response from L. Newton Thomas and twenty-two other Charlestonians who were Willkie boosters. Walter Hallanan, West Virginia's Republican National Committeeman, announced that he supported Willkie. The West Virginia Young Republican organization came out for Willkie. Lewis Welch, the *Daily Mail*'s political columnist, noted that if the convention went to a fifth or sixth ballot that the state's delegation could go for Willkie.

.   .   .

The bad news from Europe had become worse during the week before the convention. All of the first-run movies were accompanied by newsreels that showed French roads clogged with refugees fleeing the German advance and being attacked by Stuka dive-bombers. Triumphant German troops were shown parading through Paris, while the once mighty French army was depicted in disarray, either retreating or with their hands up in surrender. After Marshal Petain replaced Paul Reynaud on June 18, United Press (UP) reported "Petain's first act as the new premier of France, a plea to Germany for cessation of hostilities, was communicated through his friend and one-time military pupil, Generalissimo Francisco Franco." On the same day, UP reported that Churchill was conceding that the Battle of France was lost.

The situation was so dire, the emergency so immediate, that Roosevelt was able to persuade two prominent Republicans, former Secretary of State Henry Stimson, and Frank Knox, the publisher of the *Chicago Daily News* and the 1936 Republican vice-presidential candidate, to be secretary of war and secretary of the navy, respectively.

This news brought consternation to the Republicans beginning to gather in Philadelphia for the next week's convention where Knox had been scheduled to participate as a delegate from Illinois. The isolationists were indignantly proposing to read Stimson and Knox out of the party. But more thoughtful Republicans realized that if they did not nominate a candidate as opposed to Hitler as FDR was, then there would be more defections.

On that same Sunday, the day before the convention's start, the headline in the *Charleston Gazette* announced, "France Signs Armistice With Germany," accompanied by a "radio photo" (a term used at the time to describe the latest technology for transmitting photographs) of the actual signing in the railroad car at Compeigne that had been the scene of Germany's capitulation at the end of World War I. In Philadelphia, arriving delegates saw headlines like the *Record*'s "France Signs on Hitler's Terms." The armistice surrendered Paris and Northern France as well as a broad swath along the Atlantic coast from Belgium to the Spanish border.

The *Record* also reported that the House of Representatives had passed a record $4 billion appropriation for the navy the day before. There could be no more powerful evidence of the gravity of the world situation than that the members of the House deemed it necessary to act on a Saturday.

PART TWO

THE GREATEST CONVENTION

CHAPTER FOUR

★

"JUST THE NEXT PRESIDENT
OF THE UNITED STATES"

The Philadelphia Convention Hall stood for over seventy years.
Anyone headed south on the train from New York, could see it on
their right just after the train passed the University of Pennsylvania as
it left Philadelphia. Headed north, it would have been on the left before reaching the station and just after passing Children's Hospital.
Rectangular in shape—265 feet long and 145 feet wide—it was gray in
color, had a curved green roof, and looked exactly like what it was, a
very large auditorium. In 1936, it was the scene of Franklin Roosevelt's
nomination for his second term. In 1948, it was where Harry Truman
woke up a lethargic, defeatist convention and began to kindle the excitement that led to his surprise defeat of Thomas E. Dewey.

If the building was air-conditioned, the fact escaped the notice of
those attending the 1940 Republican Convention. Although outside
temperatures began the week on the cool side and barely reached
eighty degrees by Friday, the convention hall was totally exposed to
the sun all day, there being no tall buildings around it to provide
shade. Furthermore, a space designed to accommodate 14,000 was
often jammed with many more warm bodies. Add the hot glare of
lights that were there for the newsreel cameras—lights so bright that
some delegates began to wear sunglasses—and the building became,
in the words of Marcia Davenport, "a filthy, sweaty hell of sealed-in
heat."

Having been forewarned, Davenport says, "I went to Macy's Basement and bought half a dozen of the plainest, cheapest, white summer
dresses they had which cost about four dollars a piece. Each night I
threw one away and started out with a fresh one in the morning."

On Thursday, when the outside humidity rose and the inside heat
was at its worst, eight tons of ice were placed in the hall cooling system. "The rumor spread that now it would be cool," United Press
reported. "It wasn't. It was hot."

As for the number of people crammed into the hall, the figures
given by various newspapers range from highs of 16,000 to 22,000 for
the convention's most crowded night. Which was right? The hall's
seating capacity of 14,000 would seem to support the lower figure.
So would the fact that it was used by the Philadelphia papers, whose
readers' knowledge of local reality may have helped them resist the
tendency of their New York brethren to hype the number.

On the other hand, anyone who has attended a convention, especially one occurring before television imposed some measure of deco-
rum, knows that the number of seats is almost irrelevant. Aisles and
hallways are constantly crowded. For those who haven't been there,
it is hard to imagine the amount of milling around that goes on.
Except during the most eloquent and highly anticipated speeches,
schmoozing never stops as delegates visit other delegates and alternates, talk to reporters in the aisles, and visit food stands and rest-
rooms. Floor passes are often slipped to friends in the gallery who
get the thrill of going out onto the floor for awhile. In 1940, security
was lax to the point of nonexistence, and no one has ever figured
out just how many standing room tickets were distributed by
Willkie's man, Sam Pryor.

At the south end of the hall, there was a deep blue curtain at the
rear of a stage that had been expanded to accommodate officials and
distinguished guests. From there, a short walkway led to the speakers' rostrum, on either side of which were typewriter tables and
chairs to accommodate 851 reporters. They were separated by a ten-
foot-wide aisle from the delegates. Maine and Vermont got the best
seats because they had been the only states carried by Alf Landon in

the Roosevelt landslide of 1936. The seats for the delegates and alternates were divided into eight sections, separated by wide aisles down which delegates could parade in the demonstrations that traditionally followed the nomination of each candidate.

In front of the space reserved for each delegation was a standard with the name of the state in white on a blue background topped by a gray elephant holding an American flag in its upraised trunk. These were the standards that delegates would carry as they marched around the floor in demonstrations designed to show the strength of their candidate's support. The delegates on the floor were surrounded on three sides by a large horseshoe-shaped balcony sometimes referred to as the gallery. Traditionally, tickets to the balcony were allotted, often through the state's national committeeman, to friends and relatives of the delegates and other party loyalists. It is hard to think of any other convention in American history in which the occupants of the balcony played a more meaningful role than they did at this one—never was the identity of those who received tickets more important.

When the convention wasn't in session, the delegates adjourned to the air-conditioned lobbies and bars of their hotels. The official headquarters of the convention was the Bellevue Stratford. Taft's 102-room headquarters was at the Benjamin Franklin, Dewey's seventy-eight rooms were at the Walton, and Vandenberg's forty-eight at the Adelphia. Russell Davenport told the press that Willkie had just two rooms at the Benjamin Franklin and conned reporters into favorably comparing Willkie's modest quarters to the grander accommodations of the other candidates. But, in truth, Willkie had five rooms at the Benjamin Franklin plus his personal suite at the Warwick and separate headquarters at the Land Title building and a storefront for Oren Root's volunteers. Columnist Drew Pearson claimed that Willkie had six headquarters in all.

As for the city itself, Philadelphia had been the site of the first Republican convention in 1856, and it quickly became a GOP stronghold. Since the Civil War, only one of its mayors had not been a Republican. It was the home of the *Saturday Evening Post*, which its competitor, *Life*, described as "the biggest Republican magazine in the US." Its two million people made it the third largest city in the country. It was a conservative city with a conservative skyline dominated by the statue of Benjamin Franklin atop City Hall. Its leaders dined at conservative clubs and at the Old Bookbinders' restaurant, and their favorite dish, usually served at breakfast, was scrapple, a concoction of ground pork, pork fat, and cornmeal that has failed to find favor outside Pennsylvania.

Conventions in those days were longer, this one scheduled to last five days—Monday through Friday. The local businessmen who had helped finance the convention needed time to profit from their investment. And time had to be allowed for balloting. Back then, conventions actually chose candidates instead of ratifying the verdict of the primaries. Sometimes that process took multiple ballots during which the roll of states was called and each delegation chairman would announce his state's vote. Modern conventions are shorter because their results have been pre-determined by primaries. Although there were some primaries in 1940, there were not enough to dominate the process. The last time since then that the Republicans have even threatened to have multiple ballots was the Reagan-Ford race in 1976 and before that Taft-Eisenhower in 1952. For the Democrats, the last close race was between John Kennedy and Estes Kefauver for the vice-presidential nomination in 1956.

On Monday, the main event would be the keynote address given by Harold Stassen, the youthful governor of Minnesota. On Tuesday it would be a speech by former president Herbert Hoover. On Wednesday would come the nomination for president, followed on Thursday by presidential balloting and on Friday the vice-presidential nominations and balloting.

This convention's guests would include the wives of all the major candidates, four Taft sons, two Vandenberg daughters, three Willkie brothers, Willkie's son, Phillip (who was in transition between Princeton and Columbia Law), the widows of two presidents, Mrs. Benjamin Harrison and Mrs. William Howard Taft, and Theodore Roosevelt's daughter, Alice Longworth, and two of his sons, Archie, who was for Willkie, and Theodore Jr., who was a Dewey delegate.

Hugh D. Auchinloss, Jacqueline Kennedy's stepfather, was a delegate from Virginia. Other delegates included future Senate Republican leader Everett Dirksen and future House Republican leader Charles Halleck. Their "Ev and Charlie Show" would become one of the most regularly watched press conferences in the '50s and '60s. Halleck's successor as House Republican leader and a future vice president and president, twenty-six-year-old Gerald Ford, sat in the balcony with his girlfriend, the New York model Phyllis Brown, rooting for Wendell Willkie, for whom he had been serving as a volunteer worker in New York.

The Indiana delegation included Will Hays, better known as the man who censored the movies and was responsible for movie marrieds sleeping in twin beds and for actresses like Carole Lombard, Claudette Colbert, and Ginger Rogers having to wear bras—only Jean Harlow managed to evade the edict.

Big-foot journalists including Arthur Krock, Dorothy Thompson, Walter Lippmann, and Damon Runyon were all over the place, but also present were some unknowns who would later become prominent—Chalmers Roberts, who was to reign for several decades as the *Washington Post*'s leading reporter, paid his own way to Philadelphia to cover the convention for the *Washington Daily News*. Herbert Block, later to become the nation's premiere political cartoonist with the *Washington Post*, covered the convention for Scripps-Howard.

Prominent radio reporters, like NBC's H. V. Kaltenborn and CBS's Elmer Davis, covered the convention for the networks from booths tucked under the stage's proscenium arch. NBC, which had originally scheduled ten hours or so for the proceedings, ended up devoting twenty-nine hours and twenty-six minutes to the convention. Television made its first appearance with an estimated 50,000 viewers, who were receiving transmission in Philadelphia, New York City, Schenectady, and at the RCA exhibit at the World's Fair.

Among the thousands of other spectators was nine-year-old Tom Eagleton, whose father was a Republican from Missouri but who would later represent the state for eighteen years as a Democratic United States Senator. Tom was for Dewey because "Dewey had the best campaign buttons." Eleven-year-old James Billington, destined to become the Librarian of Congress, was then so dedicated to Willkie's internationalism that he wrote to the editor of the *Philadelphia Evening Bulletin,* earnestly advocating the Indianan's cause. Future ambassador William McCormick Blair, Jr., then just out of Stanford, came to root for Dewey but ended up chanting "We Want Willkie." Also present was Walter Johnson, considered by many to be the greatest right-handed pitcher in the history of baseball. He was a Republican candidate for congress in Maryland that year. Fifteen-year-old Gore Vidal was there with his grandfather, T. P. Gore, the blind former Democratic senator from Oklahoma whose denunciations of the New Deal had won him an invitation to sit on the speakers' platform.

The delegates had been selected in primaries or in state conventions. On the first ballot a few were pledged to vote for the candidate who had won their presidential primary. Most, however, were free to vote for the candidate of their choice, although this freedom could be subject to the wishes of a political boss or the state's governor. Most of the delegates were not well known nationally then or now. But they were usually prominent in their hometowns or were on their way to becoming prominent. The latter helps explain why they wanted to be delegates. It certified their status in the party, improving both their political and their business prospects. They also wanted to have a voice in determining the party's nominee. This motive was especially strong in 1940 when war or peace seemed to many to be the issue.

A yen to travel was another motive. This was a simpler age and going to the big city was a major event for many people. Philadelphia had tourist attractions like Independence Hall and the fancy movie palaces that did not exist in smaller towns. The director John Huston later captured what for most Americans was the magic of these theaters with the "Let's go to the movies" scene in his film version of the musical comedy *Annie* that depicts the orphan girl being taken to Radio City Music Hall by Daddy Warbucks.

Philadelphia also had two major league baseball teams—the Phillies and the Athletics—at a time when there were only sixteen in the entire country and when baseball still reigned supreme as the country's favorite professional sport. The chance to see a major-league game was a major element in the appeal of a big city, especially in the eyes of the American male.

Another attraction of considerable importance, again especially to the men, were Philadelphia's bars. In quite a few states, Virginia and Iowa among them, you could not buy liquor by the drink. It is not surprising that, when the *Philadelphia Record* interviewed delegate Hugh Edgar Exum of Amarillo, Texas, he complained that his was the only convention hotel that did not have a bar. The *Record*'s photograph of his room showed how he had adjusted to this deprivation: A quart of Old Taylor bourbon whiskey sat on the bureau.

.   .   .

On the Friday before the convention began, most delegates had not yet arrived in Philadelphia. The only convention activity was the meetings of the various committees. Friday, however, was the occasion of one important decision made by the Republican National Committee. It voted to deny delegate representation to future national conventions to any district that failed to get at least 1,000 Republican voters to the polls in the previous national or state election.

The GOP was so weak in many southern states that the main reward for its active members was to be chosen as a delegate to the national convention, where the delegate's vote could be exchanged for cash. It is thus understandable that the votes of southern delegates were often greeted with suspicion. During this convention, when one Georgia delegate failed to answer a roll-call vote, the commonly accepted explanation was that he had sold his vote to two candidates and feared retribution from one if he voted for the other.

On Saturday, the top three candidates—Dewey, Taft, and Willkie—arrived in Philadelphia, "each predicting victory and each radiating good will towards the others," according to the New York *Herald-Tribune*'s Joseph Driscoll. They arrived by train, as did most of the delegates. (Others came by automobile; only a handful by plane.) Dewey and Taft proceeded to their respective hotels, Dewey to the

Walton and Taft to the Benjamin Franklin, where Taft's supporters had placed decorative elephants wearing red and yellow circus blankets labeled "Taft" in silver letters in the lobby and in front of the hotel. Both men held press conferences. Dewey said he favored aiding Britain but only with "surplus" materials, emphasizing the word surplus. And he called Stimson and Knox "competent" but "interventionists." Taft said that he expected to be nominated after a "normal" number of ballots, which he later described as three or four, that he was not interested in making any deals, and that he would rather remain a senator than become a vice president.

Willkie was met at the 30th Street station by Charles Halleck and Russell Davenport and a half dozen other Willkie workers and a dozen or so reporters and photographers. "The book," wrote Warren Moscow, who covered this and many other conventions for the *New York Times*, "called for a cavalcade of cars to scream itself back to the candidate's hotel attracting attention by the sheer decibel count of its sirens." Instead Willkie told reporters, "[I]t's such a beautiful day I'm going to send Mrs. Willkie on to the hotel to unpack and I'm going to walk there to see what this convention city looks like. If you have any questions, why don't you walk along with me?" His first stop was his headquarters on the seventh floor at the Land Title Building on Broad Street. "There was a crowd waiting," wrote Joseph P. McLaughlin of the *Philadelphia Record*. "They broke into a loud cheer as Willkie, straw hat in hand, stepped off the elevator."

By the time Willkie departed, word of his presence had spread and a crowd had gathered in front of the Land Title Building. Willkie walked from there to Oren Root's storefront in a former Child's restaurant at Broad and Market "with photographers scurrying ahead and a rapidly growing throng at his side," reported Ernest Crozier of the *Herald Tribune*, who explained the growth of the crowd with this dialogue.

"What's all the excitement," a passing pedestrian asked. "The next president of the United States," came the reply. "That's all—just the next president of the United States."

Willkie's regard for the press was high—witness his cultivation of

Van Doren, Davenport, the Reids, the Luces, and the Cowles—so he sought to charm reporters with frank answers to their questions as they tagged along beside him. It seems unlikely that he did not recognize Damon Runyon in their midst. Runyon had earlier that week predicted a Dewey victory but Willkie seemed to sense what he had to do to change the reporter's mind.

When the crowd reached the convention headquarters at the Bellevue Stratford hotel, Willkie, Runyon later wrote, "headed right to the bar."

He was so big and tough that he never budged an inch from the bar while everybody was scrimming and scrounging trying to get something . . . then he said "let's have another" and began shaking hands all around and every time he shook hands he ruined somebody's dukes. He had a handshake like a guy squeezing an orange. He left the Bellevue and went all over town and he left hundreds of guys so they couldn't pick up a fork for a week.

Later in his life, Willkie's drinking would be considered a problem, but that day it endeared him to Runyon and others in the crowd; it was an era when hard drinking was seen as a sign of masculinity.

Runyon quickly revised his opinion that Dewey would win. In an article published the next day he wrote "[E]ven the most enthusiastic supporters of the young New York District Attorney have to admit that there has been a distinct veering away from him in sentiment among the voters in the past forty-eight hours."

After leaving the bar, Willkie met with delegates that he was trying to win over, with leaders from Pennsylvania (then the second largest state in the union, the state that offered the prize of seventy-two of the convention's 1000 delegates) preeminent among them. They were pledged on the early ballots to Governor Arthur James as a favorite son and were supposed to be leaning toward Taft on the later ballots. Although the favorite son designation was usually intended as an honorific, James took his candidacy more seriously. He told the *Philadelphia Inquirer* "Pennsylvania delegates will be for me on the first ballot and for many more after that." Willkie however was said to have significant support in the western part of the state.

John Wise, editor of the *Butler Eagle,* published in a town near Pittsburgh, for example, reported that fourteen of the state's seventy-two votes would ultimately go to Willkie, citing the example of one delegate, who "indicated he may stay with James for several ballots to see what happens but after that, if the Governor's chances fail to improve he will switch his vote to Willkie." The *Philadelphia Record* reported that two Pennsylvania delegates had come close to fisticuffs in the lobby of the Bellevue Stratford—"What's this I hear about you being off the reservation?" said a James loyalist to Frank Harris of Pittsburgh, a rumored strayer to Willkie.

"I'll have you know sir, I keep my pledges," replied Harris.

"What kind of poker game are you trying to play with me," asked the James man. "If you're off the reservation, get off. Look here, you're not looking at me straight," he added as he chucked Harris under the chin.

"Hands off me Sir, keep your hands off me," replied Harris, who the *Record* reported was "trembling with anger."

Willkie, however, did not appear to have enhanced his prospects of winning Pennsylvania when, speaking of the state's reputed Republican boss, he told the *Evening Bulletin*: "I don't like Joe Pew's brand of politics and would not allow myself to become part of this policy of returning to the days of Harding and Coolidge." His feelings seem to have been reciprocated. The *Record* reported that Pew was leading a "Stop Willkie" movement.

That night, Willkie and his wife Edith were leaving his headquarters at the Benjamin Franklin when they ran into Arthur Krock and Turner Catledge of the *New York Times*. Krock and Catledge were journalistic heavyweights, worthy of special attention as Damon Runyon had been earlier in the day. So Willkie invited them to come to his suite at the Warwick for a drink. When they got there, Edith withdrew to the bedroom, where Krock recalls seeing through the half-open door her stocking feet as she lay resting on the bed. Krock and

Catledge brought up Willkie's need for a floor manager. Then Willkie asked, What's that? Krock and Catledge patiently explained that the floor manager was the man who represented the candidate at the convention and handled communication between the candidate, who by custom could not go to the hall, and his delegates, and who supervised the other campaign aides as they tried to persuade fence-sitting delegates to come down on their candidate's side.

Krock tells the story as an illustration of Willkie's innocence, but it is entirely possible that Willkie was feigning innocence as part of Davenport's strategy of presenting him as the anti-politician. Remember, Willkie attended two previous conventions, actually serving as an assistant floor manager for Newton Baker in 1932. Obviously he knew what a floor manager was, so it is not unlikely that he was attempting to flatter the two newsmen. Krock in particular was known for his propensity to offer counsel to prominent public figures, so Willkie was aware that Krock would be pleased to be treated as his mentor. Krock seems to have assumed that Willkie attended to his advice, for on Sunday he wrote a story entitled "Willkie forces seek strategist" that appeared in the *New York Times* on Monday. It said that Willkie was doing exactly what Krock had told him to do.

The fact is that the Willkie forces were already on the case. That same Saturday night, they gathered in Hamilton's hotel room to plot a floor strategy. Present were Charlie Halleck, Charlton MacVeagh, Sam Pryor, West Virginia's Walter Hallanan, New York's Kenneth Simpson, and Massachusetts's Sinclair Weeks and Henry Cabot Lodge Jr. Using "MacVeagh's Bible," a compendium of details about each delegate that MacVeagh had been compiling since April, they identified the delegates from each state that should be their contacts. Then each member of the group was assigned his share of the delegates with whom he was to keep in touch and try to convert to Willkie's cause or, in the case of the already converted, make sure those delegates did not stray.

For many delegates, Sunday was a day to have fun, maybe taking in Independence Hall or visiting the zoo in Fairmont Park. Bob Hope was appearing at the Steel Pier an hour away in Philadelphia's favorite seaside resort, Atlantic City. The Philadelphia Phillies were playing a doubleheader against the Chicago Cubs. Just one game out of last place, the Phillies were definitely not among the National League's elite teams, but that day they had a chance because their star pitcher, Hugh Mulcahy, would be on the mound for one of the games. Unfortunately, the optimism inspired by his presence had to be balanced by the grim foreboding caused by the Phillies pitcher in the other game, Walter "Boom-Boom" Beck, whose nickname testified to his propensity for yielding extra base hits in profusion.

As for the movies, playing in Philadelphia that day were: Fred Astaire in *Roberta,* Jean Arthur in *Too Many Husbands,* and Charles Boyer and Bette Davis in *All This and Heaven Too.* But, even at the movies, escape from the headlines was impossible. Not only did the newsreels feature bedraggled French troops in chaotic retreat, but two of the feature films dealt with peril abroad. *Waterloo Bridge,* starring Vivien Leigh and Robert Taylor, was set in wartime London, and *Mortal Storm,* with Margaret Sullivan and James Stewart, told the story of Jews fleeing Nazi persecution. The *Record* called it one of the season's "most impressive movies."

Although the main headlines that Sunday morning were about the fall of France, most of the other prominently displayed stories were about the convention. Among them was the *Herald Tribune*'s "Dewey and Taft deny deal as Republicans gather," under which ran a report of a stop-Willkie movement that was part of a deal between Taft and Dewey or was being led by Joe Pew or by Alf Landon. Reporters were having a hard time pinning down which rumor was true.

Arthur Vandenberg arrived in Philadelphia on Sunday, to be greeted at the train station by supporters carrying signs reading, "Welcome Van, you're the man." He was taken to his headquarters at the Hotel Adelphi, where he announced to the press that he expected to win nomination on the sixth ballot. He said he opposed conscription, declaring "[W]e can't get into this war under any circumstances, and we should be careful not to take steps that may lead us into it." When asked about Roosevelt's appointment of two Republicans, Stimson and Knox, to the cabinet, he asked, "What Republicans?"

He went on to say that if Stimson stuck to his conviction that America's ships should convoy aid to Britain, then Vandenberg would oppose his confirmation.

Taft also had a press conference that Sunday. He too described himself as against compulsory military training. A few days earlier he had said of the appointment of Stimson and Knox: "This is another indication that the Democratic Party is becoming a war party."

Dewey spent Sunday meeting delegates at his headquarters at the Walton. Using two connecting rooms, Dewey would meet with one group of delegates in one room while another group was being ushered into the other; every fifteen minutes Dewey changed rooms.

Like Taft and Vandenberg, Dewey felt it was important to appeal to the isolationists. Speaking to 500 supporters in a room off the hotel's lobby, he was asked, "How about throwing out the warmongers?"

Dewey replied: "We won't have to. There won't be any of them left when we're finished here."

There was increasing speculation among the delegates about a Taft-Dewey or Dewey-Taft ticket. The *Record*'s Thomas P. O'Neil reported "Hotel corridors buzzed with Taft-Dewey talk."

Willkie seemed to be gaining momentum all through the day. On Sunday morning he attended a breakfast in honor of Frank Harris, that delegate from Pennsylvania who had almost gotten into a fight the day before because of the rumor of his defection from James to Willkie. At the breakfast, Harris confirmed the rumor and said he would bring fourteen of Pennsylvania's delegates with him into the Willkie camp. News also came from the Sunday *Philadelphia Inquirer* that "a substantial number of New Jersey's thirty-six delegates [pledged to Dewey] are expected to desert him after the first ballot in favor of Wendell Willkie." Other defections from Dewey were reported coming from his own state's delegation, including Syracuse's mayor Rolland B. Marvin who announced his support for Willkie. And the *Herald Tribune* reported that, among delegations leaving New York's Pennsylvania Station for Philadelphia that Sunday, there was "a growing sentiment for Wendell Willkie in the New England states." That night, at a rally at Philadelphia's Academy of Music, Willkie announced to a cheering crowd of 3,500 that Governor Raymond Baldwin of Connecticut was not only supporting him but would second his nomination. Willkie, however, was only predicting that he would get "upward of seventy-five votes" on the first ballot. With 501 needed to nominate that left him with a long way to go—even with momentum.

CHAPTER FIVE

★

MONDAY, JUNE 24, 1940

Monday morning, at between 5:00 and 5:30 AM, a seven-car presidential train passed through Philadelphia. It was carrying Franklin Roosevelt back to Washington from Hyde Park, where Eleanor had seen him off the previous evening after what she described as "three sunny, beautiful days" of escape from the cares of state.

Within hours of his return to the White House, however, FDR found himself right back in the eye of the storm. Although his meetings with Senate majority leader Alben Barkley and New York's Mayor Fiorello La Guardia dominated news accounts from the White House that day, of much greater significance was a meeting Roosevelt held late that morning with army Chief of Staff George C. Marshall, Chief of Naval Operations Harold Stark, and Undersecretary of State Sumner Welles. These men and their subordinates had been working on recommendations for how US national security policy had to change in light of the fall of France. In essence, they told him "We can't give anything more to Britain without jeopardizing our own defenses." They were acknowledging a widespread fear within the defense establishment of what would happen if the United States was attacked and the public discovered that the weapons of our own defense had been squandered in a futile attempt to save the

British. "Those who were found to be party to the deal," Major Walter Bedell Smith observed, "might hope to be found hanging from a lamppost."

It even appeared that Roosevelt was following his military's advice later that day, when he announced the cancellation of the sale of twenty torpedo boats to Britain, a sale he had been known to favor. Actually, the cancellation was compelled by an opinion from Attorney General Robert Jackson that the sale was illegal, but Senate isolationists "hailed the order as a sign that the administration is backing down from its policy of aiding Germany's enemies," according to the *Philadelphia Inquirer*.

Despite all this, Roosevelt told his national-security advisors that he wanted to continue giving Britain as much help as he could get away with. Now, of course, it was clear that what he could get away with depended in large part on the identity of his Republican opponent. If the opponent turned out to be an isolationist who would exploit the leaks sure to flow from the defense establishment about its reluctance to send more weapons to Britain, then Roosevelt would not be able to get away with very much. He needed Wendell Willkie to be the nominee.

At eleven that morning, the opening session of the convention was scheduled to begin. As delegates arrived outside the hall, they were greeted by a fifty-piece band that blared away on behalf of Thomas E. Dewey. Small boys passed out Dewey buttons, Willkie buttons, and Vandenberg fans reading "Get on the Vanwagon with Van." Taft supporters were given red carnations. Inside the hall there was a band at one end and an organ at the other. Some delegates from Buffalo walked down the aisle wearing Uncle Sam outfits and of course there were Texans with ten-gallon hats. The major celebrities were Alice Roosevelt Longworth and Alf Landon. Landon strolled over to the press section to chat with H. L. Mencken but had to return to his seat when Chairman Hamilton gaveled the convention to order.

Philadelphia's Mayor Robert E. Lamberton made a short welcoming speech. Albert J. McCartney, a Presbyterian clergyman from

Washington, DC, gave the invocation, reminding the delegates that they were gathered in "a solemn hour of world tragedy." Warren Moscow of the *New York Times* said, "The atmosphere of this convention was different, delegates approach their tasks with far greater solemnity. Even with their wives and friends, they talked as though the fate of the nation depended on their discussions."

They were not, however, too solemn to shout "Louder!" when they couldn't hear Mayor Lamberton. The problem—it was thought to be a defective microphone—would reappear later in the convention. Another problem that would come to the fore later was a shortage of balcony tickets—something that delegates were complaining about that first morning: "I've never seen anything like it" a veteran delegate told the *Record*, "delegates can't even get an extra ticket for a friend."

As delegates emerged from the convention hall and returned to their hotels, the talk was of Dewey's failing strength and of what was described as the rising tide of sentiment for Willkie. The morning papers brought good news for Willkie from two prominent columnists—the conservative Mark Sullivan and the liberal Drew Pearson. Sullivan said Dewey had "peaked" in March. Pearson said Dewey was "washed up." Pearson saw the race as between Taft and Willkie. Sullivan noted that Willkie's "good fortune was that the peak of the people's turning toward him coincided with the sitting of the convention. . . . [Mr. Willkie] has strong popular appeal . . . and the advantage is that his appeal is new while Mr. Roosevelt has necessarily suffered some tarnish from use."

The *Evening Bulletin* featured the news of Willkie's Sunday breakfast with Frank Harris: "Willkie promised 14 Penna. votes." Governor Ralph L. Carr of Colorado announced he would support Willkie and was expected to bring twelve votes with him. The New Jersey delegation attended a reception given by Willkie, "[M]any of them," the *Herald Tribune* reported, "wearing Willkie buttons." They were among the two hundred delegates Willkie managed to see that Monday. Charlie Halleck predicted Willkie would get fifteen of California's votes. Cyrus McCormick, the national committeeman from New Mexico, said that Willkie would win on the fourth ballot. Perhaps most hopeful of all, although it was buried at the end of a long *Herald Tribune* article and not reported by the other papers, was a rumor from "reliable sources" that "returns from all sections of the country received in the last few days and now being tabulated for a nationwide poll indicated that Mr. Willkie would overhaul and pass Mr. Dewey as the leading Republican candidate."

This news was hard for the few who saw it to credit—only last Friday, a Gallup poll had shown Dewey leading with 47 percent to Willkie's 29 percent—but clearly attention was being paid in some quarters. The New York oddsmakers made Willkie the betting favorite at even money and, on the New York Stock Exchange, utility stocks soared. Dewey, however, seemed unperturbed. At a news conference, he predicted he would have 370 to 420 votes on the first ballot and that he would have the 501 needed to win the nomination no later than the third ballot. Dewey talked to delegates from sixteen states on Monday. He also got some welcome news from the credentials committee deciding a contest between Dewey and Taft factions in Florida. It voted to seat a predominantly pro-Dewey delegation. As for the so-called "Willkie boom," Dewey said, "I have difficulty in finding where the Willkie talk is being translated into delegate strength."

As for Taft, this headline from the *Herald Tribune* told the story: "Taft support holds firm in raids of Willkie." Willkie's visit to the Texas delegation in the Robert Morris Hotel, for example, failed to pry away even one Taft vote. That afternoon, eight Republican congressmen from five different states—Ohio, Indiana, Wisconsin, South Dakota, and Michigan—issued a statement that, if not explicitly pro-Taft, was definitely anti-Willkie: "The Republican Party will win in November if it selects from its ranks a leader with a past record of consistent support of Republican policies and principles and whose recent pronouncements are a guarantee to the American people that he will not lead the nation into war." The eight congressmen said that they were speaking for more than half of the Republican members of the House of Representatives. It seemed that the rising tide of pro-Willkie sentiment was getting backs up among the Republican regulars.

Monday night, the convention assembled to hear Governor Harold Stassen's keynote speech, but first came what those present described as a "stirring rendition" of Earl Robinson's "Ballad for Americans" performed by the Philadelphia symphony orchestra, the singer Ray Middleton—he was to star on Broadway with Ethel Merman in *Annie Get Your Gun*—and the Lynn Murray Chorus. What was a bit odd about this was that the ballad had been written for the WPA, the GOP's least favorite New Deal agency, and its sentiments were decidedly left and hardly appropriate for Republican ears. But, just like the southerners who loved to hear Paul Robeson sing "Old Man River," the delegates ignored the message and enjoyed the music.

Harold Stassen was later to become a national joke for hanging on too long in his futile, but repeated, campaigns to become president. Back in 1940, however, the governor was a hot political commodity. Just thirty-three, he was regarded as the "boy wonder" of Republican politics.

Stassen carried a copy of his speech to the podium but did not read it. He had memorized the whole thing. This was the ambitious young governor's moment to shine in the national spotlight and he intended to make the most of it. He launched into an attack on the Roosevelt administration, which, he said, "Instead of keeping its eyes statesmanlike on the welfare of the nation, has turned its political eye upon a third term."

That line had delegates cheering, as did Stassen's reaction to Roosevelt's appointment of Stimson and Knox to his cabinet. Instead of attacking the appointments, as the GOP had been doing, Stassen said his only regret was that the Republicans weren't replacing the rest of Roosevelt's "New Deal incompetents." With those words, he won what the *Herald Tribune* described as his "first real ovation." Stassen went on to make two points that promised trouble for Roosevelt. He opposed compulsory military service "as the method of Hitler and Mussolini and Stalin" and declared that "we are too woefully weak to give the Allies the material assistance this nation wants to give them."

Stassen concluded by quoting George Washington, "Let us raise a standard to which the wise and honest can repair—the event is in the hands of God," and raising both his arms. "The gesture brought the delegates under every standard to their feet," the *Herald Tribune* reported. As the band struck up "Hurrah for the U of M," the University of Minnesota's fight song, the audience cheered, with many people standing on their chairs and waving small American flags. Although one reporter, noting that the speech had gone on for an hour, said that the audience was bored, he was probably describing his own reaction, not the audience's. Even though a jaded journalist might have found the speech tedious, delegates at the beginning of a convention are usually excited, optimistic, and eager to be an enthusiastic audience.

Later that night, Harold Stassen and Wendell Willkie got together. The meeting had been arranged by their mutual friends the Cowles brothers. Stassen, who it will be recalled had begun to lean toward Willkie after the latter's stirring speech in St. Paul, now offered to support him. He had only one condition: He wanted to be named Willkie's floor manager. Willkie agreed. As things worked out, Stassen actually shared the floor manager role with Pryor and Halleck, but his support proved unwavering and it was important. Indeed, one reporter would call it "a crushing blow" for Taft and Dewey. Although that may have been an exaggeration, the endorsement had undeniable impact coming as it did from a man who symbolized the party's future and represented the Midwest where, except in Indiana, Willkie was seen as being weak. Indeed, at the moment, Willkie had the support of only about a third of the Indiana delegation. Even more significant than Stassen's support may have been another development that Monday: Shouts of "We want Willkie!" began to be heard in Convention Hall. They were sporadic and failed to ignite the crowd. But they had begun.

CHAPTER SIX

★

TUESDAY, JUNE 25, 1940

Tuesday morning's headlines featured Stassen's speech; "Key-
noter hits third term" was the *Record*'s. But war news also got its
share of attention. The *New York Times* reported "Nazi fliers strike
widely in Britain," and the *Herald Tribune* devoted the banner to
"France signs Italian truce, fighting ends." Inside the *Herald Tribune*,
Walter Lippmann asked: "What is the record of Messrs. Taft and
Dewey and of the isolationists who have shaped the policy of the Republican Party in the past eighteen months? It is a record of having
been deaf, dumb, and blind in the presence of every warning and of
every epoch-making development . . . of being always surprised, always unprepared, and always confused by the course of events."

Lippmann described Dewey as a man who "changes his views
from hour to hour . . . always more concerned with taking the popular position than he is in dealing with the real issues." The columnist who liked to compare Robert Taft to Neville Chamberlain did so
once more: "The same complacence, the same incapacity to foresee,
the same apathy in action" and concluded "Mr. Taft has admirable
qualities but to nominate and elect him would be to invite for the
nation a disaster of unpreparedness and for Mr. Taft personally a
tragic ordeal."

The Associated Press reported that Hitler had decreed a ten-day festival to celebrate the conquest of France. "Bells throughout Germany pealed out the tidings, their notes picked up by a radio network of all stations in Germany and those of conquered Paris, Amsterdam, Warsaw, Copenhagen, Prague, Oslo, and Brussels . . . the strains of 'Deustchland Uber Alles' filled the air."

The German government's announcement of the celebration ended with "We will sail against England." The AP explained that "Germany was ready, single-minded to turn its energies toward the remaining enemy—England—in an onslaught that 'will be like nothing the world has ever seen.'" It is difficult, if not impossible, to think of any other convention for which the daily news had greater impact then it did as the Republicans gathered in Philadelphia in 1940. Delegates closely followed reports from Europe. Like practically everyone else, they had been fascinated and astonished by Hitler's conquests. Unlike the average citizen, however, their interest was intensified by their need to understand the effect the war news was having on the voting public. Clearly minds were being changed, but which candidate would benefit? So it was that not only the news from abroad, but the news of each day's political developments—and what the columnists had to say about them—was carefully scrutinized for an indication of which way the wind was blowing, for any sign that might point to the candidate who would win the nomination.

Some thought that the winner could be former president Herbert Hoover, the man who was scheduled to be Tuesday evening's main speaker. That morning, the lead item in Drew Pearson and Robert Allen's "Washington Merry-Go-Round" column in the *Record* reported that

> Hoover has been pointing out to "Republican leaders" that Roosevelt had been staking everything on an Allied victory. But now it was no use for the United States to go down with them. . . . Hitler was going to rule the world and the United States would have to do business with him. What the country needed was a man in the White House who had not alienated Hitler and who had contacts in Germany.

Was Hoover describing Dewey, Taft, or Vandenberg? None, according to Pearson and Allen: "It was obvious he had himself in mind."

If that was the case then there was much to buoy his spirits that Tuesday. The morning had begun with a story in the *Herald Tribune* that quoted G. E. Carpenter, the national committeeman-elect from Nebraska, saying that he intended to vote for Dewey on the first ballot as a result of Dewey's winning the state primary, but that "after the first ballot I wouldn't be surprised if Nebraska's delegation voted for Mr. Hoover."

Later, when Hoover arrived at the Bellevue Stratford Hotel, according to the *Herald Tribune*, "automobile traffic was stopped as the crowd surged into the street and surrounded his automobile. As he stood in the car waving his hat, the crowd chanted 'Hoover Hoover Hoover.'"

The *Evening Bulletin* reported "Herbert Hoover is not a candidate and his name will not be placed in nomination according to a close associate of the former president." But Hoover's friend mentioned the possibility that a movement to draft him might "originate spontaneously" on the floor of the convention. Nothing Hoover did that week was designed to close the door on that possibility. Indeed, it seems possible that a United Press story that morning had expressed his fondest hope when it reported that "[T]onight former president Hoover delivers a speech that may pull the plug on the other candidates and give the nomination again to the man from California."

Many of the more experienced delegates assumed that the opening session would be dull, and so they didn't arrive in Philadelphia until late that day, in time for the keynote speech. Tuesday was their first full day at the convention. There was nothing important scheduled until Hoover's speech that night, so many of the delegates spent the day in the business center of Philadelphia, where most of their hotels were located. John O'Reilly of the *Herald Tribune* captured the scene—"[M]arching clubs, bands, and live elephants moved through yelling crowds. Supporters of every candidate were trying to out-do the others as the time for voting approached."

Vehicular traffic was halted time and again as parades moved through the streets and crowds gathered in front of hotels to cheer one candidate or another. "Hotel lobbies, which had been busy for several days, were packed today with masses of people who sang, marched, danced, shouted, and chanted the slogans of their favorite candidates," O'Reilly added. In the bar of the Bellevue Stratford, a large group began chanting "[W]e want Willkie, we want Willkie," and the bartenders joined in, shaking cocktails in time with the chant.

While most of the delegates were enjoying the show on the streets and in the lobbies, the members of the platform committee, which was supposed to report to the convention that day, were still locked in debate over the foreign affairs plank. The committee's fifty-three members met behind closed doors in the Bellevue Stratford's penthouse. The argument was fierce. "Tempers were short and voices were loud," noted one reporter stationed outside the room. They were, after all, debating the major issue of the day: Should America aid the Allies? And if so, how far should it go?

Little news was seeping out from the closed door, so the Associated Press did its best with this report:

2:47 PM Three waiters carry in three trays leaving four tuna fish sandwiches, three ham, two combination, one western and one fried egg.

2:50 PM The waiters come out. Somebody forgot the cheese on rye.

5:03 PM Waiter enters leaving a tray of soda pop.

8:19 PM Electrician enters with a radio so that members can hear Herbert Hoover's speech.

9:13 PM Waiter enters with soft drink.

10:56 PM Waiter enters with more sandwiches.

12:04 AM Delegates come out.

Of course, the politicking went on all day. Dewey spent the day trying to staunch the flow of delegates from his side to Willkie's. His headquarters issued a statement from former Governor Henry J. Allen of Kansas who said, "Delegates do not slip away from the top candidate. I've never seen more solid forces than those in back of Dewey." Mrs. M. E. Noriss of Burlington, Washington, who was to second Dewey's nomination, said, "There is no excitement for Willkie in the Far West. No utility tycoon could get to first base in the West."

But some slippage seemed to be occurring. In New Jersey, delegate David Albright claimed that Willkie would get eighteen of the state's thirty-two votes. Dewey's man David Pomeroy conceded that there was a "strong undercurrent" for Willkie but insisted, "We're going to put Dewey over." Arthur T. Vanderbilt, another Dewey delegate, sent a telegram to Dewey's supporters back in Newark urging them to send telegrams to the delegation in favor of Dewey.

The reason that Vanderbilt did this was because the New Jersey delegates had received more than 100,000 letters and telegrams urging them to vote for Willkie. Other delegates from states all over the country also found themselves swamped by pro-Willkie messages as the enthusiasm of Oren Root's Willkie clubs spread. Average citizens had caught the Willkie fever.

Willkie himself was a whirlwind of activity. He had breakfast with the Indiana delegates, who indicated that he would get at least ten of their votes. Then he met with the entire Connecticut delegation, all of whom were now enthusiastically committed to him. Then came meetings with groups from Washington, Oregon, North and South Dakota, New York, North and South Carolina, Illinois, Minnesota, Georgia, California, New Hampshire, Arizona, and Arkansas. The reaction of Governor Frank Merriam of California was typical: He said that he was "greatly impressed by Mr. Willkie."

Willkie also met with a group of Negro delegates and invited them to visit him in the White House in 1941, reminding them "I led a fight against the Ku Klux Klan in 1924 in Akron when every judge on the bench was a member of the Klan." The GOP, it should be noted, was still enough the party of Lincoln that the Mississippi delegation was led by a black man, Percy Howard.

That afternoon, Stassen turned over the convention gavel to permanent chairman Joe Martin, who was welcomed by cheering delegates as the band played "There'll Be a Hot Time in the Old Town Tonight." After Martin made a brief address, during which he called the Democrats "the war party," the convention adjourned until evening.

Although Hoover did not use Martin's words that night, his speech made clear that he not only thought of the Democrats as the war party, but that he was even more of an isolationist than Joe Martin.

That Hoover enjoyed the warm regard of his own party was evident when he entered Convention Hall. As he walked down the center aisle to the accompaniment of perhaps the most exultant of all campaign songs, "California Here I Come," the delegates leapt to their feet cheering. When he reached the rostrum, John D. M. Hamilton went to the microphone and said, "Mr. Chairman, it is a great pleasure and honor for me to present the Honorable Herbert Hoover." Once again the delegates were on their feet roaring. The ovation went on and on until Joe Martin pounded the gavel and warned the crowd that their cheers were taking up the time the radio network had scheduled for the speech.

Hoover's words appealed to the isolationist heart of the Republican Party, and its hatred of the New Deal. As for the latter, he said, "[W]e are faced with the task of saving America for free men," and argued that if he had continued in office, he would have ended the depression that the New Deal had only perpetuated.

As for the danger Hitler posed to America, Hoover said,

Every whale that spouts is not a submarine. The 3,000 miles of ocean is still protection. The air forces, tanks, and armies of Europe are useless to attack us unless they can establish bases in the western hemisphere. To do that, they must first pass our Navy. It can stop anything in sight now.

Radio listeners were puzzled that this speech was not interrupted by more cheers from the crowd. The problem was that, in the convention hall, the former president's remarks were scarcely audible. Gore Vidal was sitting on the speaker's platform, five or six rows behind Hoover. He could hear Hoover but he could also tell that the delegates out front could not. "There was," he says, "the dull rumble that tells you they're talking to themselves." Shouts of "Louder!" could be heard.

There had been trouble with the microphones during the opening session. In addition, Hoover had a soft voice and had a tendency to stand a foot or so away from the microphone. Engineers sent him notes urging him to speak up and stand closer but the notes either were not delivered or were ignored.

Hoover and his associates suspected that he had been given a defective microphone, or that the sound system had been tampered with and that the guilty party was Willkie's friend, Sam Pryor, Chairman of the Committee on Arrangements. Whatever the cause, it is clear that the speech failed to electrify the delegates as Hoover had hoped.

"The ex-president received an ovation, timed officially at eleven minutes," writes Warren Moscow.

> But to those in the hall at the time, it was less than over-powering. Hoover's friends from his home state of California marched the California standard around the convention hall, the traditional gambit for starting a stampede. A few other state standards were similarly flaunted by single delegates. No one stopped them, no one joined them.

The next day, the top headline on the front page of the *New York Times* was "Hoover bids for nomination to fight New Deal." But, in the story that followed, Jim Hagerty called the demonstration "mild."

Mild is not the kind of word a candidate wants to have used in this situation. These demonstrations in which delegates march around the floor waving states' standards while the band plays and the crowd cheers were the traditional way of showing the intensity of feeling for a candidate. If the feeling is not intense, then it's not very helpful.

As in the early days of almost every convention, much of the action took place off the floor as each candidate and his supporters maneuvered to improve their delegate totals. Although attempts were made to keep the negotiations secret, it seems clear that, by Tuesday night, the following offers and counteroffers had been made by the candidates or their close associates.

Willkie asked for Vandenberg's support and was turned down by the senator, who said he thought the convention choice would come down to the two of them.

Taft offered the vice presidency to Vandenberg, who countered with the same offer to Taft with the roles reversed.

Taft asked for Hoover's support but the former president clung to the hope that his party would turn to him once again.

Dewey offered Vandenberg the vice presidency in return for Vandenberg's support. Vandenberg's answer: "Tell Dewey that I think my place on the Senate Floor is more important than on the Senate rostrum. Also tell him that if he will take the vice presidency with me, I shall be a pre-pledged one termer [Dewey would then be in direct line for the White House in 1944]. Also tell him if this is too much for him to swallow at once, I'll make him a sporting proposition. I'll meet him at 11:00 to flip a coin to see which end of the ticket we take." That was the end of the conversation. Vandenberg later said, "I never heard from Dewey again until it was too late. He missed the boat."

Vandenberg's proposal to flip a coin was another indication that he took his candidacy less seriously than his rivals did theirs. He simply wasn't working as hard as they were. But his support was important to the other candidates because of the size of the Michigan delegation. And, although Vandenberg was not going to exert himself, he wanted to leave open the possibility that the convention would ultimately turn to him.

The negotiations that were most closely watched were between Taft and Dewey. Their delegates combined would constitute clear control of the convention. These negotiations culminated on Tuesday night after Hoover's speech, when two of Dewey's top aides, J. Russell Sprague and Ruth McCormick Simms, called on Taft's campaign manager, David Ingalls, and Taft's brother, Charles, at the Benjamin Franklin Hotel. They offered Taft the vice presidency in return for his support. Taft's people reacted just as Vandenberg had, except for the coin toss, and proposed the same ticket in reverse. Neither side would budge.

It may be that Dewey's endorsement of another candidate would have been worthless. His delegates were wavering and more likely to follow their own instincts than his instructions in the event that he withdrew. Dewey didn't even have the enthusiastic support of some of his own staff. An inkling of their sentiment is supplied by an eminent historian, Yale's John Morton Blum, who, as a young college student, was a paid Dewey worker. He says that, in his heart, he was 100 percent pro-Willkie.

Kenneth Simpson, the leader of New York City Republicans as well as the Republican National Committeeman for the state of New York, was now helping Willkie win delegates. Many observers credited Simpson with Dewey's election as district attorney and with his impressive showing against Herbert Lehman in the 1938 gubernatorial race.

When Dewey had been quoted several months before the convention as saying that he "would have done as well without Simpson," relations between the two took a downward course. Furthermore, Simpson fit the early Willkie supporter profile. He was a liberal who had gone to Yale and then to Harvard Law School. And, far from being a typical politician, he was a socialite and art collector whose friends ranged from Gertrude Stein and Alexander Kerensky to the eminent literary critic Edmund Wilson, with whom he had attended the Hill School.

For Taft, the bargaining brought good news in the form of emerging signs, if not firm commitments, that he would ultimately receive the support of several states that were pledged to favorite sons on the first ballot. These included Oregon, where Senator Charles McNary was the favorite son, Iowa (Hanford J. McNider), South Dakota (Governor Harlan J. Bushfield), and most of all Pennsylvania

(Governor Arthur James), whose boss Joe Pew had spoken those kind words about Taft earlier in the day and who was said by Damon Runyon "to be leaning to Taft after having his delegates cast a couple of courtesy ballots for Governor James."

CHAPTER SEVEN

★

WEDNESDAY, JUNE 26, 1940

The politicking continued. Dewey backers claimed that they had attracted fifty-two new votes that would show up on the second ballot. Taft's people were predicting victory on the fourth ballot. The Taft and Dewey camps still couldn't get together on a stop-Willkie program. One problem was that the two men delegates most looked to for leadership in bringing the Taft-Dewey forces together—Herbert Hoover and Alf Landon—were not offering clear counsel. Hoover, of course, hoped for a deadlock that would propel him into the nomination. Landon was involved in the work of the platform committee well into Wednesday afternoon. Besides, he didn't like Hoover, who had threatened to take the nomination away from him in 1936. He was also distinctly more for aid to the Allies than Hoover, though still less so than Willkie.

"[Landon] is opposed to Willkie, but he is very hostile to Hoover. The feeling between them is so strong," the *Record*'s Robert S. Allen reported, "that it is feared that if Hoover throws his weight against Willkie, Landon may rally to him."

Willkie's people had little hope of getting Hoover on their side. He was too much of an isolationist and was almost certain to go for Taft, Vandenberg, or Dewey, in that order, if he abandoned his own hope for the nomination. The Willkie camp's strategy was to keep

Hoover's hopes alive and prevent him from endorsing any other candidate by holding out the possibility that he might get Willkie's delegates if Willkie's campaign faltered. To that end, William Allen White, the pro-Willkie editor of the *Emporia Kansas Gazette*, announced to the press after leaving a meeting with Hoover: "If they don't nominate Mr. Willkie I think the man who will be nominated then will be Mr. Hoover."

The Wednesday morning papers carried the news of Stassen's endorsement of Willkie. The GOP's New Jersey gubernatorial nominee, Robert Hendrickson, also came out for the Indianan, as did former senator David Hastings of Delaware. The *Inquirer* reported, "Willkie boom gains strength in west."

Nevada delegates talked of a poll taken in their state on Monday and Tuesday that showed 62 percent for Willkie among the Republican voters. "There is no question that Willkie is the most mentioned man in Philadelphia," reported the *Herald Tribune*.

Willkie's early afternoon press conference was attended by more than 100 reporters. In answer to a question about finances, Willkie said that he had spent just $4000 on his campaign. Of course, the volunteer groups had raised and spent more, and the value of the free publicity Willkie had gotten from his publisher friends would be impossible to calculate. Still, the modest sum he cited is evidence that campaign finance was not a major problem in those days. When the conference ended, the reporters, in a scene right out of a Frank Capra movie "broke into applause, then a chorus of cheers," according to the *Herald Tribune*. The Willkie-Davenport strategy of wooing the media had paid off. First he had won over the most powerful of the media barons. Now he had the ink-stained wretches on his side as well.

All this good will may have led reporters to be a bit too indulgent of one Willkie statement. When asked about reports that bankers and utility executives were behind the deluge of pro-Willkie letters and telegrams that had descended on the convention—just one delegate from New York said he had received 22,500 wires—Willkie not only denied the charge but added, "There hasn't been one wire or phone call or one letter sent out from any of the volunteer groups here requesting anybody to wire, write, or communicate with any delegate in my behalf." None of the reporters pointed out that the only remaining explanation was immaculate conception.

At midday, there was good news for Taft. A headline in the *Evening Bulletin* proclaimed "Taft leading Willkie and Dewey; victory on the fifth ballot planned." John C. O'Brien reported that, after a personal visit from Herbert Hoover, "confidence soared to new heights at Taft headquarters." Hoover's support, the Taft people said, would assure at least twenty to twenty-five votes from the California delegation. The Taft supporters also questioned the value of Stassen's and Hendrickson's endorsements of Willkie, claiming that Taft would still get support in Minnesota and Delaware. Furthermore they claimed previous Willkie endorsements by governors Baldwin of Connecticut and Carr of Colorado had inspired resentment in those delegations and that there would be support for Taft from each.

When Wednesday's session began at 2:10 PM, Joe Martin announced that the resolutions committee still had not finished the platform. He recognized Senator Charles Tobey of New Hampshire, who moved that the convention adjourn until 4:45. When Martin called for a vote, there was a loud chorus of "Nays"; he pounded his gavel and announced the motion had carried. (Convention chairmen, it should be noted, rarely hesitate to interpret a voice vote as agreeing with the chairman's wishes. One memorable example would occur the night during the 1944 Democratic Convention when it was clear that the delegates, heavily dominated by the labor unions, were ready to choose Henry Wallace, even though the party leaders favored Harry Truman. When Chairman Sam Rayburn entertained a motion to adjourn and the "ayes" were drowned out by a thunder of "nays," Rayburn declared the convention adjourned until the next day to give the leaders time to get the troops in line.)

During the adjournment, the plaza in front of Convention Hall teemed with activity. Delivery trucks arrived filled with posters, placards, and banners. In a scene reminiscent of the preparation for a circus, campaign workers unloaded their candidates' signs and carried them into the hall along with cowbells, horns, and other noise-makers needed for the demonstrations that would follow the nominating speeches. The stage was being set for the evening show.

When the convention resumed at 4:45, delegates were told that the session would continue straight through the evening without a recess for dinner. As the evening session proceeded, delegates would filter downstairs to the basement hot dog stands. By 8:00 PM the supply of frankfurters had been exhausted, even though they sold for twenty-five cents at a time when the going rate was a nickel or a dime.

The invocation by Rabbi Michael Aransohn of Cincinnati suggested that the cause of his fellow Ohioan, Robert Taft, was not far from his heart:

> Of what will it avail us if we offer up our sons and daughters on the altar of Moloch? Is it not better to fight in our own land against the more hideous Huns and fiercer vandals in our own midst [although here he seems a Deweyite]—the bands of gangsters and racketeers who flourish everywhere. Let us not let ourselves be sucked into the maelstrom of war.

Now at long last came the platform, presented by Herbert K. Hyde, the chairman of the Resolutions Committee. As Hyde proclaimed that the GOP stood for "America, preparedness, and peace," the vigor of his delivery combined with the heat of the auditorium to bring sweat to his brow and his hair fell down over his forehead. The audience applauded most enthusiastically when he declared that, "[T]o ensure against the overthrow of the American system of government, we favor an amendment to the constitution providing that no person shall be President of the United States for more than two terms." For the delegates, no prospect was worse than a third term for Franklin Roosevelt.

The 3000-word platform relied heavily on generalities. One of its authors confided to a reporter for the *Record* that it was designed to "step on no toe and to placate everybody." Indeed, it could be said that specificity had been successfully avoided on every issue but the third term and on one other for which the GOP could take legitimate pride.

> We pledge that an American citizen of Negro descent shall be given a square deal in the economic and political life of the nation. Discrimination in the civil service, the Army, the Navy, and all other branches of the government must cease. To enjoy the full benefits of life, liberty, and the pursuit of happiness, universal suffrage must be made effective for the Negro citizen. Mob violence shocks the conscience of the nation and legislation to curb this evil should be enacted.

The platform committee did not resolve the disputes between the internationalists and the isolationists that had been the major factor in drawing out their deliberations. In the end, they straddled, but with one leg planted more firmly in the isolationists' camp. The bone tossed to the internationalists: "[W]e favor the extension of aid to all people fighting for liberty or whose liberty is threatened as long as such aid is not in violation of international law or inconsistent with the requirements of our national defense."

H. L. Mencken said the foreign affairs plank was "so written that it will fit both the triumph of democracy and the collapse of democracy, and approve both the sending of arms to England and sending only flowers."

Hans Thomsen, the leading Nazi diplomat in Washington, told Berlin in a memo that was discovered after the war that the foreign affairs plank "was taken almost verbatim from the conspicuous full-page advertisement in the American Press which was published upon our instigation." That ad, which had appeared in the *New York Times* and a dozen or so other major papers, had been signed by Congressman Hamilton Fish and other isolationists and had been paid for by the Nazis. A German agent, George Sylvester Viereck, wrote the ad while in Fish's office.

Thomsen described Viereck's effort as "a well camouflaged blitz campaign," and asked for money to finance a three-day visit to the Philadelphia convention by fifty isolationist Republican congressmen, "so that they may work on the delegates of the Republican party in favor of the isolationist foreign policy." He said the congressmen would be invited by a "well-known Republican congressman who works in close collaboration with [the German Embassy]." In fact, the fifty were invited by Congressman Hamilton Fish and did go to Philadelphia to testify before the platform committee.

It would be wrong to assume that British intelligence was not equally active. In his book *Desperate Deception*, Thomas Mahl implies that the apparent heart attack of Ralph Williams, the Taft-leaning chairman of the Arrangements Committee, may have actually been a poisoning arranged by British agents, a speculation that had little evidence to support it but was nonetheless sufficiently intriguing to be adopted by Gore Vidal in his novel *The Golden Age*.

Certainly, British intelligence was not without its influential American helpers. British agents described Helen Reid and Walter Lippman of the *Herald Tribune*, Walter Winchell and Drew Pearson, among those "who rendered services of particular value." And, as we've learned, Mitzi Sims, the wife of the British military attaché, was Vandenberg's mistress in the 1939–1940 period. Indeed, Walter Trohan, a *Chicago Tribune* reporter, said that insiders called Vandenberg "the Senator from Mitzigan." Another woman known to be a British agent, Betty Pack, also appears to have cultivated Vandenberg. Although Mitzi and Betty did not seem to have any effect on his isolationism, which endured until Pearl Harbor, it is possible that their attentions may have sapped the energy from Vandenberg's bid for the presidency. He had been in front until the beginning of 1939; now, in 1940, he ranked fourth among the candidates.

There is no evidence that these Americans were paid agents. Hamilton Fish was a dedicated isolationist; Helen Reid openly urged helping the British. Each had a large area of common purpose with either Germany or Britain.

The platform was adopted by acclamation. Martin then announced that the roll call of states would begin to determine which states would nominate a candidate and in what order.

Alabama yielded to New York, which declared it intended to nominate Tom Dewey; Arkansas yielded to Ohio, which would nominate Taft. When Indiana passed there was a gasp from the audience. Why wasn't it nominating Willkie? The delegation had been split, and those opposed to Willkie were for the moment in a slight majority. The dispute was finally resolved while the roll call proceeded by a threat from John D. M. Hamilton, who, in addition to being chairman of the national committee, was a delegate from Kansas, to nominate Willkie himself. That embarrassed the Indianans into agreeing to put Willkie's name forward. But, before Indiana's decision was announced, the role call had proceeded. Several states announced their intention to nominate favorite sons. At the end of the roll call, Indiana asked to be recognized. The convention fell quiet. Then, when the crowd heard the words Wendell Willkie, the cheering exploded. Some of it came from the delegates but most of it came from the balcony, in what a reporter described as "one steady deep-throated roar."

Now the actual nominating speeches began. "The delegates grinned and sat back expectantly," wrote Sidney Shalett of the *New York Times*; "they were like old fire horses sniffing smoke, their fun was about to begin and they knew it." What was different about this convention was that much of the rest of the country shared the delegates' excitement. Interest in the convention had grown to the point that the networks were canceling regularly scheduled programs to increase their coverage.

That night, Dewey, Taft, and Willkie were to be nominated, the other candidates would come the next day. Dewey's name was presented by the prominent attorney John Lord O'Brian. His first applause came when he said Dewey could "be trusted to keep the country out of war." He also described Dewey as "a life-long" Republican in implied contrast to Willkie.

O'Brian finished and a big floor demonstration for Dewey began. Among the state standards in the parade were those of New York (carried by Colonel Theodore Roosevelt Jr.), Idaho, New Jersey, Illinois, Washington, Wisconsin, South Carolina, West Virginia, California, Tennessee, Alabama, Florida, Montana, Missouri, Utah, Kentucky, and Colorado. The band played Columbia's "Roar Lions Roar" in honor of the institution whose law school Dewey had attended. Football fight songs were much favored by convention demonstrators.

The delegates paraded up and down the aisles, shouting, ringing cowbells and a variety of noisemakers, and holding aloft placards bearing photographs of Dewey and messages like "Dewey Can Beat Roosevelt," "Tom Dewey is a vote-getter," and "Nominate a Winner, Tom Dewey." The demonstration had lasted twenty-five minutes when Chairman Martin gaveled it to a close.

Taft's name was presented by Grove Patterson, the editor of the *Toledo Blade*: "Ohio, mother of Presidents, brings this convention a great American, an amazing vote getter, and he has always been a Republican . . . he wears through life's sun and storm the durable fabric of character." The Taft demonstration began on an even more enthusiastic note than Dewey's, with the ceiling opening to let hundreds of toy balloons—red, white, and blue—float down to the delegates on the floor. Led by silver-haired John W. Bricker, the governor of Ohio, delegates paraded down the aisles carrying banners and placards that read "We want Taft," "No glamour, no sarong, just a man who won't go wrong—Bob Taft," "He'll put the New Deal boys to rout—Bob Taft knows what it's all about." The hall was transformed into a forest of red, white, and blue Taft banners, with the band joining in to add to the tumult. When the demonstration had gone on for sixteen minutes, Chairman Martin pounded his gavel in an attempt to restore order. Gradually the crowd simmered down. Only a few bells and horns could be heard. "Finally, there was only one horn player," the *Herald Tribune* reported. "Martin glared down at him. The tooter stopped. The demonstration had lasted 19 minutes." Although Dewey's demonstration had been longer, it was, according to the *Evening Bulletin*, "weaker in volume than Taft's."

After Taft's seconders had their say, Charles Halleck stepped to the microphone to nominate Wendell Willkie. Halleck took on the main charge against Willkie, that he was not a lifelong Republican, by asking: "[I]s the Republican party a closed corporation? Do you have to be born into it?"

One answer to this question had been given earlier by James E.

Watson, a former Senate majority leader: "You know that back home in Indiana we think it's alright for the town whore to join the Church, but we don't let her lead the choir on the first night." That was certainly the way Taft and Dewey delegates felt; they frequently interrupted Halleck's speech with boos that competed with applause from Willkie delegates and cheers from the gallery.

The battle between the boos and the cheers testified to the strength of feeling between isolationists, passionate about avoiding America's involvement in another slaughter like World War I, and the internationalists, who were equally passionate about the need to stop Hitler. Another factor was the split between liberals and conservatives, which had within it an element of culture clash between small-town America and the cities of the northeast. Most of the people on the floor, the delegates themselves, represented conservative, isolationist small-town America. Most of the people in the gallery were on the other side, although there was enough overlap among these groups—and enough underlying cultural unity in a country where practically everyone still admired Will Rogers—to produce the possibility of movement back and forth and make it difficult to predict the winner.

When Halleck finished, what followed was described, by the *Evening Bulletin,* as "the most terrific demonstration ever heard in Convention Hall." Both the *Record* and the *Bulletin* used the word "riot" in their headlines to describe the event.

A tremendous cheer filled the great auditorium. Although the gallery began to chant "We want Willkie," a floor demonstration did not start immediately. But then the spectators saw the New York banner waved back and forth. Mayor Rolland B. Marvin of Syracuse was trying to seize it, but several Dewey delegates were trying to hold it in place. An Associated Press photograph showed six hands gripping the pole. Mayor Marvin, however, weighed 220 pounds and was built like a linebacker. With the help of a shove from Frederick Courdert of Manhattan, Marvin prevailed and started the parade, where he was quickly joined by delegates from Connecticut.

Two more scuffles ensued as Marvin passed the New York delegation twice while circling the hall and a dozen or so Dewey delegates tried to snatch back the standard, but proved no match for Marvin. Marvin's New York and Connecticut's standards were joined by standards from New Jersey, Rhode Island, Delaware, Minnesota, California, Washington, and Virginia. The last two states also saw fights between delegates who wanted to join the parade and those who definitely did not. In all, a half dozen fist fights broke out on the floor. One paper said that 100 policemen were needed to sort things out. Twelve of them came to the rescue of the Pennsylvania standard as former Senator George Wharton Pepper, loyal to the candidacy of Governor Arthur James, resisted attempts by Willkie delegates to seize it.

"None of the previous demonstrations approached the ear-splitting roar that swept down from the galleries which appeared to be 90 percent for Willkie," according to the *Evening Bulletin*.

"The Willkie demonstration lasted 20 minutes—5 minutes less than the demonstration for Thomas E Dewey," wrote Thomas P. O'Neil of the *Record*. "But there was more passion packed into one minute of the Willkie demonstration than in the entire 25 of the carefully manufactured Dewey parade."

After the demonstration came the Willkie seconding speeches. The seconders included Bruce Barton, the advertising man who was a New York congressman. He told the audience "[W]e don't mind the boos," which of course inspired more boos from the Dewey and Taft delegates. Barton was followed by Connecticut Governor Raymond Baldwin, who spoke the line that pleased the crowd the most when he said that Willkie had proved that it was possible to take power "away from the politicians and give it back to the people."

The fact that the crowd in the balcony was distinctly pro-Willkie had not escaped the notice of observers. The other candidates felt that they had been cheated by Sam Pryor's distribution of the tickets. There had been complaints about a shortage of tickets as early as Monday. Some tickets were given to each delegation, but delegates who were not for Willkie did not feel they had received their fair share. Damon Runyon said "Anyone wearing a Willkie button can get a ticket." Martha Taft called Pryor "a despicable worm." Angered by the chants of "We Want Willkie" from the balcony, Colonel R. B. Creeger of Texas, a leader of the Taft delegates, rushed to the platform and asked to be recognized so that he could protest Pryor's chicanery. Chairman Martin persuaded Creeger not to speak. This was the first of a series of favors Martin performed for Willkie that may have been responsible for his being rewarded after the convention with the chairmanship of the Republican National Committee.

After the last of the Willkie seconding speeches, the convention adjourned at 11:10 PM and the exhausted delegates headed back to their hotels.

CHAPTER EIGHT

★

THURSDAY, JUNE 27, 1940

On Thursday morning, the New York *Herald Tribune* published an editorial urging Willkie's nomination. Run at the top of the front page, it was the first front-page editorial in the paper's long history—a move so unprecedented that the *New York Times* devoted an article to describing what its rival had done. The *Tribune*'s editorial, also noted by Philadelphia's morning papers, declared that Willkie "seems to us to be heaven's gift to the nation in its time of crisis. Such timing of man and the hour does not come often in history."

Inside the *Herald Tribune* that Thursday morning, a column by Walter Lippmann, after observing that Taft and Dewey "had their heads buried deeply in the sand," proclaimed Willkie "as the man obviously best fitted to the circumstances of the hour." Later that morning, as tardy delegates drifted into the convention hall, still recovering from the hoopla of the night before, newsboys outside were hawking early editions of the *Evening Bulletin*. Its front page carried news that quickly spread among the delegates. The latest Gallup poll had been leaked to columnists Joseph Alsop and Robert Kintner. It confirmed a rumor that had earlier appeared in a back page of the *Herald Tribune*, and what the chants and cheers from the gallery and the letters and telegrams from back home were already telling the delegates: Willkie was now in the lead, having passed Tom Dewey in the poll.

Later that day, Dr. George Gallup issued a statement declaring that his poll would not be ready until Friday or Saturday but acknowledging that "the Willkie trend has been sharply upward." When the poll was later released, the actual figures would show that Willkie had 44 percent to Dewey's 29 percent and Taft's 13 percent.

The news however wasn't all good for Willkie. "Willkie's Drive Is Stopped, GOP's Old Guard Claims," was the headline in a story by the *Record*'s Robert S. Allen, who reported that "a secret canvass showed that [Willkie's] maximum strength was 290 votes. 501 are needed to win." This emphasized the hard fact that Willkie still had to translate all that enthusiasm into actual votes by delegates.

There were only three or four thousand people in the hall at the scheduled starting time of ten AM, and it wasn't until 10:44 that the session actually got under way. Verne Marshall, the editor of the *Cedar Rapids Gazette*, nominated Iowa's favorite son Hanford McNider. He began by observing, "This is a Republican convention," with his strong emphasis on "Republican" suggesting that he was not a potential convert to the Willkie camp. The Iowa delegates did not attempt to demonstrate. Nor did any of the other delegations nominating favorite sons that day. Not even Michigan, whose Arthur Vandenberg was the only one of that day's nominees deemed to have even an outside chance of being his party's choice. The Michigan delegates did sing "God Bless America" and "The Battle Hymn of the Republic," and the organ belted out Michigan's football song.

Other candidates nominated were Senator Styles Bridges of New Hampshire, Governor Harlan Bushfield of South Dakota, publisher Frank Gannett, Senator Charles McNary of Oregon, and Governor Arthur James of Pennsylvania. James's name was put forward by Senator James S. Davis, who said "We want a president who has experience as a government executive. Government should be efficient and businesslike, but government is not industry." In other words, "we don't want Willkie." This was a message similar to that of a handbill that had mysteriously appeared in delegates' seats before the session began. It said Willkie was the candidate of the private utility interests.

After Davis finished, the Pennsylvania delegates did not parade, but managed to shout "We want James" for fifteen minutes, with George Wharton Pepper as the main cheerleader. They concluded by going to the rostrum and singing a rousing "Fight fight fight for James." The only problem was that the band at the other end of the hall was playing something else.

Delegates were impatient for the balloting to start. They "milled around the hall and created a tumult of chatter over which [speakers] had difficulty making themselves heard," a reporter wrote. "The delegates and alternates were so noisy that Chairman Martin had to gavel them down." Word began to leak out that the convention would be adjourned after the last nominating speech for South Dakota's favorite son, Governor Harlan Bushfield, and restless delegates and spectators began to leave. The actual recess came at 2:47 with the convention scheduled to resume at 4:30.

The delegates had all returned to their seats by 4:40 when the moment they had all been waiting for arrived. At precisely 4:41 Chairman Martin announced, "[W]e will now vote on the candidates for the presidential nomination." Now numbers became the name of the game. All the managers kept score as the roll call of the states proceeded.

Alabama was the first state called. Its chairman reported, "Alabama casts seven votes for Thomas E. Dewey, and six votes for Taft." Willkie's name was not heard until Arkansas gave him two votes, but Dewey got the same number, and Taft led with seven. In California, Willkie, Taft, and Dewey were in a dead heat with Herbert Hoover, each getting seven votes. (Hoover had not been nominated but delegates were free to vote for him, or for anyone else for that matter.) But Connecticut brought a roar from the gallery by casting all sixteen of its votes for Willkie; then Delaware gave Willkie three of its six with one each for Taft, McNary, and Joe Martin, even though Martin, like Hoover, hadn't been nominated.

Willkie, however, led in only four other states: Indiana, where he was narrowly ahead with nine votes to seven each for Dewey and Taft; Wyoming, where he had four votes to one each for Dewey and

Vandenberg; and Nevada and Rhode Island, where he and Taft were tied with two votes each in the former and three in the latter. Dewey's big states were New York, which gave him sixty-one votes, and Illinois, where he garnered fifty-two. Ohio's fifty-two and Texas's twenty-six were Taft's best.

The good news for Willkie was that he did better than most observers had expected by getting a total of 105 votes from twenty-four different states. The bad news was that Dewey's 360 and Taft's 189 combined to give them a total of 549, or well over a majority—enough, it seemed, to put them in control of the convention.

A second ballot began immediately after the first was finished and each candidate's total vote had been announced. Willkie scored some significant gains, his biggest haul being nine new votes from Maine. His total rose to 171. Taft also gained and was now at 203. Dewey still led, but his 338 votes represented a loss of twenty-two. A major error in Dewey's strategy became evident. His managers had claimed he would get fifty-two new votes on the second ballot; instead he had lost twenty-two. Similarly, they had said that they would have 400 votes or more on the first ballot, only to receive just 360. Gerald B. Lambert, a Republican pollster, tells of meeting with Dewey's top advisers early in the week. "I said one thing to do was to hold back about 50 or more delegates on the first ballot, so that they could be sure of increasing the number on the second ballot. If that happened, everybody would jump on the Dewey bandwagon." But it hadn't happened. Lambert's suggestion had been met "with the most annoying, patronizing air I have encountered in my political life."

It was 6:49 when the result of the second ballot was announced. Chairman Martin then recessed the convention until 8:30. Most delegates chose to grab a quick meal at nearby restaurants, which were jammed. Those who returned to their hotels found their mailboxes stuffed with pro-Willkie messages, which only added to the impact of the 40,000 telegrams delivered to the convention hall that day, the great majority of which were also pro-Willkie.

During the recess for dinner, both Taft and Willkie's forces went to work trying to persuade favorite sons to switch to their candi-

date. They tried to convince Dewey to drop out, but he was determined to continue. Harold Stassen asked Alf Landon to give Willkie
the Kansas delegates that had been voting for Senator Arthur Cap-
per, but Landon said the votes would go to Dewey. Taft tried to persuade Hoover to give him his delegates, but Hoover stubbornly clung
to the hope that he would ultimately prevail when the convention
deadlocked on the other candidates. Taft's aides tried to reach Joe
Pew to ask for the Pennsylvania delegates that had been supporting
Arthur James, but Pew's butler said that he was taking a bath and
could not be disturbed.

After the delegates returned from dinner, a third ballot was taken.
Dewey lost twenty-three votes more and Taft gained nine, leaving
their combined total at 529, still more than a majority. But the big
story was Willkie's gain of eighty-eight votes, which put him in second place at 259.

The most dramatic moment for Willkie came after New York had
announced that he had thirteen votes, the count was challenged, and
the delegation was polled. When the revised count gave Willkie
fourteen additional votes, making a total of twenty-seven, a mighty
cheer went up from the crowd and "We want Willkie" was chanted
with renewed vigor.

Willkie's largest gain, however, was in Massachusetts, where he
picked up nineteen votes that had previously been cast for its son Joe
Martin. He also got ten new votes from Pennsylvania, taking them
away from Governor James, giving him a total of fifteen, confirming
the Butler *Eagle*'s prediction and actually exceeding it by one. James,
however, continued to hold on to fifty-seven votes, and they remained
one of the two great prizes devoutly sought by the main candidates.
The other was Michigan, which still was loyally giving Vandenberg
thirty-six of its thirty-eight votes. Since Vandenberg's chances of
emerging as a compromise candidate were slim—his strength had declined from seventy-six to seventy-three to seventy-two votes on the
first three ballots—it seemed almost certain that his followers would
ultimately have to choose another candidate.

Dewey, realizing that he was in deep trouble, at the end of the third ballot tried to get the convention adjourned. He asked Vandenberg for help and the Michigan senator was willing, but the Willkie forces, sensing victory, wanted to go on. Dewey and Vandenberg, joined by Hoover, begged the Taft people to support adjournment, but Taft, like Willkie, felt he was on the way to winning. He expected to get McNider's, Bushfield's, Hoover's, and McNary's voters. Taft was also convinced that his friend and colleague Arthur Vandenberg would ultimately give him Michigan. And, either believing that Joe Pew really was taking a bath or that at worst Pew was signaling that he wanted to stick with James for a ballot or two longer, Taft still thought that he would get the lion's share of Pennsylvania's votes.

The fourth ballot began just after 10 PM. There was hardly any change through Georgia, but California passed, which ignited rumors about what it might do. The speculation became more intense when Illinois also passed. Together they represented 102 votes, almost as many as the Pennsylvania-Michigan combination that had been talked about so much.

As the roll call proceeded through Montana, Willkie had gained only thirteen votes. The "We Want Willkie" chants were not as loud or as frequent. They came back in full throat, however, when New Jersey gave him twenty-three votes and New York thirty-five, both substantial increases. The chants grew even louder when Pennsylvania was reached, and the gallery was hoping that Willkie's fresh momentum would sweep it into his column. He did get four new votes for a total of nineteen, but James held on to fifty-three.

As the fourth ballot was coming to a close, Willkie's supporters crossed their fingers, hoping that California and Illinois would give their man the boost that James's delegates had failed to supply. But, after all the delay, California did not change its vote from that on the previous ballot. And Illinois, while providing four new votes for Willkie, gave Taft twenty-three new votes, raising his total to twenty-seven and bringing forth an enormous cheer from the Taft delegates.

When the final tally was announced, Willkie had gained forty-seven new votes, but Taft was close on his heels with forty-four. The totals now stood at 306 for Willkie, 259 for Taft. Dewey had fallen to third place. His managers urged him to withdraw, and word spread that he was coming to the hall to announce his support for Taft.

Willkie was discouraged. He had spent the evening in his suite at the Benjamin Franklin, dining on steak and French fries, asparagus, and raspberries, chain smoking Camels or any cigarette he could bum from his colleagues, and constantly conferring with his managers at the convention. For most of the evening the news had seemed hopeful, but the latest reports were decidedly less so. John Cowles, who was with him, later recalled: "Willkie turned to me and said 'Apparently Taft is going to be nominated on the next ballot.'"

As the fifth ballot began—only four times in its history had the GOP gone beyond a fourth ballot—the big question was how Dewey's vote would be split between the two remaining leaders. The first big break came with Kansas. Between the fourth and fifth ballots, Alf Landon had asked convention chairman Joe Martin's advice on what to do. Martin told him, "It looks like it's going to be Willkie." This was another important moment when Martin acted in Willkie's favor. Landon and Kansas voted accordingly, which ignited the loudest "We Want Willkie" chants yet heard. The gallery believed Landon would influence other delegates. The Willkie troops turned the volume even louder when New York awarded seventy-five votes to the Indianan, ten to Taft, and six to Dewey. "The Willkieites made the rafters ring with joy," the *Herald Tribune* reported.

Taft, however, kept chipping away. His ten votes from New York represented a gain of five. He also gained three new votes in Arkansas, Illinois, and Minnesota; four each from Georgia and Nebraska; five from North Carolina; six each from Louisiana and West Virginia; twelve from Oklahoma; and thirteen from Washington, whose chairman cast them "for a real Republican." Taft also picked up nineteen votes from Iowa and South Dakota that had gone to their favorite sons. The result was, when the final vote was announced, an even split between Taft and Willkie. Each added 123 votes.

Now Taft's total was 377. But Willkie's 429 put him just seventy-two votes from victory. It was a little too close for the Taft people, so they tried to persuade Martin to adjourn the convention until Friday morning. Willkie's managers, sensing victory, wanted to continue. Once more Martin sided with Willkie and refused to adjourn.

Meanwhile, the delegates had spilled out into the aisles arguing with one another, with their discussions often becoming heated. One reason for the frayed tempers was that they were tired, bone tired. It was midnight. They had stayed up most of the night before and "had spent most of their days in meetings, parades, demonstrations, and stood for hours chewing the fat in hotel lobbies" the *Herald Tribune* explained. The delegates' faces were drawn.

Floor managers and their assistants on both sides were even more exhausted. Not only were they worn out, but temperatures inside the hall had reached the point where it was now one vast Turkish bath. But most of them felt that this next ballot was going to be it. They had to get themselves up for one last great effort. After all, this wasn't the usual political struggle where victory and patronage were the only concerns. Also at stake was the choice between stopping Hitler and preserving the peace. So they moved frantically from one delegation to another, attempting to shore up support here, win over a new delegate there. The noise from the gallery made it almost impossible to be heard. And the pressure on them grew as the roll call got under way at 12:30 AM, and moved relentlessly from one state to another. They knew each vote lost was probably lost forever.

Alabama passed.

Arizona gave Willkie 6 votes.

Arkansas cast 10 for Taft and 2 for Willkie.

California gave 22 to Taft and 17 to Willkie.

Colorado gave Taft 6, Willkie 5.

At this point, Taft was leading 38 to 30.

Then came Connecticut with 16 for Willkie.

Delaware: Willkie 6.

Florida: 10 for Willkie, 2 for Taft.

Now Willkie seemed to be running away from Taft but the pendulum swung again.

Alabama now reported: 7 for Taft, 6 for Willkie.

Georgia: Taft 7, Willkie 6.

Idaho: Taft 6, Willkie 2.

Illinois: Taft 33, Willkie 24.

Then back and forth it went. Marcia Davenport called the tension unbearable as another of her white dresses wilted in the heat.

Indiana: Willkie 23, Taft 5.

Iowa: Taft 15, Willkie 7.

Kansas: Alf Landon continued to cast its 18 votes for Willkie.

But now Taft took two entire delegations in a row.

Kentucky: Taft 22.

Louisiana: Taft 12.

The margin was now just one vote with Wilkie ahead 148–147. It appeared either candidate could emerge the nominee. Maine passed, then Willkie began to increase his lead.

Maryland: Willkie 15, Taft 1.

Massachusetts: Willkie 30, Taft 2.

Michigan was next. Vandenberg had returned to Washington for a Senate vote. After the fifth ballot, he told his wife to ask Frank McKay, the national committeeman from Michigan who controlled the delegates, to switch to Taft. But McKay owed a favor to Willkie's supporter John D. M. Hamilton. Hamilton told McKay now was the time to deliver. McKay, however, insisted on a condition: "Some of my boys are worried about the picking of judges. They want to know, if your man Willkie is nominated and then elected, whose word will he take on recommendations for the federal bench—the organization's or the amateurs' running the Willkie clubs?"

Hamilton reported the problem to Sam Pryor, who called Willkie. What would Willkie do? Earlier in the evening he had told John Cowles that he had refused to make any deals to get delegates to switch to his side. But now it was clear that Michigan could be a turning point of the convention. The moment was reminiscent of Willkie's college days when, after sticking to his anti-fraternity principles for three years, he finally caved in during the fourth to Gwyneth Harry's ultimatum. He now told Pryor, "To hell with the judges, get the delegates."

Willkie may not have been aware of McKay's reputation. In an interview in 2001, former president Gerald Ford, who was from Grand Rapids just as McKay was, and knew him well, put it bluntly: "McKay was a crook." To put it more gently, McKay was not a fan of competitive bidding. When Michigan state agencies bought tires for their vehicles they bought them from Frank McKay's dealership on Frank McKay's terms.

The acting chairman of the Michigan delegation announced that the vote would be Willkie thirty-five, Taft two. The gallery exploded—everyone knew Michigan was crucial.

Although Taft was staggered by Michigan, he seemed to recover a bit by winning Minnesota eleven to ten and Mississippi nine to two. But then came a series of heavy blows that came close to finishing him off. Willkie won Missouri twenty-six to four, New Jersey thirty-two to zero, and New York seventy-eight to seven. Ohio's fifty-two delegates remained loyal to Taft, but then Oklahoma and Oregon went for Willkie. Pennsylvania was Taft's last hope of stopping the stampede.

Pennsylvania passed. The suspense continued. The delegation had been in a room off the floor caucusing since the intermission between the fifth and sixth ballot. Arthur James was begging the delegates to vote for him one more time. He was the favorite son who took his chances too seriously. On the fifth ballot he had received only seven votes from other states. His delegates saw that he couldn't possibly win. They were not, however, leaning to Taft, as Taft had been hoping. Twenty-one of them had already defected to Willkie. Joe Pew had hoped to save the rest for Taft but, above all, he wanted to beat Roosevelt. Many of the delegates shared that feeling. Seeing Willkie as a winner and wanting to board his train before it left the station, they rebelled, rushing to the floor. One, David Reed, seized the microphone and announced seventy-two votes for Willkie. James managed to get the microphone back and declared that the state was still with him. By the time the dispute had been settled, the roll call had proceeded and Virginia had put Willkie over the top with its sixteen votes. Pennsylvania had missed the bandwagon, but it was significant that, at the end, even the conservative Joe Pew wanted to get aboard.

Governor John Bricker of Taft's home state moved to make the nomination unanimous. The final count on the sixth ballot was 988 for Willkie and zero for everyone else. The convention adjourned at 1:30 AM.

CHAPTER NINE

★

FRIDAY, JUNE 28, 1940

Early Friday morning the people of Elwood, Indiana, ordinarily sound asleep well before midnight, filled the streets celebrating the triumph of the hometown boy. Anderson and Main Streets swarmed with honking automobiles and cheering crowds. "Factory whistles sounded shrill blasts, citizens afoot blew horns, beat drums, pans and cans," according to the Associated Press. Soon a torchlight parade began. "Jubilant Hoosiers piled into the center of town to join the main parade," the *Herald Tribune* reported; "neighbors slapped each other on the back, asking whether they had ever expected such an honor and achievement for 'Wendell.' Those who could collect their wits to answer vowed that they had 'known it all along.'"

While Elwood celebrated, the editors of the nation's leading paper, the *New York Times*, prepared an editorial for its Late City Edition that morning.

> Willkie did not need either Hitler's invasion of Holland or the latest returns of the Gallup survey to convince him there is a difference between democracy and dictatorship in Europe. . . . We find it highly reassuring that in this critical hour the Republican Party has chosen to put its best man forward.

Willkie, who had stayed up celebrating with friends, finally got to bed at 4:30 AM. Just half an hour later, his sleep was interrupted by a phone call from Ralph Cake. Cake, the Republican National Committeeman from Oregon, wanted Willkie to select Senator Charles Mc-Nary as his vice-presidential running mate. The same idea had already been proposed by publishers Roy Howard, Helen Reid, and Gardner Cowles. But Willkie had a problem: He had already promised the vice presidency to Governor Baldwin of Connecticut. Willkie called Baldwin's friend, Sam Pryor, and asked for advice. Pryor told Willkie that Willkie himself would have to talk to Baldwin.

The arguments for McNary were that he made a much better balance for the ticket than Baldwin. McNary was a westerner who, like Willkie, had a rough-hewn Will Rogers image but came unadulterated with any of the gloss of the eastern establishment. He had become dean of the Willamette Law School in 1909, but he was also a farmer, gaining a reputation as a leading horticulturist with his experiments, which included the development of the imperial prune. A United States senator since 1917, he was a public power advocate, which balanced Willkie's history with the private utilities. He was also highly regarded by the isolationist wing of the party, with which he often agreed and which Willkie desperately needed to woo.

When Willkie called Baldwin, Baldwin saw the logic of having McNary on the ticket and agreed to withdraw. All the rest of Willkie's team of advisors, including Henry Luce, Russell Davenport, Charles Halleck, John Cowles, Joe Martin, and Pryor joined Helen Reid, Gardner Cowles, and Roy Howard, in agreeing on McNary. When Martin called McNary, however, McNary was reluctant, saying, "Hell no, I wouldn't run with Willkie." When McNary had arrived in Philadelphia, he had denounced Willkie as a tool of Wall Street. But he gradually yielded to the persuasion of Martin and Ralph Cake and finally agreed to join the ticket.

"I remember the scene as if it were yesterday," Joseph Alsop wrote years later. "I knocked patiently on the door and after a brief time, Senator McNary himself let me in. Before I could even sit and make myself comfortable, the Senator produced a bottle of bourbon, pouring three full fingers, taking a strong restoring draft and cursing roundly into his drink. Party loyalty counted for a great deal more in those days than it does now. And if the Republicans agreed that McNary's candidacy would give them the best chance, then he would have no choice but to accept it. He called Willkie—as Roosevelt's Secretary of Interior Harold Ickes had earlier described him—'That damn barefoot boy from Wall Street' which was indeed largely accurate. And he said that the vice presidency even under the best of circumstances was 'no better than a god-damned spare tire.'"

Most of the delegates slept late that morning. For three days they had been immersed in the convention with hardly a moment to spare for anything else. Now, as they gradually got out of their beds, their minds were at last free to think about matters outside the realm of politics. Looking at the sports section, for example, they could see that in the American League Cleveland was leading Detroit by two games and the Red Sox by three. In the National League, Cincinnati led Brooklyn by one and a half and the Giants by two. Locally, the Phillies had lost last night to the Giants, seven to zero, and were now in their accustomed position at the bottom of the National League.

The stock market was up. Packard and Willkie's company, Commonwealth and Southern, led the Most Active List. The financial editor of the *Herald Tribune*, C. Norman Stabler, got carried away as he wrote of the "new hope" Willkie's nomination brought to investors and to the country:

> The results last night, when popular demand overrode political considerations and the Republican Party re-won the name of Grand Old Party by nominating the outstanding individual in the country to pilot the nation through the turbulent years immediately ahead, would be greeted this morning with a sigh of relief and a prayer for ultimate victory at the polls.

Delegates who were thinking of going to the movies must have been discouraged by the *Bulletin's* review of a new film that was opening that day. Called *Four Sons* and starring Don Ameche: "It will only depress and probably bore you." The *Bulletin* was a bit kinder to the other new film of the day, *I Was An Adventuress,* starring Vera Zorina and Richard Greene, which it said "would have been an ordinary meller about clever jewel thieves" had it not featured an accomplished supporting cast, including Erich von Stroheim, Peter Lorre, Sig Ruman, plus Zorina dancing an excerpt from *Swan Lake* choreographed by her husband, George Balanchine.

The ballet audience, small in any event, in those days must have been infinitesimal among the delegates to the convention, so that this was not a movie to tempt more than a handful to stay over Friday night. And, since neither the Phillies nor the Athletics, the other Philadelphia baseball team, were playing that day, most of the delegates were packing their suitcases, making travel arrangements for the trip home, and getting out of the hotel before check-out time. Some would go straight to the train stations since the vice-presidential choice was generally not considered to be one for the delegates to make but for them to be informed of by the new presidential nominee. The great majority, however, would wait until evening to depart and instead attend the convention's final session.

That afternoon, Charles McNary became his party's vice-presidential nominee. His only opponent was Representative Dewey Short, an extreme isolationist who had come to the convention as the only announced vice-presidential candidate. McNary got 890 votes, to Short's 108. Then, at 4:35 PM, Willkie made what at that time was an unprecedented appearance by a presidential nominee before a Republican convention. He and Edith walked down the center aisle to a thunderous ovation, and the band played Willkie's campaign song to the tune of "Hi Ho Hi Ho It's Off to Work We Go," from Walt Disney's *Snow White,* a movie that had been immensely popular during the preceding year. The Willkie version changed the word "off" to "back" to remind voters of the millions left unemployed by the New Deal.

After being introduced by Joe Martin as the next president of the United States, Willkie spoke briefly to the convention. Apparently suffering from amnesia about his agreement with Frank McKay for the Michigan votes, he declared "I stand before you without a single pledge, promise, or understanding of any kind, except the advancement of your cause, the preservation of American democracy." Concluding the speech, Willkie uttered some words that would haunt him in the future: "So, you Republicans, I call you to join, help me. The cause is great, we must win."

Hard-core party members would recall with resentment the words "you Republicans" as revealing that Willkie was still a Democrat at heart. But that afternoon in Philadelphia, those who noticed the gaffe ignored it, as Willkie received another ovation and everyone sang "God Bless America."

At a cabinet meeting the next morning, FDR said, "I have the general opinion that the Republicans have nominated the strongest ticket."

"Strongest" had to have two meanings for the president, one bad, one good. The bad was that of all the possible Republican choices, Willkie was the most likely to beat him in November. The good was that Roosevelt could now count on support for his foreign policy from the Republican nominee instead of the implacable opposition that he would have received from Taft.

Remember, just that Monday, Roosevelt had been confronted by Marshall, Stark, and Welles, with the enormous risk he would have to take to continue aiding Britain. Now he had the comfort of knowing that if he chose to take the risk, he would have the support of the person who would have been in the best position to eviscerate him for leaving this nation stripped of its defenses.

Another pressing issue that would require Willkie's help had been raised by a Friday news report that New York's governor Herbert Lehman had come out in favor of a military draft. Another story the same day underscored the need for the draft by showing that, despite vigorous efforts to recruit and a large pool of the unemployed, the regular army still had only 250,000 men. But the political danger of a draft remained great. After all, the country had never had one except when it was at war.

Would the country's rapidly rising sympathy for Britain and dislike of Hitler—illustrated by the increasing sentiment, 53 percent in the most recent Gallup poll, in favor of a third term for Roosevelt, and the amazing escalation of support for Willkie, both of which happened after Hitler had launched his blitzkrieg against Western Europe on April 9—endure the threat that their sons might be called for military service?

The answer to that question depended on whether Willkie would be able to maintain his independence from the party regulars who were mainly committed isolationists. So far he had done a remarkable job. Only the deal with Frank McKay marred his record of refusing to compromise with them.

His campaign had been based on skillful public relations, the favor of media giants, and volunteers attracted by his personality, his independent spirit, and his fierce opposition to Hitler. It is also true that the power of Wall Street helped. In those days, the influence of Wall Street banks and law firms over bankers and lawyers in the rest of the country was much greater than it is today. This meant that a call from a New York banker or lawyer to their counterparts in smaller localities could be assured of sympathetic attention. Thomas L. Stokes, who was a Scripps-Howard columnist at the time, told of meeting a woman on a train leaving Philadelphia after the convention. Her husband was a delegate who had arrived at the convention favoring Hoover, but "[M]y husband's banker called him and told him we should switch to Willkie, which we did." Stokes added, "Her husband certainly knew, whether she did or not, that his own banker's call was the result of a long-distance call to him by a representative of international finance in New York." It is also true that the tentacles of the Edison Electric Institute, the utilities' trade association, reached into cities and towns all over America.

And it should be added that those letters and telegrams were not all genuine. Alf Landon tells of responding to them, only to get a sackful returned marked "addressee unknown." Still, the volume of letters and telegrams was so great that it is impossible to believe that anything like all of them were manufactured. That last Gallup poll showed that real people were behind most of the messages.

I knew the Willkie people in my hometown. They were independent souls who did not march to any drummer but their own. What had started among a small coterie of the elite had become a genuine peoples' movement, creating what the *Kansas City Star* called "a huge tidal wave of popular acclaim" coming from what the *Los Angeles Times* described as "living rooms, crossroad grocery stores and street corners" throughout America. The "nomination of Mr. Willkie," wrote the *Philadelphia Inquirer* "stands as a shining demonstration to all the world of democracy at work." *The Nation's* Robert Bendiner called it "a genuine popular revolt." The *Washington Post's* Edward T. Folliard called it "a tremendous and historical revolt of the people against the politicians." The weight of the evidence is with them.

PART THREE

"SAVING FREEDOM

AT A MOMENT OF GREAT PERIL"

CHAPTER TEN

★

"I STILL DON'T WANT TO RUN"

Willkie now began a retreat from the center of the stage that would be interrupted briefly by his mid-August acceptance speech in Elwood, Indiana, and then would resume until after Labor Day when, as was the custom in those days, he began his campaign. After the convention, he traveled from Philadelphia to New York on publisher Roy Howard's yacht. Howard was one of the most conservative of Willkie's supporters and this trip may have been part of an effort Willkie needed to make to reach out to the right wing of the party. The Howard yacht left Philadelphia on Saturday and traveled down Delaware Bay, turning into the Atlantic at Cape May, and arriving in New York on Monday.

The excitement generated by his come-from-behind victory in Philadelphia followed Willkie to New York, where his appearances at the Radio City Music Hall and at the Empire Theater to see *Life with Father* were greeted by cheers from the audience. His main activity in New York was organizing a staff for the campaign. The big question was what to do about John D. M. Hamilton. Should Willkie ask him to continue as chairman of the Republican National Committee? Sam Pryor and Charlie Halleck said "Yes," reminding Willkie of the help Hamilton had been in getting the nomination—after all it was he had who called in that favor from Michigan's Frank McKay—

and of Hamilton's popularity with party regulars throughout the country. "No," answered Helen and Ogden Reid, Russell Davenport, and Oren Root, all of whom thought Hamilton too conservative and too isolationist. Furthermore, Alf Landon, who was still a force within the party, did not like Hamilton.

Willkie chose Joe Martin. Martin was, like Hamilton, popular with Republican regulars. He was also less conservative and less isolationist—but only by a few degrees. He also had another job, as a Republican leader of the House, that seemed likely to be a distraction from his campaign duties.

Cynics might have suspected that Willkie chose Martin as a reward for Martin's friendly rulings at the convention, and that a deal might well have been made before the rulings were given. But Martin himself says that he did not want the job, that he had to be talked into it by Alf Landon, the Reids, Colonel Robert McCormick of the *Chicago Tribune*, and most of all by Willkie himself, who invited Martin to his Fifth Avenue apartment. "I've never known a man so hard to say no to. He had a great Midwestern simplicity and enthusiasm. As he talked on, I became conscious of the fact that I like Willkie."

With Martin on board as RNC chairman, Hamilton was given the consolation prize of the title of executive director of the committee, and a salary of $25,000 at a time when senators got only $10,000. It was also decided that Root would continue as head of the Willkie clubs and that Russell Davenport would be designated Willkie's "personal representative." Even if the title may have been a trifle vague, Davenport remained Willkie's closest advisor.

Willkie also flew to Washington to confer with his running mate Charles McNary. McNary's response was much like Martin's: "I like Mr. Willkie very much. He is open, forthright and able." McNary agreed to campaign in rural areas where his Will Rogers quality, even more marked than Wilkie's, made him unusually popular. In fact, *Life* magazine said that small-town movie audiences would applaud when McNary appeared in the newsreels, a tribute that they did not give Willkie or FDR.

On July 8, Willkie resigned from Commonwealth and Southern. His son Phillip had urged him not to, fearing that Willkie would be left penniless if he lost the election. But Willkie told him not to worry, that something would turn up. Willkie and his wife then left New York for Colorado Springs, where they spent six weeks at the Broadmoor Hotel, a famous resort where Willkie received Republican luminaries like Herbert Hoover and planned the fall campaign but made only a handful of public appearances.

As Willkie retreated from the spotlight, Franklin Roosevelt moved to center stage. Not only was he the principal player in the events of the summer, but in terms of the story told by this book, understanding the wrenching choices that he faced that summer of 1940 is the key to understanding the significance of Willkie's nomination. Only if we realize how close a call those days were for Roosevelt, the United States, and Britain can we comprehend how essential was Willkie's role in the steps the president took to prevent Britain's collapse and to prepare this country for its entry into World War II.

Of all the choices facing FDR after the fall of France, none was more daunting than choosing between arming Britain and arming the United States. Remember that on June 24, his national-security advisors had counseled no more aid, saying that the United States needed everything we had and everything we could produce for our own defenses. In deciding whether to follow their advice, the first question Roosevelt had to ask was: Did Britain have the will—and the ability—to withstand the coming Nazi onslaught?

Although there was little doubt about the sincerity of Churchill's defiant stand against the Nazis, there was considerable concern that the architect of Munich, Neville Chamberlain, might still harbor thoughts of placating Hitler. His longtime allies in the Conservative Party, Lord Halifax and Sir Samuel Hoare, were also suspected of preferring a peace that would spare England the horrors that would surely accompany a German invasion.

Concern about a British collapse began to recede on June 30th, when Chamberlain laid to rest any fear of his participation in further appeasement by making a radio address firmly supporting Churchill and denouncing talk of peace. Earlier, Churchill outmaneuvered an effort by Halifax and Hoare that might have produced a more accommodationist Whitehall, one that would accept the status quo in Europe in return for Hitler's assurance that England would not be invaded and that the British Empire would be preserved.

Then on July 3rd and 4th, the British either seized or destroyed enough of the French fleet that it no longer presented the threat that it had posed of being combined with the Italian Navy to dominate the Mediterranean. This action enraged the Petain government and ended any possibility of even a lukewarm relationship between Britain and Vichy. By such a radical step, however, the British demonstrated they were willing to fight on—whatever the cost.

Roosevelt had pushed the law to its outer limits to rush military equipment to Britain and France. Indeed, the attorney general had ruled that the sale of the twenty torpedo boats would exceed those limits, forcing FDR to cancel it. Since the torpedo boat negotiations had begun before France fell, the navy had supported the sale, but it seemed clear from Admiral Stark's stand at the June 24 meeting that such support was unlikely to be forthcoming in the future. To make matters worse, Senator David Walsh, an Anglophobic Irishman from Massachusetts who was chairman of the Senate Naval Affairs Committee, had managed to attach an amendment to the navy appropriations bill that added another obstacle to letting Britain have American ships.

For Churchill, the torpedo boat decision had to be very bad news indeed. On June 15 he had cabled Roosevelt reiterating in the strongest terms an earlier plea that the United States let Britain have fifty U.S. destroyers that had been mothballed since World War I. England needed them to protect its shipping against U-boats and itself against the cross-channel invasion threatened by Hitler. The extent of Churchill's sense of the desperate need for these destroyers became clear when it was followed on June 26 by an unprecedented personal letter from King George VI to Roosevelt repeating and endorsing Churchill's request in the most urgent language.

To prepare the country for possible war against the Nazis, Roosevelt knew he would need a military draft. The Burke-Wadsworth bill providing for such a draft had been introduced in mid-June. With the fall of France having greatly heightened the country's sense of peril, the bill's prospects were reasonably bright at the moment. But Roosevelt feared that, as the sense of danger diminished, opposition to the bill would grow.

The pending draft bill had affected Roosevelt's thinking about a third term. He saw that, if he proposed drafting others, he could not refuse a draft himself. This both helped him understand his duty and inspired a political strategy. The best way to handle the third-term issue, without his seeming to want to overturn the precedent against the third term dating from George Washington, was to have the nomination not appear to be something he sought but a call to duty from his party.

No one knew for sure what was in the mind of a man a contemporary cartoon depicted as the Great Sphinx, with a cigarette holder jutting from its mouth. But the consensus seems to be that, until April 1940, he was tending toward retirement when his second term expired in January 1941. He had signed a $75,000-a-year contract to write for *Colliers* magazine. To his friends and family he talked longingly of retiring to Hyde Park to preside over his library, which he formally dedicated in a ceremony held between the conventions, to finish his retreat cottage just above Eleanor's Val-Kill, and to oversee the operation of his farm. He had a good reason for not ruling out a third term, however: He would have seen a relentless erosion of his power if Congress and the bureaucracy were certain he was a lame duck.

There is, nonetheless, some merit to the argument that Roosevelt had all along intended to seek a third term. The argument's strongest point is that FDR had failed to groom a successor. At various times he had hinted to James Farley, Cordell Hull, Paul McNutt, and Henry Wallace, the secretary of agriculture, that he would support them. Hull was probably the recipient of the most hints, but Roosevelt's detractors agree that he suspected Hull, at age sixty-nine, lacked the drive to really go after the nomination. Friendly historians argue that Roosevelt's real first choice, Harry Hopkins, had been disqualified by a serious illness in 1939 that the president could not have anticipated. The man who would have been Roosevelt's second choice, Robert Jackson, had been soundly whipped by Willkie in that Town Meeting debate. His third choice, Wallace, could not possibly win the presidency on his own in 1940, as was to become clear from the reaction of the convention to Roosevelt's insistence that Wallace be the vice-presidential nominee.

Roosevelt thought James Farley, the popular postmaster general and chairman of the Democratic National Committee, was too conservative, but he owed Farley a tremendous debt for Farley's efforts in the 1932 and 1936 campaigns. He definitely did not want Farley as an enemy, but Farley was opposed to a third term and had urged supporters to nominate him at the convention with the hope that a Hull-Farley ticket would emerge. In early July he also leaked word to the *New York Times* that he was leaving politics to accept a job with the New York Yankees baseball organization.

Roosevelt, by this point in the summer of 1940, had clearly decided on a third term. Judge Sam Rosenman, FDR's longtime speechwriter and confidant, believes the final decision was motivated by the British evacuation of Dunkirk. That sounds right, as this is when it became clear that France would fall and that Britain's plight was desperate. Roosevelt's sense of duty combined with his strong ego convinced him that the country and the world needed him to continue at the helm. If any doubt about running lingered in Roosevelt's mind, it was surely eliminated when, on July 1st, Willkie challenged him, saying that he wanted Roosevelt to run for a third term because "I want to beat him."

Assuming that Roosevelt did not want there to be any hint that he was seeking a third term and that he wanted to be drafted by a unanimous convention, the main obstacle in his path was James Farley. The president already had the pledged votes of a majority of the delegates but he didn't want there to be any floor fight, and that was sure to happen if Farley was nominated. Additionally, valuing Farley's political skills as highly as he did, Roosevelt wanted Farley's wholehearted support during the coming campaign. Handling Farley would be a major challenge to the president's human and political skills. He invited the party chairman to lunch at Hyde Park on July 7th.

Jim Farley left Manhattan for Hyde Park that morning. The day was already warm, well on its way to being a scorcher. Instead of heading directly north on the east side of the Hudson he crossed the George Washington Bridge and took Route 9W north through Rockland County, where he had been born. The journey brought back warm memories of his family and of growing up. Soon, however, his thoughts turned to his impending meeting with FDR.

Widely considered to have been the political mastermind of Roosevelt's great victories in 1932 and 1936, Farley had begun to disagree with the president during FDR's second term. He was not enthusiastic about the court-packing plan, in which Roosevelt had unsuccessfully attempted to add up to six new justices to the Supreme Court, that had sabotaged much of his New Deal program.

Then, in 1938, Farley was again not happy with FDR's effort to aid liberal Democrats and purge conservatives, which, though it had a few successes, notably in Alben Barkley's victory in Kentucky and Lister Hill's in Alabama, had more defeats—by Walter George in Georgia, Joseph Tydings in Maryland, Guy Gillette in Iowa, and Cotton Ed Smith in South Carolina. Farley was also becoming more conservative himself, less of a New Dealer and more sympathetic to the Garner wing of the party.

Farley had epitomized the big-city boss–practical politician side of the Democratic Party, to which winning elections and party loyalty reigned far above ideology. Ideologically, the party was split between liberals, mostly Northern, and conservatives, mostly Southern. The conservatives and liberals came together to some extent on agricultural policy, where helping the farmer was a cause shared by both sides, and on foreign policy, where the party had only a handful of isolationists like Senator Burton Wheeler of Montana. Practical politicians helped bring the factions together by reminding them that they all wanted to win elections. Because Farley had played this uniting role he was highly regarded throughout the party.

Farley also harbored political ambitions for himself, but he had rejected Roosevelt's advice that he follow FDR's path to the White House by seeking the governorship of New York and demonstrating that he could run the nation's largest state. Farley apparently felt his experience as postmaster general and as chairman of the Democratic National Committee was all he needed to qualify himself for the presidency. Moreover, the governor of New York, Herbert Lehman, was a Democrat and would not leave office until 1942.

Their disagreements led to Farley and Roosevelt becoming increasingly distant from each other. Roosevelt relied more and more on Harry Hopkins and Ed Flynn, a Democratic leader from New York City, for political advice—and less and less on Farley.

Farley had told Roosevelt that he was opposed to a third term. Now he was determined to make clear that that stand was unalterable, that he would not continue to serve as chairman of the national committee, and that his own name would be presented to the convention as a candidate for president.

Early that July afternoon, Farley crossed the bridge at Poughkeepsie and proceeded up Route 9, the old Albany Post Road, for five miles to Hyde Park, actually arriving before FDR had returned from church. He was met by FDR's mother, Mrs. Sara Roosevelt. She did not beat around the bush, immediately telling Farley that she hoped there was no truth to the rumor in the morning's *New York Times* that he intended to leave politics to take an executive position with the New York Yankees baseball club.

"You know," she said, "I would hate to think of Franklin running for the presidency if you're not around. I want to be sure you help my boy."

Farley's answer was noncommittal. An awkward moment was salvaged by the appearance of Harry Hopkins. Soon they were joined by Roosevelt's press secretary Steve Early, Hopkins's secretary Victor Scholis, and Roosevelt's personal secretary Missy LeHand. Then Eleanor Roosevelt came downstairs. She immediately followed up on her mother-in-law's comment by saying that she was both pleased and shocked by the news in the morning paper that Farley was going into business and leaving politics: "Of course I'm pleased to have anything happen to you which would be personally beneficial but I am shocked at the thought you may not direct things in the coming campaign." After all their years with a son and husband in politics, neither Sara nor Eleanor Roosevelt were innocents. They were clearly co-conspirators in the plot to keep Farley on board.

The president then joined the party and the group went in for lunch. Conversation around the table had both light and serious sides. The former concerned whether Andrew Jackson was justifiably attacked about the legality of his wife's divorce. Roosevelt loved gossip, whether it be about historical figures or Wendell Willkie's mistress, Irita Van Doren.

The serious talk was about Britain's attack on the French fleet a few days earlier, in which Britain had destroyed or seized most of the French navy, killing 1250 French sailors. Many Americans were shocked. Just a few weeks before, these dead French sailors had been Britain's allies. How could the British now murder them! Churchill himself said, "This was heartbreaking for me." It was an action born of desperation and of necessity. England had to keep the French fleet from falling into Nazi hands. Roosevelt understood this. Indeed, there is evidence that he had secretly approved the action beforehand. And Harry Hopkins later told Churchill that it was this action that convinced the president that Britain would continue to fight. However Roosevelt also knew that it left a bad taste in the mouths of many of his countrymen, and would for a time at least make it more difficult for him to give Britain the aid that he wanted to give.

After lunch, Roosevelt invited Farley into his study for a talk. The study, a small, dark, high-ceilinged room, was dominated by FDR's large Victorian desk. It was just off the front porch, which was on the shady side of the house, where the other guests had repaired after lunch. Farley could hear snippets of their conversation as he and FDR talked.

It was so warm in the study that both men took off their coats. Farley was so angry that he "looked like a thundercloud," Roosevelt later recalled. FDR tried to soothe him with small talk. After a half hour of aimless chitchat, Roosevelt finally got to the point: "Jim, last July when we canvassed the political situation, I indicated definitely that I would not run for a third term. I believe we decided that on or about February 1st, I would write a letter to one of the states which has an early primary stating that I would not be a candidate for re-election."

"It was North Dakota," Farley replied.

"Well, after that conversation of ours and when it got along to February 1, I could not give that statement. It [being a lame duck] would have destroyed my effectiveness. . . . I still don't want to run . . . I want to come up here. . . . Jim, what would you do in my place?"

"In your position, actually, I would do exactly what General Sherman did—issue a statement saying I would refuse to run if nominated and would not serve if elected."

This suggestion could not have delighted Roosevelt. He had decided that he must run—Tommy Corcoran said "[T]he Democratic nominee was decided in Copenhagen"—but he wanted to be drafted. FDR wanted the country to understand that what he had just told Farley was true, that, as far as his personal preference was concerned, he wanted to retire to Hyde Park, but that he felt it was his duty in light of the precarious world situation to accept a call to serve another term. So Roosevelt said, "I could not in these times if nominated and elected refuse to take the oath, even if I knew I would be dead within 30 days."

"This statement made a powerful impression on me," Farley later recalled, "and it has been deepened in my mind by what happened five years later"—FDR was to die on April 12, 1945—"I can see him now with his right hand clasping the arm of his chair as he leaned back, his left arm bent at the elbow to hold his cigarette and his face and eyes deadly earnest."

Farley then made another statement not designed to please his host: "I'm going to allow my name to go before the convention."

This meant that Roosevelt would have opposition, that delegates would have another, and very popular, candidate to vote for, and that Roosevelt's nomination would not be unanimous. Before Roosevelt had a chance to try to change Farley's mind, the party chairman slammed the door shut, saying "My decision is irrevocable."

Farley's determination to run for president is a little hard to understand, because he knew he had no chance of winning. His real hope had been to be the vice-presidential nominee in a ticket headed by Cordell Hull: "Hull would have been a very strong nominee and could have been elected," Farley explained, pointing out that "the last Gallup poll showed Hull to be even more popular than the president."

Farley was probably right in believing that, if FDR had stuck to his promise to announce in February that he would not seek a third term, then Hull would have been the nominee and Farley would have had a good shot at getting the vice presidency, which would have given the country a chance to adjust to the idea of having a Catholic like Farley as president. So, Farley may have been angry enough at Roosevelt for having broken his promise—and for having shut him out of the inner circle—that he decided out of spite to throw a monkey wrench into Roosevelt's hoped-for draft.

Despite his anger, however, Farley struggled to remain objective in advising the president. When Roosevelt sought his counsel on possible vice-presidential nominees and asked what he thought of Henry Wallace, Farley replied: "Boss I'm going to be very direct. Henry Wallace won't add a bit of strength to the ticket. He has always been most cordial and cooperative with me, but I think you must know that people look on him as a wild-eyed fellow."

Farley got the impression that Roosevelt wanted Wallace. Still, Farley said, "I told the president that in my judgment there was only one man with whom he should run. And that man was Hull."

But, when Roosevelt asked him to urge Hull to take second place, Farley says, "I refused saying I knew how Hull felt about both the third term and the vice presidency adding that I certainly was not going to urge him to change his attitude."

This wasn't totally reasonable. Why recommend Hull to Roosevelt if he wouldn't urge Hull to run? But Farley was angry, so angry in fact that Steve Early had to drive him around for an hour after the meeting to give him a chance to cool off. The drive calmed Farley down enough that when he was interviewed by reporters as he was leaving he gave no hint that he was upset.

Farley's impression that Roosevelt favored Henry Wallace was shared by Roosevelt's speechwriter and adviser Judge Sam Rosenman, who, when confiding to Wallace that he thought FDR would seek a third term, added, "In that case you'll have to be vice president." In addition, Wallace was told by Harry Hopkins that in the event Hull would not accept the vice presidency, "the President might come as close to agreeing on you as anyone." An even stronger endorsement could be inferred from the fact that Hopkins and Wallace traveled to the Democratic Convention together, leaving Washington for Chicago on July 11 on Baltimore and Ohio's Capital Limited.

Wallace had the disadvantage of being a former Republican from Iowa and the son of a Republican secretary of agriculture. He was also a mystic, which helps explain Farley's characterization of him as "wild-eyed." His biographers, John Culver and John Hyde, write of "the dedicated enthusiasm with which he plumbed the occult during the 1920s and 1930s. All manner of exotic phenomena fascinated him, seances, symbols, rituals, astrology, Native American religion, Oriental philosophy." Wallace described himself as "a searcher for methods of bringing the inner light to outward manifestation and raising outward manifestation to the inner light."

On the plus side, he was widely considered to have been an outstanding leader of the Department of Agriculture. He had compiled a distinguished record as a scientist: "One of the true galvanizers of scientific research in agriculture" is the way a contemporary described him. Wallace created a hybrid corn that revolutionized farming. His constantly probing mind asked questions that made other scientists stop and think. Once, for example, he wondered, since rats are so important to scientific research, Why hasn't anyone considered the possibility that "genetically unequal rats would give unequal results?"

He was a sports enthusiast and a virtual fitness fanatic. He walked three miles through Rock Creek to his office from the Wardman Park, an apartment hotel much favored by Washington officialdom where his fellow residents included Colonel Dwight Eisenhower and Attorney General Robert Jackson. He was a spirited participant in a wide variety of athletic activities including Indian wrestling, boomerang throwing, tennis, badminton, and boxing. His approach to the last sport was so vigorous that he once knocked out Senator Allen Ellender.

Wallace's performance as secretary of agriculture was impressive enough that, in the late '30s, both *Look* and the *Saturday Evening Post* had run articles featuring him as a good bet to win the Democratic presidential nomination in 1940. The columnist John Franklin Carter had called him "the great liberal hope for 1940."

One thing that distinguished him from his fellow Midwestern progressives like George W. Norris and Robert LaFallotte was his early internationalism. Wallace was outspokenly anti-Nazi. His combination of staunch opposition to Hitler and dedication to the New Deal naturally had great appeal to Franklin Roosevelt, but his combination of mysticism and a Republican past—this was before he joined the Roosevelt administration in 1933—left him with little appeal for party regulars like Farley and promised a giant headache for FDR at the convention.

As the Democratic Convention drew near, the mood in the country was not good. The reason was probably a combination of the British attack on the French fleet and Roosevelt's silence on the third term issue. The death of all those French sailors who just weeks ago had been England's comrades in arms was depressing to Americans who were still not far removed from the "Lafayette, we are here!" spirit of World War I. And FDR's refusal to say whether he would seek re-election was both puzzling and frustrating. In particular, delegates who were preparing to attend the convention felt that decision making was going on out of sight and without their voices. This meant that they approached the convention with the usual excitement replaced by a glum sense that they were going to be puppets.

The only spirits that didn't seem to have sunk were FDR's. The

Great Optimist refused to let life get him down. During the week before the convention, he laughed his way through a White House showing of *The Ghost Breakers* with Bob Hope, Paulette Goddard, and Anthony Quinn. FDR told Harold Ickes a joke that made fun of himself. Roosevelt's critics often alleged that he confused himself with the deity. So FDR's story concerned a psychiatrist who had just gone to heaven. After making his obeisance before the great white throne he hurried back to St. Peter and begged to be allowed to return to Earth. It seemed that the being on the throne thought he was Franklin D. Roosevelt.

On the Saturday before the convention, Roosevelt took a weekend cruise on the presidential yacht, the *Potomac*. FDR loved the *Potomac* for many reasons, not least of which was the food. Prepared by Filipino stewards, it was delicious and a welcome contrast to the dull menus at the White House, where the tasteless cuisine, featuring such delicacies as overcooked canned string beans and tuna casserole, may well have constituted Eleanor Roosevelt's revenge for Lucy Mercer.

On this trip, Roosevelt was joined by Judge Sam Rosenman, Dr. Ross McIntire, Missy LeHand, and two of her friends. "We had a quiet, uneventful journey down the river and back," wrote Rosenman. "One would never imagine that significant political history was being made by the calm, thoughtful man sitting in the stern playing with his stamps or reading the newspaper. We did a little fishing. In the evening after dinner the President caught one rock bass and one eel."

CHAPTER ELEVEN

★

"THE CONVENTION IS BLEEDING TO DEATH"

When they finished fishing, Roosevelt and Judge Rosenman worked on a message to be read to the Democratic Convention on the following Monday evening, July 13th, stating that the president did not want a third term and telling his delegates that they were free to vote for the candidate of their choice.

Sunday night, after they had returned to the White House, Rosenman had gone to bed when the phone rang. It was Attorney General Robert Jackson and Frank Walker, one of the president's political advisers, calling from Chicago to tell Rosenman that it was the consensus of Roosevelt's friends in Chicago that he should not release his delegates. Harry Hopkins called at 7 AM to reiterate the point. They knew they had enough delegates for Roosevelt to beat Farley but they were afraid that, if released, enough of the delegates would defect to create an embarrassingly close race. Hopkins said he would call back to make the point to the president personally.

"I hurriedly dressed and went into the president's bedroom down the hall while he was still having his breakfast," Rosenman later recalled. "He had apparently spent a restful night and he looked very fit and was in a fighting mood. I told him his friends in Chicago were going to call him soon to urge him not to send the message at all. While I was still in the president's bedroom the call came through from Chicago and the president asked me to listen in on the telephone extension."

Harry Hopkins spoke first, followed by Walker, South Carolina Senator Jimmy Byrnes, and Chicago Mayor Ed Kelly, the head of the Kelly-Nash machine and one of the most powerful of the big-city bosses. All argued that the message should not be sent.

Roosevelt stood his ground. He gave two reasons, according to Rosenman, "first a personal feeling that if he was nominated he wanted it to be a free and open nomination by delegates released from any pledge or commitment, second for purposes of history he wanted to make it clear that he was not actively seeking a third term. He wanted that stated as part of the permanent written record of the convention."

The Chicago group then tried to persuade FDR not to have the message delivered by Speaker William Bankhead that night as planned, but instead to wait until Tuesday night when it could be read by Alben Barkley, whose devotion to FDR was deemed considerably less questionable than Bankhead's.

Roosevelt resisted even this point. "I have never seen the President more stubborn," recalled Rosenman. FDR finally yielded, however, when it was pointed out that Bankhead wouldn't speak until 10 PM and that Barkley would have a larger audience when he spoke at an earlier hour Tuesday evening. "On that basis, and that basis alone, the president gave in."

But Roosevelt was more worried than he wanted to admit. What if Farley did get enough votes to embarrass him? There was one sure way to prevent that: persuade Farley to forgo balloting and let the president be nominated by acclamation.

So, Roosevelt picked up the phone and put in a call to the Democratic National Committee headquarters at the Stevens Hotel in Chicago. Mrs. Duffy, Farley's faithful secretary, answered. She buzzed her boss to tell him that the president was on the line.

"Is everything going all right?" asked the president.

"Everything is okay with me. I'm just on my way to the convention hall. Have you got that letter we talked about ready?"

"Good that you brought it up, Jim. I just got back from my weekend trip and am going to tackle it this afternoon. I may have it ready for you tonight."

"I'll be right here if you want me."

Pause.

"By the way, Jim, there are a lot of stories in the paper. They're writing stories about there being no need for a ballot."

"That's perfectly silly. There just has to be a ballot. You and I both know there must be a ballot and that any effort to prevent a ballot or a roll call will be the one thing that's needed to wreck the Democratic Party in November. It's just too ridiculous to discuss."

"Of course," FDR muttered, giving up. "Take care of yourself."

After talking to FDR, Farley left the Stevens for the Chicago Stadium, where the convention was to be held. Larger than the Philadelphia Convention Hall, it could accommodate a crowd of 25,000. But, as in Philadelphia, whatever air conditioning the stadium possessed stood little chance against the heat generated by a full house on a hot day. By happy coincidence, however, a cold front moved through Chicago that afternoon, and the temperature dropped from eighty degrees at 1 PM to sixty-eight an hour later.

At noon, Jim Farley banged the gavel and opened the 1940 Democratic Convention. The first session was brief, lasting just fifty minutes, and featured welcoming addresses by Farley and Mayor Kelly. It was sparsely attended. Veteran delegates knew that nothing would happen at the first session—and Chicago offered a variety of more alluring attractions.

That afternoon, the Cubs, with Larry French pitching and Gabby Hartnett catching, were playing the New York Giants at Wrigley field. (The Cubs won 5-to-3.) Later that week the Brooklyn Dodgers would come to town. At the movies, *Andy Hardy Meets a Debutante*, with Mickey Rooney and Judy Garland, was playing at the Chicago, Nelson Eddy and Jeannette McDonald were starring in *New Moon* at the United Artists, Cary Grant and Irene Dunne appeared in *My Favorite Wife* at the Garrick and the long-run showing of *Gone with the Wind* was in its final weeks at the Wood. At the Apollo was *The Mortal*

Storm, the movie about Jews escaping Nazi persecution that had been showing in Philadelphia during the Republican Convention. A more sympathetic view of the Nazis could be found at the Little German, a neighborhood theatre, which featured *Der Felzug in Polen,* a film about the Nazi blitzkrieg in Poland. It was a reminder that there was a substantial German community in the nation's heartland that was, if not pro-Hitler, firmly opposed to aiding Germany's enemies.

For shoppers, Chicago offered Marshall Field, one of the nation's great department stores and mecca for my mother and millions of other women. For those who preferred the stage, Al Jolson and Ruby Keeler were starring in *Hold onto Your Hats* at the Grand Opera House, and Percy Warram and Lillian Gish led the Chicago company of *Life with Father* at the Blackstone. Wendell Willkie, it will be recalled, was cheered while attending the show's New York production shortly after the Republican Convention.

Next door to the Blackstone Theatre was the Blackstone Hotel, a splendid turn-of-the-century building with red-carpeted marble corridors, where Harry Hopkins's suite 303 was the nerve center of the convention. By unhappy coincidence, it was the same suite that had been the scene of the "smoke-filled room" plot to nominate Warren Harding. Hopkins had a direct line to FDR at the White House, and it was through him and his lieutenants, Jimmy Byrnes, Ed Flynn, and Ed Kelly, that the convention learned what the Boss wanted. *Time* magazine called them "the Janizariat" after the sultan's legendary palace guard.

Hopkins's suite consisted of a large living room with a fireplace, a bedroom with twin beds, and a bathroom—which, in addition to serving the usual function, also housed the phone with a direct line to the White House, assuring privacy for any conversation with Roosevelt. In addition to his suite at the Blackstone, Hopkins also had a room at the Ambassador East to which he could escape from the clamor of the convention.

Henry Wallace had a couple of rooms across the street at the Stevens, staffed at first by just one aide, Claude Wickard, joined on Wednesday by Paul Applebee, who had to resign his civil service position at the Department of Justice to participate in the politicking in Chicago. Harold Ickes tartly noted that Hopkins's aides were not similarly sensitive. They were there, he observed, "Hatch Act or no Hatch Act," referring to the recently enacted law designed to keep Roosevelt from using the civil service for political purposes.

Also located in the Stevens was the headquarters of the Democratic National Committee, where Jim Farley was ensconced. Farley, too, had a direct line to the White House, but it was Hopkins, the delegates quickly learned, to whom the president was confiding more frankly.

Harry Hopkins was not a physically attractive man. Stomach cancer had deprived him of any chance of succeeding Roosevelt and had left him looking one step removed from the undertaker. His thin hair was carelessly combed above a pale face, his chest appeared to have been caved in, and beneath protruded a small potbelly. His unprepossessing appearance made him an easy target for everyone who hated the New Deal and even for some, like Harold Ickes, who loved it but distrusted Hopkins's bureaucratic maneuvering and closeness to FDR. For Ickes it was especially galling that, although he had been the first cabinet member to come out for a third term, here in Chicago it was Hopkins who was speaking with Roosevelt.

Hopkins had become so close to Roosevelt that he now lived on the second floor of the White House. Now that the presidency was out of his own reach, he seemed to have dedicated his life to Roosevelt, and the president's awareness of the devotion gave him a special place among Roosevelt's advisers. He was also a firm believer in the New Deal. The son of an Iowa harness maker who had gone to New York to work in a settlement house, Hopkins became Federal Relief Administrator in the early days of the Roosevelt administration, then head of the WPA, and finally secretary of commerce.

He and Farley would lead the opposing camps throughout the convention, first fighting over whether FDR was to get the nomination by acclamation, and then about who would be the vice-presidential nominee.

All day Monday the Janizariat pressed Farley to stop seeking the presidential nomination. Governor Herbert Lehman of New York and Boss Ed Crump of Memphis were among the many dispatched to try to persuade the chairman. "They all felt that if the president was at the head of the ticket they would get more votes for their local ticket," Farley explained. "It was as simple as that."

Farley, however, was determined to be nominated. His last act before leaving for the convention on Monday was to call Carter Glass, an elderly and frail—but widely respected—conservative senator from Virginia, known as the father of the Federal Reserve and scheduled to nominate Farley on Tuesday night. "I was aware of the pressure being put on him by the acclamation boys to have him sit out the convention at his home and leave me without my chosen nominator:

"Are you coming?" I ask him.
"It's a fight, ain't it, try to keep me away."
"I still hope you'll place my name in nomination."
"Nothing can stop me, and I mean nothing."

On Monday night, Farley got another chance to speak at the convention. At the conclusion of his speech, he received an ovation that could not have brought joy to the Janizariat. They, however, had to be pleased that they had persuaded FDR not to entrust his message to Speaker William Bankhead, who followed Farley to the platform and as temporary chairman of the convention delivered the keynote address. There was a full house on hand. Unfortunately, the father of the very lively actress Tallulah Bankhead was less than lively in his speaking, and less than ardent in his advocacy of another term for Roosevelt. Even Farley, who shared Bankhead's moderate conservatism, thought the speech "lacked fire" and that Bankhead appeared "tired and worn." There was no chance that he could have ignited a demonstration for Roosevelt that could have led to a nomination by acclamation.

Tuesday morning did not dawn brightly for the Janizariat or any of the other pro-third-termers. They realized that, although Roosevelt's name had only been mentioned sparingly on Monday, on the few occasions it was spoken, mainly in Mayor Kelly's opening address, it had not generated an enthusiastic response from the audience. Was it, wondered those who remembered Sam Pryor's machinations during the Republican Convention, because Farley controlled the distribution of tickets to the Chicago stadium? If that had been the case, Mayor Kelly resolved to correct the problem. After all, his police force could control who had access to the building—whether they had tickets or not. Other third-term supporters feared that the problem was not just tickets but a more serious malaise sapping the spirits of the delegates. "The situation," Secretary of Labor Frances Perkins told FDR over the phone, "is just as sour as can be." Secretary of the Interior Harold Ickes telegraphed, "The convention is bleeding to death. Your reputation may bleed to death with it."

Perkins urged Roosevelt to come to Chicago immediately to speak to the delegates. FDR didn't think that was a good idea, but thought his wife might be the answer. He asked Perkins to call Mrs. Roosevelt. Perkins understood the marital situation in the White House well enough not to suggest that FDR ask her himself.

Tuesday morning, a cartoon on the front page of the *Chicago Tribune* had depicted a bunch of cigar-smoking fat guys parachuting into the convention. They were labeled "political spenders," "machine politicians," "New Deal experimenters," "payroll padders," "tax eaters," "political bosses," and "theorists" under the overall banner of "our (meal) ticket: Roosevelt." The *Tribune*, to be sure, was no friend of FDR's. Conservative and isolationist, it was run by the autocratic Colonel Robert McCormick, and stridently opposed both FDR's New Deal and his internationalism. On Monday, the front-page cartoon had depicted the Democratic donkey smoking a pipe labeled "Roosevelt's Peace Promises" while seated on a powder keg labeled "Roosevelt's war-like utterances" identified as "all measures short of war," "stab in the back speech," "enmity of most of Europe," and "quarantine speech."

If the *Tribune* seemed indifferent to the danger from abroad, the same cannot be said for the *Chicago Daily News*. On the front page of its Tuesday afternoon edition was the headline "Nazi Troops Mass on Coast, Blitz Looms." The *Daily News* was still owned by Colonel Frank Knox, who had joined Roosevelt's Cabinet as secretary of the navy in June.

Also on Tuesday afternoon, word began to circulate among the delegates and reporters that a statement from Roosevelt would be read that night. Would it release his delegates or not? Jim Farley heard from one source that it would, and from another that it wouldn't. When Frances Perkins came to his office that afternoon, wearing her trademark tricorne hat, Farley told her about the contradictory reports he was getting. "Jim, has the president talked to you about it?"

"No."

"That's incredible."

Perkins must have called FDR, because just after eight that evening, as Farley was getting ready to leave for the stadium, he was buzzed once more by Mrs. Duffy and picked up the phone.

"Jim, I've been trying to reach you all afternoon," said Roosevelt. "And I haven't been able to catch up with you. What are you up to out there?"

"Oh I'm a pretty busy fellow out here," replied Farley, who had been in the office throughout the afternoon and knew that Roosevelt hadn't called.

"Jim, I wanted to tell you that Alben has that statement we talked about."

Roosevelt, however, did not explain what the statement would say. So Farley went to the stadium like practically everyone else, not knowing the contents of the message.

Not only was Senator Alben Barkley, the man chosen to deliver FDR's message, an ardent Roosevelt loyalist, he was also one of the party's greatest orators. It was he who would be the first to stir the 1948 Convention with the hope that Truman just might be able to win.

That Tuesday night in 1940 Barkley was dressed in a white suit— in that era white was much favored by politicians as summer attire. Farley, Bankhead, and Hopkins (among many others) wore white suits during the convention. Introduced to the strains of "My Old Kentucky Home," Barkley at first appeared nervous to the *Tribune's* Arthur Henning, but "when Barkley mentioned the magical name of Roosevelt for the first time the Convention went wild." The organist played "Franklin D. Roosevelt Jones," a lively song of that year inspired by the craze of giving children the president's name. A twenty-five-minute demonstration ensued, and state standards were paraded around the hall with North Dakota and Arkansas in the lead.

After he gaveled a halt to the demonstration, Barkley, all traces of nervousness gone, resumed his speech in full command. Frequently interrupted by applause as he built to his conclusion, he declared that the Roosevelt administration was the "greatest instrument for the good of the American people since the Declaration of Independence."

After he concluded his address, Barkley paused and said, "I have a message for you from the President of the United States." He proceeded to read these words:

> The President has never had and has not today any desire to or purpose to continue in the office of President, to be a candidate for that office, or to be nominated by the convention for that office. He wishes in all conviction and sincerity to make it clear that all of the delegates at this convention are free to vote for any candidate.
>
> That is the message which I bear to you tonight from the President of the United States by the authority of his word.

The crowd was silent for a moment and then erupted, realizing that "any candidate" could include Roosevelt himself. In the words of a next day's headline, "Bedlam broke loose." A voice came over the public address system booming, "We want Roosevelt." Delegates rushed into the aisles, with the state standards held high. The parade was led by New York, followed by North Carolina, West Virginia, Pennsylvania, and Alabama.

A fight erupted over the Massachusetts standard. Farley supporters, including John Kennedy's older brother Joe, didn't want to join the demonstration. Roosevelt's delegates won out, however, and soon the Massachusetts standard was carried down the aisles with all the rest. In fact, only Maryland (whose senior senator, Joseph Tydings, FDR had tried to purge in 1938), Virginia, Nevada, Louisiana, and Puerto Rico did not join the parade.

The roar of the crowd of 25,000 was joined by two bands and a much-amplified organ. Dominating everything was a voice from the loudspeaker shouting, "We want Roosevelt." Warren Moscow of the *New York Times*, realizing that the chant was not coming from the microphone on the rostrum, decided to track down its source. He found it in a small office in the convention basement. Speaking into a microphone down there was one Thomas D.—the D, he explained, was for Democrat—Garry. The media's version of his official title did not add luster to the reputation of the convention. It was "Superintendent of Sewers."

Mayor Kelly had not only stationed his minion at the microphone in the basement but had filled the auditorium with loyal members of Chicago's Kelly-Nash Democratic organization. "The stadium gates were manned by Kelly henchmen," wrote Jonathan Mitchell in the *New Republic*. Ward and precinct workers streamed in. "The city organization called in the boys for the big moment and packed the balconies," wrote Sam Fuller of the *Chicago Daily News*, including, a *Tribune* columnist added, "several thousand rounded up late in the evening by Johnny Touhy from the 27th Ward of which he is lord."

Back in Charleston, the Peters family followed the convention on the radio. We listened to Barkley's speech with admiration and growing excitement. My father decided we should go to the convention. He did not have tickets. Although he had attended the 1936 Convention in style—accompanying the governor and the governor-elect— now he was out of power, his faction having been defeated in the May primary. But he still had friends in the delegation and was confident that they would come up with tickets for us.

The next morning we piled into the car and left Charleston at 8:00 AM bound for Chicago. In those days without interstates it was a long drive through the western part of West Virginia to the Ohio River and all the way across Ohio and Indiana. My father mapped out a route designed to avoid cities. The largest we went through was Marion, Ohio, which numerous signs identified as the birthplace of Warren Harding. Cities were avoided because there was no fast way through them. It was one traffic light after another. There was nothing my father could do, however, to avoid those lights once we reached the Chicago suburbs. So it was not until about midnight that we got to our hotel.

On the way, we listened to the radio. I remember hearing Frank Sinatra singing "I'll Never Smile Again" with Tommy Dorsey's orchestra. (The most popular song of the year, it anticipated World War II's haunting songs of separation, "You'll Never Know," "I'll Be Seeing You," and "Long Ago and Far Away.") Most of the time we listened to broadcasts of the convention. The afternoon session was dull but included one important event, the adoption of the platform, in which a relatively isolationist foreign affairs plank saying that we wouldn't go to war was modified at Roosevelt's request to include the words "unless we are attacked."

Listening to the radio while traveling could be maddening in those days. The sound would fade and be interrupted by static and we would frantically change the dial for a clearer channel. The sound got better at night, especially, it seemed, on Chicago's WGN. We heard Senator Lister Hill nominate Roosevelt in a speech that was lame compared to Barkley's of the night before.

Then the venerable Carter Glass rose to nominate Jim Farley. Glass had left a sick bed to come to Chicago. At first, his gravelly voice sounded weak. There were scattered boos from the Kelly-Nash crowd in the audience. Then, either because the boos angered him or his microphone was adjusted or both, "the faint voice surged into a fighting roar." Glass described Farley as "a man of character and intelligence, a man on whose word every human being can always rely, a man who never in his lifetime violated a pledge once given," and definitely not seeking to please Roosevelt, said that Farley was "a man who believes in the unwritten law of the Democratic Party, as advocated ever since before the days of Thomas Jefferson, who less than three years before his death appealed to the party which he established never to nominate a man to the third term for the presidency." There was an ovation for Glass at the end of his speech, but it was short, not prolonged by the organ or the band—which remained under Kelly's orders.

Edward Colgan nominated Senator Joseph Tydings of Maryland, who remained resentful of FDR's unsuccessful effort to purge him. Then Dwight Morrow, a former ambassador to Mexico and curiously enough the father-in-law of Charles Lindbergh, nominated John Nance Garner. By this time, temperatures in the hall had risen to the point that delegates were nodding off. There was only a brief demonstration by the Texas delegation as the band played "The Eyes of Texas are Upon You."

Then the balloting began. It wasn't close. Roosevelt got 946½ votes, Farley 72½ , Garner 61, and Tydings 9½ . Unlike in Philadelphia, where Willkie needed six ballots to gain a majority, Roosevelt had his on the first ballot with plenty of votes to spare. The result should not have been surprising. A Gallup poll taken before the convention indicated that 92 percent of the Democrats wanted Roosevelt to seek a third term.

Why had Farley, knowing that he could not win, insisted upon being nominated? What my father used to call the "human" reason was that, for Farley, simply being nominated was the pinnacle of his life. It was in Farley's own words, "[M]y greatest thrill in politics . . . the greatest scene of my life . . . never in my wildest dreams had I thought I would live to see my name presented to a Democratic convention for the office of the president of the United States." It was enough for an Irish boy with only a high school education to have come so far, to have his wife and children present as his name was put forward by Carter Glass, a man he revered as a "great and noble American."

There was also little doubt that Farley wanted to give FDR a hard time, that he was mad at all the slights—real and imagined—from the president, and that he just didn't want this to be easy for FDR. In insisting on being nominated he also probably inspired an overreaction by the Janizariat. Their efforts to win the nomination by acclamation angered many delegates, especially those whose friends and family members were denied admission to the gallery on Tuesday and Wednesday nights because of the Kelly-Nash people who got in, as Jonathan Mitchell noted, by just "showing a white slip of paper."

The resulting bad feeling was clear even to a kid like me as I circulated through the hotel lobbies Thursday morning trying to glean the inside dope by eavesdropping on conversations among the delegates. Their mood worsened during the day as the news began to circulate that Wallace was going to be the vice-presidential choice.

On Wednesday evening, after Roosevelt called Cordell Hull to offer him the vice-presidential nomination, and received the negative reply he had expected, Hopkins's bathroom phone rang. It was FDR saying, "It's Wallace." Sam Rosenman called Wallace at 2 AM to tell him he was the president's choice.

Thursday morning, Roosevelt called Farley: "Now Jim, we have to give some consideration to the selection of a vice president. I have thought it all over and have come to the conclusion Wallace is the best man to nominate in this emergency."

Once again, Farley was going to thwart Roosevelt.

"Mr. President, I'm going to vote for Jesse Jones."

"I think Henry is perfect. I like him. He's the kind of fellow I want around. He's honest. He thinks right. He's a digger."

"Mr. President, there is no use fooling around. The nomination of Wallace won't help the ticket in any way. While I have personal regard for Wallace as a man for his integrity, for his courage, and for his energy, and the rest you say, the people look on him as a mystic and I think you'll regret it. I think you're unfair to your country and your party in forcing Wallace's nomination and you'll live to regret it."

"He's not a mystic. He's a philosopher. He's got ideas. He thinks right. He'll help the people think."

They proceeded to discuss other candidates. Farley told Roosevelt that Assistant Secretary of War Louis Johnson was telling everyone "The president has given me a green light."

"Oh my God," Roosevelt replied.

"Looks like Louis will run into a red light."

"He'll run into a red light about the next block."

"By the way," the president added, "you were great last night." The conversation thus ended on a light and friendly note, but the president now knew that Farley was not only *not* going to help him with Wallace but, in fact, had a candidate of his own—Jesse Jones, the conservative head of a government agency called the Reconstruction Finance Corporation (RFC).

Farley was far from being Wallace's only opponent. Harry Hopkins called and tried to persuade Roosevelt to switch to a less controversial candidate. Speaker Bankhead and Jimmy Byrnes called with the same message. Harold Ickes sent FDR a telegram offering himself as a candidate. "Dear old Harold," Roosevelt said to Rosenman. "He'd get fewer votes even than Wallace," a comment that, while seeming to speak to Ickes's lack of political appeal, revealed that Roosevelt worried about Wallace's shortage of the same ingredient.

Roosevelt should have been worried, if what I was hearing from hanging around the hotel lobbies was any sign. Sitting in one stuffed chair after another blackening my fingers with the ink of one Chicago newspaper after another, I tried to overhear what the delegates were saying. They complained about Harry Hopkins and the "bossed convention." They didn't like Wallace. The Peters poll indicated that Paul McNutt would have been the unbossed choice of an open convention.

Frances Perkins had followed FDR's suggestion and called Eleanor Roosevelt, urging her to come to Chicago. Mrs. Roosevelt checked with Farley:

"I don't want to come before the convention unless you think it's all right."

"Why it's perfectly all right with me."

"Please don't say so unless you really mean it."

"I do mean it and I'm not trying to be polite. Frankly the situation is not good. Equally frankly, your coming will not affect my situation one way or another. From the president's point of view, I think it desirable if not essential that you come."

This was Farley at his best, letting Mrs. Roosevelt know that she wasn't going to con him into following FDR's wishes but also giving her the sound, objective advice that she might save the day for her husband.

Farley met Mrs. Roosevelt at the airport. She was accompanied by Franklin Jr. and Farley drove them to the Stevens, where she planned to stay. Along the way he told her that he opposed Wallace: "Willkie will get liberal financial support. It would be important to attract contributions to the Democratic campaign and I don't know where they are going to come from with Wallace on the ticket."

According to Farley's account of the conversation, Eleanor Roosevelt agreed. When they reached the hotel she called FDR.

"Franklin, I've been talking to Jim Farley and I agree with him, Henry Wallace won't do. . . . I know, Franklin, but Jesse Jones would bolster the ticket and win it business support." (Mrs. Roosevelt's memory of this part of the conversation is different. She says she merely passed along Farley's views without injecting her own.)

Farley also suggested she mention Bankhead and Barkley as alternatives to Wallace. Roosevelt didn't like either idea and asked to speak to Farley directly.

"I've given my word to Wallace, Jim. What do you do when you've given your word?"

"I keep it. But you made a mistake to give it. I'm going out to vote for Jesse Jones and if he won't run I'll vote for Bankhead."

"I am committed," Roosevelt replied.

"Why not McNutt?" Farley asked.

"Apparently you still have your sense of humor."

When he reached the convention, Farley told Jesse Jones what Roosevelt had said. Jones, wanting to keep his job at the RFC, decided that he had to withdraw. Only Wallace, Bankhead, and McNutt remained in the race for vice president.

Delegate sentiment was clear. Perhaps its most succinct expression came from Governor Leon C. Phillips of Oklahoma. When asked about Wallace by Governor Eurith Dickinson Rivers of Georgia, Phillips replied, "Henry's my second choice. After anyone else—black, white, or yellow—who can get the nomination."

The Thursday afternoon session of the convention was adjourned before nominations for vice president could be made. The Janizariat wasn't sure it had the votes to put Wallace across at that point. The evening session got under way at 7:30, just after Farley had escorted Mrs. Roosevelt to a seat on the platform. Congressman Henry Steagall nominated Speaker Bankhead. At first the demonstration on Bankhead's behalf seemed mild with only South Carolina, Louisiana, and Virginia joining Alabama in marching around the floor. But then they were joined by Texas, Maryland, and North Carolina. "Rebel yells grew in intensity," reported the *New York Times*. The demonstration's second wind was based on a determination to, according to one reporter, "demonstrate for anyone not pushed by the White House."

The demonstration had lasted for twenty minutes when Chairman Barkley pounded his gavel and the roll call continued. Wallace's nomination was greeted by a mixture of cheers and boos, with the latter predominating. The first mention of the name of Paul McNutt brought cheers from the floor. *Time* magazine called it "the greatest ovation of the convention" and, even though the band remained silent, the *New York Times* called the demonstration "the best so far." Chants of "We want McNutt" filled the hall. But before it could continue McNutt came to the platform. Knowing of the pressure on him from the Hopkins gang, the crowd realized that McNutt was going to withdraw and did not want to let him. He began, "In the first place," and was shouted down before he continued. Finally the crowd let him speak. He could not bring himself to endorse Wallace by name, saying Franklin Roosevelt "is my leader and I am here to support his choice for vice president."

After the nominating speeches and before the balloting, Eleanor Roosevelt was introduced. My father, who had succeeded in his search for tickets, and I had taken the long cab ride from downtown to the Chicago stadium just in time to watch as Jim Farley escorted her to the rostrum. The obvious warmth of their feeling for one another had an immediate healing effect on the convention. She and Farley had been friends and allies for almost twenty years and now their friendship was paying off for her husband, whose own relationship with Farley had so badly deteriorated. She began her speech by paying tribute to Farley. "I think nobody could appreciate more what he has done for the party, what he has given in work and loyalty and I want to give him here my thanks and devotion." The word devotion struck just the right grace note. The stadium that had rung with boos for Wallace as the nominations were made now listened respectfully to the first lady and her simple but eloquent plea, "[T]his is no ordinary time, no time for thinking about anything except what we can do best for the country." When she finished, there was warm applause from the audience.

And then the balloting began. There were still boos for Wallace but they were a little less raucous.

Alabama, Arizona, and Colorado went for Bankhead; California, Connecticut, Delaware, and Florida for Wallace. Then Kentucky, Louisiana, and Maryland went for Bankhead while Illinois, Iowa, Indiana, and Kansas joined the Wallace column. At this point, the vote tallied 197 for Wallace and 127 for Bankhead. The Janizariat led by Jimmy Byrnes scurried down the aisles asking, "Do you want a vice president or a president?"

Byrnes breathed a bit easier when Massachusetts, Michigan, and Minnesota all went for Wallace. But then Bankhead won Mississippi, Missouri (including Harry Truman), Montana, Nebraska, and Nevada. The vote stood at 271 to 188. Wallace's name was still being booed enough to reduce Mrs. Wallace to tears. The vote was still close enough to make the Janizariat sweat. They were also sweating in the White House, not only because the vote was close but because it was a typically hot and humid July evening in Washington and Roosevelt, because of his sinuses, did not like to have air conditioning in the rooms he was using.

The White House was "an exceptionally quiet place" that night because, explained Rosenman, "nearly every Washington official who would normally call the president was at the convention or was at the radio in his own office or living room listening to the proceedings."

A small group had gathered in the Oval Room, on the second floor of the White House (not the Oval Office in the West Wing). It included Rosenman, Missy LeHand, Grace Tully, Press Secretary Steve Early, and a few others. Together they listened to the radio as FDR played solitaire. "His face was grim" as it became clear that Wallace might be defeated. Roosevelt put aside his cards and asked Missy LeHand for pad and pencil. He wrote in silence for five full pages, then handed them to Rosenman, saying: "Sam, take this inside and go to work on it. Smooth it out and get it ready for delivery. I may have to deliver it very soon so please hurry it up."

It was a speech declining the nomination. Jimmy Byrnes had been telling the delegates the truth. If they didn't nominate Wallace they wouldn't get Roosevelt. As Rosenman worked on the draft, Roosevelt turned to keeping score as the ballots were being cast. Soon it became clear that the Janizariat would prevail.

New Hampshire, New Jersey, New Mexico, and New York went for Wallace and, after North Carolina gave Bankhead seventeen votes, Wallace took eight states including the giant delegations from Ohio and Pennsylvania. Showing his continued strength in the south, Bankhead came back to win Tennessee, Texas, and Virginia, but it was too late. At eight minutes after midnight, Wallace was declared the winner with 627 votes to Bankhead's 329. Sixty-six delegates stuck by McNutt despite his withdrawal.

Wallace "started forward to be ready to deliver his acceptance speech," reported the *Tribune*, but Jimmy Byrnes "rushed up and intercepted the senator. Byrnes was fearful of what would happen if Wallace were to face the booing convention.

'Don't do it Henry,' cried Byrnes, 'don't go out there. You'll ruin the party if you do.'"

A crestfallen Wallace retreated to his chair, his acceptance speech undelivered.

"For sheer force of personality and character ... Willkie makes the greatest impact of any man I've ever talked to. He rings true."

Russell Davenport and Wendell Willkie. Henry Luce said, "The man who made Willkie, next only to Willkie himself, was Davenport."

The post-convention Willkie campaign team. Rear center is Oren Root, at the far left is Sam Pryor in front and Russell Davenport in rear, on Willkie's left is Joe Martin and on his right John D. M. Hamilton, who lost his job as Republican National Committee Chairman to Martin.

Robert Taft, a conservative isolationist called "Mr. Republican." The race was between him and Willkie during the final three ballots of the convention.

Thomas E. Dewey led the Republican candidates in the polls from early 1939 until the Republican convention, but "he was cold, cold as a February iceberg."

A friendly moment between two adversaries, FDR's liberal, internationalist Treasury Secretary Henry Morgenthau and the conservative, and then isolationist, Republican Senator Arthur Vandenberg.

"The plaza in front of Convention Hall teemed with activity."

Delegates struggle for the New York standard. "A half dozen fist fights broke out on the floor . . . policemen were needed to sort things out."

Wendell and Edith make their way through cheering delegates the day after his nomination.

Wendell, Edith, and son Philip wave from the campaign train, "The Willkie Special."

With the thermometer at 102 (degrees), Willkie arrives in Elwood to receive the Republican nomination.

"One would never imagine that significant political history was being made," by this fisherman.

Roosevelt looks on as War Secretary Henry Stimson draws the first draft numbers, just two weeks before the 1940 election.

Another fisherman. Willkie relaxes after the 1940 election at Sam Pryor's vacation home in Florida.

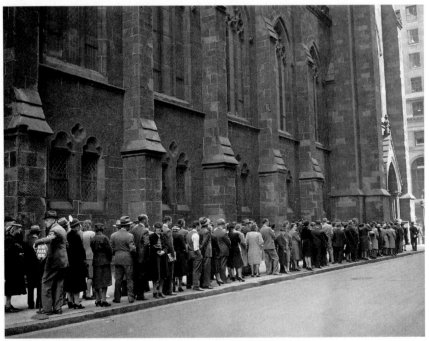

The end of the journey. Average citizens wait in line to say farewell.

Back at the White House, Roosevelt's speech declining the nomination also went undelivered. "The President by this time looked
weary and bedraggled," Rosenman recalled. "His shirt was wilted
from the intense heat of the oval room." Still, FDR decided to give
his acceptance speech that night or, to be more precise, that morning. "He was wheeled into his bedroom where he washed, changed
his shirt, combed his hair and in a few minutes came out smiling,
looking his usual jaunty, imperturbable self." He was wheeled to the
broadcast room and began to speak.

> I found myself . . . in a conflict between a deep personal desire of
> retirement on the one hand and that quiet invisible thing called con-
> science on the other.
>
> Lying awake as I have done on many nights, I have asked myself
> whether I have the right as Commander in Chief of the Army and
> Navy to call on men and women to serve their country . . . and at
> the same time decline to serve my country in my personal capacity
> if I am called upon to do so by the people of my country.

The delegates listened to the president with the same quiet attention that they had given his wife earlier in the evening. As he spoke,
eyes turned toward the huge flag-draped photograph of the president that dominated one end of the balcony and on which a blue
and white spotlight was shone. "Then it was over," wrote Sidney
Shalett in the *New York Times*, "the crowd rose to its feet and roared.
It was a mighty roar of approval for the man who was to lead their
battle this campaign year." There was no demonstration, however,
the delegates were too tired.

Despite the success of the president's acceptance speech, the verdict on the convention as a whole was far from favorable. "Angrily,
sourly, in grave disunion, the convention adjourned," reported *Time*.
Life reported that "[M]any an observer who had thought he was
completely reconciled to the idea of a third term came away from
the Chicago convention last week shocked and sick at heart" at "the
shabby pretense that this was a genuine draft" engineered by a "cyn-

ical ends-justify-the-means alliance of New Deal reformers and self-seeking big-city bosses."

Henry Luce's pro-Willkie publications could have been expected to take a jaundiced view, but many liberals agreed. The *New Republic*'s Jonathan Mitchell called the proceedings "a shambles" and deemed the New Dealers' performance "fearful, panicky, and weak." "What could have been a convention of enthusiasm and high spirits ended almost like a wake," wrote Harold Ickes. "If there was a cheerful happy delegate in Chicago on Friday I did not run across him." The liberal columnist Raymond Clapper lamented, "something has gone out of American life this week. At least I have lost something. It was faith in President Roosevelt." Polls that had shown Roosevelt leading Willkie 53 percent to 47 percent going into the convention now showed him losing New York and Pennsylvania—then the nation's two largest states. The convention made FDR seem weak at a time when the challenge he faced from the world seemed to grow greater by the day.

The headlines, as the convention came to a close, underscored the gravity of that challenge. "Give up Gibraltar! Spain to Britain: Two million men ready to back me up—Franco." This ominous threat from the Spanish dictator couldn't have come at a worse time for Great Britain. To have its most important naval base invaded at the same time that the home island was being assaulted by Germany would be more than it could handle. That headline on Thursday, the 18th, was followed the next day by another that was even more ominous: "Peace Now: Hitler warns England it's final offer" over a story describing Hitler's threat of terrible consequences if Britain did not surrender immediately.

The departing delegates also had to face defection by Democrats who were either isolationists or opposed to a third term. The day after the convention, Democratic Senator Edward Walsh of Nebraska announced that he would support Willkie, and Rush Holt of West Virginia demanded that the Senate vote on his resolution opposing the third term. FDR now had the daunting task of trying to help Britain survive its extreme peril while struggling to unite his party against the challenge of the most dynamic Republican nominee since the other Roosevelt.

For FDR and, indeed, for the world, the big question was this: Would Wendell Willkie, who continued to rest and plan in Colorado Springs, go on backing Roosevelt's foreign policy; or would he, in an understandable effort to reach out to the isolationist base of the Republican party, moderate or abandon his defiance of the Nazis?

CHAPTER TWELVE

★

THE DEAL AND THE MUSTER

Franklin Roosevelt now faced two of the most difficult chal-
lenges of his presidency: (1) how to get a military draft enacted even
though this country had never had a draft in peacetime; and (2) how
to give Britain the fifty destroyers it was pleading for even though
laws seemed to forbid such a transfer. What's more, both of these
challenges had to be met in a short time. The threat of Nazi invasion
made the British need immediate, and each day the November 3rd
election grew nearer, Congress would be less likely to vote for a
draft and risk facing retribution at the polls from angry mothers.
Taking two such controversial actions between a convention and an
election was unprecedented in American political history.

Polls showed that a majority supported the draft. But, since the
opponents felt strongly enough that they were likely to vote against
a candidate on that ground only, theirs was comparable to the power
of the National Rifle Association today, only greater because of all
those worried mothers. There were also formidable legal obstacles in
the path of a destroyer deal, including Attorney General Jackson's
ruling that stopped the torpedo-boat sale. Then there was the Walsh
amendment passed in June at the insistence of Senator David Walsh,
the chairman of the Senate Naval Affairs Committee. Walsh was
loyal to Roosevelt on domestic issues but he was also a Boston Irish-

man whose profound dislike of the British made him an isolationist in foreign affairs. The Walsh Amendment prohibited the disposal "in any manner whatsoever" of US military equipment or supplies unless the army or navy chief of staff certified that the equipment was not essential to the defense of the United States.

A tiny loophole was inserted by Senator Lister Hill. Walsh's original amendment had added the words "and cannot be used" after "essential." Hill pointed out that even an obsolete old musket might still be used. Walsh agreed and "cannot be used" was dropped. This was to prove fateful.

Of course, there also was the worry not only that equipment sent to England would not be available to defend the United States, but also that it could arrive too late or be too little to prevent a Nazi victory. The story of the French aircraft carrier Brean did not inspire confidence. Remember that, while the Brean was at sea, France surrendered and the carrier was diverted to Martinique, where it and its precious cargo of American aircraft sat out the war.

The sense of imminent danger that gripped the country in June and may have led to Wendell Willkie's nomination had begun to diminish in July. Indeed, on July 2, a headline in the *New York Times* said "War Sentiment Found Declining."

For FDR, however, this bad news was balanced by the good news of Willkie's nomination. Now the Republicans were led by a man who shared FDR's views on helping Britain and on preparing this country for war. Legislation authorizing a military draft had already begun to wend its way through the congressional thicket. On July 24, the *Times* reported that "The Senate Military Affairs Committee has approved major details of the Burke-Wadsworth selective service compulsory training bill."

As for the destroyers, two groups were campaigning in favor of giving them to England. One, the Committee to Defend America by Aiding the Allies, had been formed in mid-May of 1940 and was led by William Allen White, the white-haired editor of the *Emporia Kansas Gazette*. "With a round face open as a sunflower, blue eyes shining with honesty, and a twangy voice innocent of affectation," he was "revered" as "the uncommon spokesman for commonsensical America." White was loved by liberals, including FDR, for his support of their causes and by Republicans for his steadfast loyalty to the party at election time. Roosevelt joked that he appreciated White's support for three and a half out of every four years. White's folksy manner and grassrootedness gave him the Will Rogers quality so prized in that era. Indeed, one has to wonder just how often life imitated art, as so many public men cultivated the Rogers image. It is equally likely, however, that it was Rogers, himself an actor after all, who adopted the image of an admirable type of American exemplified by men like White. Probably the truth is that both things were happening: Art was imitating life and life was imitating art.

White's influence was suggested by a letter Roosevelt had written him the preceding fall:

Dear Bill,

I have had a few quiet weeks with a chance for more thought than I had during the neutrality bill period and I have gradually been getting to the point when I need a few helpful thoughts from the philosopher of Emporia. That is why I hope the next time you come East, you will come and spend the night at the White House and let me sit on the sofa after supper and talk over small matters like world problems.

Willkie, too, valued White's counsel. White had supported him at the Republican Convention. And now White asked one of Willkie's most powerful backers, Thomas Lamont, to join him on the Committee to Defend. He also enlisted Lewis Douglas, the head of Democrats for Willkie. Other Democrats who joined White included the future governor and senator from Illinois, Adlai Stevenson and Paul Douglas. Also on board were the presidents of Yale, Harvard, and Dartmouth—A. Whitney Seymour, James Bryant Conant, and Ernest Hopkins—and the theologian Reinhold Niebuhr.

White's group was to generate more than two million letters and telegrams to the White House and countless more to members of

Congress. The committee's first major public declaration, a full-page ad entitled "Stop Hitler Now" was drafted by the playwright Robert Sherwood. It appeared in major newspapers across the country on June 12. It concluded: "Send a postcard, letter or telegram to the President of the United States, to your Senator and your congressman urging that the real defense of our country must begin NOW—with aid to the Allies!"

At his next press conference, Roosevelt displayed the ad on his desk so that all the reporters could see it. When the expected "Do you care to comment on this ad?" came, Roosevelt replied: "It's a great piece of work. Certainly educational for the country."

By setting up the question and giving the answer he did, Roosevelt displayed his regard for both White and Sherwood, who had been invited to the White House in January for a showing of the movie based on his play, *Abe Lincoln in Illinois,* but it also showed his eagerness to advance the cause of aid to the Allies.

The other group lobbying for the destroyer transfer was the Century Group, headed by Francis Pickens Miller, an official of the Council on Foreign Relations.

Miller, who was reared in the Shenandoah Valley of Virginia, graduated from Washington and Lee in 1914, fought in France in the field artillery in World War I, and after the war became a Rhodes Scholar at Oxford. Having, in the words of one writer, "fallen in love with England" he returned to Oxford for his marriage to Helen Hill, who later became the Washington correspondent of the *Economist.* He was made executive director of the Century Group in July 1940.

The group's name came from the Century Association, a New York club where the meetings were usually held, and that had many members who were involved. The Century Group included writers, editors, lawyers, educators, theologians, and businesspeople. Many were, like Miller, veterans of World War I. They were not chicken hawks; they knew what war was. Many had also been educated in Europe, four at Oxford.

The man who had called the first meeting of the Century Group, and who became the first chairman, was Lewis Douglas, the former New Deal official who came to disagree with its economic philosophy and was now supporting Willkie. Douglas's access to the GOP nominee would prove an invaluable asset. He was one of several members of the Century Group who also served on William White's Committee to Defend.

Henry Luce was another Century member and the immense influence of his publications made him an important one, as did the compelling case he made that the United States should get something in return for the fifty destroyers the group wanted to give England. This quid pro quo would later become the key to selling the destroyer deal.

Other important Century members included two editorial writers from the New York *Herald Tribune*—Walter Millis and Godfrey Parsons—and Herbert Agar, the editor of the *Louisville Courier Journal*. Agar was a friend of Harold Ickes and thus had access to the Roosevelt administration.

Other members reeked of academic respectability, such as Dartmouth's Hopkins and Harvard's Conant from the Committee to Defend, and the president and dean of the Union Theological Seminary, Henry Sloane Coffin and Henry Van Dusen. Others provided authority in matters of national security, including former chief of naval operations William Standley and future secretary of state Dean Acheson, future head of the CIA Allen Dulles, and the *Herald Tribune* and CBS's military expert Major George Fielding Elliot. Elmer Davis, the popular CBS newscaster, was another powerful media figure on the committee. But perhaps the most active, even though he attended just one meeting, was the columnist Joseph Alsop.

One of three sons of a Connecticut farm family of modest means but impressive connections (he was a distant cousin of both Roosevelts), Alsop had attended Harvard, had become a member of Porcellian (the super-exclusive club that had rejected FDR), and had had his career in journalism jump-started by his mother's friendship with Helen Reid of the New York *Herald Tribune*. He soon launched a column with Robert Kintner, which was to continue until Alsop joined the war effort in 1941. After the war he carried it on with his brother Stewart, Kintner having become an NBC executive who was later to be featured as a villain in the movie *Quiz Show.* During Vietnam, Alsop would become the object of ridicule because of his hawkish columns based on "captured enemy documents," but in 1940 he was a hero.

Alsop, like Luce, did not think that the destroyer deal could be sold unless the United States got something in return. They convinced the rest of the group; and so members were sent to talk to the British ambassador about what kind of deal could be made. In addition, the group felt that Willkie's support was essential, so Lewis Douglas was assigned to get that support. And no one felt that the deal could be sold without the navy's support, so Alsop was dispatched to get the support of the chief of naval operations, Harold Stark.

One member of the Century Group, Colonel William Donovan, a prominent lawyer and World War I hero, performed an essential fact-finding mission for Roosevelt that summer. Donovan had been the Republican candidate for governor of New York in 1932 and had supported Dewey in 1940 until the Republican Convention, when he switched to Willkie because of Willkie's internationalism. Donovan had gone to Columbia Law School with FDR and was a close friend of Colonel Frank Knox, the new secretary of the navy. Indeed, when Knox arrived in Washington for his confirmation hearing, it was Donovan who met him at Union Station, and in whose Washington home Knox stayed during the hearings.

When Roosevelt expressed frustration over the reports he was getting from Ambassador Joe Kennedy that were relentlessly defeatist about Britain's chances of holding out against Hitler, Knox suggested that Donovan would be a more reliable reporter. Roosevelt summoned Donovan to the White House, where he found himself in a meeting not only with the president but with the top national security team: Secretary of State Cordell Hull, Secretary of War Henry Stimson, and Knox.

Roosevelt said that he did not trust Kennedy's reports, and that he desperately needed a reliable independent observer to take a good look at the situation in England. Could Britain survive a Nazi attack? What were the most effective ways we could help?

Donovan arrived in London on July 14. Joe Kennedy was not told the true purpose of his trip, but Kennedy still objected that Donovan's visit would "simply result in causing confusion and misunderstanding on the part of the British." Roosevelt commented that "someone's nose seems out of joint" and ignored the ambassador's concerns.

The British knew that Donovan's mission was important. Within an hour of his arrival he was whisked to Buckingham Palace to be welcomed by King George VI. William Stephenson, the head of Britain's secret intelligence service in America, had cabled the king: "The American government is debating two alternative courses of action. One would keep Britain in the war with supplies now desperately needed. The other is to give Britain up for loss. I urge you to bare your breast to [Donovan]."

Stephenson had sent similar messages to Sir Stewart Menzies, the head of the secret intelligence service, and to Churchill. George VI showed Donovan a recent message from Hitler that had just been intercepted by British intelligence and decrypted. Hitler's message said:

> Since England in spite of her hopeless military situation shows no sign of being ready to come to an understanding, I have decided to prepare a landing operation against England to eliminate England as a base for prosecution of the war against Germany.
>
> First, the English Air Force must be so reduced morally and physically that it is unable to deliver any significant attack against the German crossing.

Donovan next had breakfast at Claridges with the American military attaches: navy captain Alan Kirk, army brigadier general Raymond Lee, and army air force lieutenant colonel Carl Spaatz. He asked, "Could the RAF hold off the Luftwaffe?" Kirk and Spaatz agreed that it could. The British had better planes, especially the Spitfire. Besides, Spaatz added, "The young RAF flyers had such amazing morale they would probably be the victors." When Donovan said that he was giving odds of sixty to forty that Britain would survive, Lee said he would "do a little better, say two to one."

Donovan did not rely solely on the experts' opinions. He confirmed them by personally visiting RAF bases, observing Spitfires in combat. Knox also arranged for the *Chicago Daily News* correspondent Edgar Ansel Mowrer, fresh from reporting the debacle in France, to come to London to assist Donovan in appraising the British situation. Together Mowrer and Donovan interviewed scores of British officials, journalists, businessmen, and everyday citizens.

"To Donovan, it now appeared," writes his biographer Richard Dunlop, "that the greatest danger came . . . from mounting submarine warfare that was choking off vital supplies. If America could transfer its overage destroyers to the British Navy, this would probably be the most valuable aid the New World could give the old." This was the conclusion that he gave Roosevelt and Knox on his return. Nothing could have pleased the Century Group more.

On July 29th, Churchill sent FDR another message about the destroyers. This was the most urgent yet: "Mr. President, with great respect, I must tell you in the long history of the world this is a thing to do now."

On August 1, Agar and two other members of the Century Group visited Roosevelt to urge trading the destroyers for bases. He told them to concentrate on building public support for the deal. Luce had already met with Roosevelt on July 25 and received essentially the same message, "Harry, I can't come out in favor of such a deal without the support of the entire *Time-Life* organization." Luce felt that Roosevelt still needed convincing, but Roosevelt's own memorandum of the August 2 cabinet meeting shows otherwise: "There was a long discussion in regard to devising ways and means to diverting 50 destroyers to Great Britain. It was the general opinion without the dissenting voice that the survival of the British Isles might possibly depend on getting these destroyers."

That afternoon, at 2 PM, Roosevelt had wheeled himself from the Oval Office through the small room where Missy LeHand and Grace Tully worked and into the Cabinet Room, which looked out from the West Wing to the Rose Garden and the south entrance of the White House. He took his place at the center of the table with Cordell Hull on his right and opened the meeting that Henry Stimson would later describe as "[O]ne of the most serious and important debates that I have ever had in a cabinet meeting."

Frank Knox began the destroyer discussion by recounting a conversation he'd had with Lord Lothian the day before, during which the British ambassador had told him that his country's navy was down to seventy usable destroyers from the War World I total of more that 400. Knox, like Alsop and Luce, favored a trade of the American destroyers for British Islands in the West Indies and told the Cabinet that he had suggested a deal to Lord Lothian.

Hull pointed out that such a trade would violate the agreement reached at a recent Pan-American conference in Havana that had ruled against takeovers of one Western Hemisphere country's possessions by another. Roosevelt suggested that that problem could be avoided by a lease. The lease idea had been in Roosevelt's mind for at least a year, and seemed to offer a solution to Hull's problem.

But then Hull raised another issue. What would happen to the destroyers—and the British fleet, of which they would become a part—in the event Germany won the war? The United States needed assurances, everyone then agreed, that the British fleet would be sent to the United States. Hull was assigned to seek this assurance through Lord Lothian.

Roosevelt brought up a political problem. He needed Willkie's help in persuading congressional Republicans to go along with the deal. He wanted an intermediary to approach Willkie to see if Willkie would lend a hand. Stimson, Knox, and Hull agreed that this was a good idea. But Henry Wallace, Robert Jackson, and Harold Ickes thought it dangerous. Willkie could refuse in a way that might embarrass Roosevelt. Anyway, if the deal proved popular, why have to share credit with the opposition?

Jim Farley weighed in on the president's side, saying it would be "good for the country" to approach Willkie. Unsurprisingly, the president's view prevailed.

Who, then, would be the intermediary? William Allen White was the answer, everyone agreed. That evening, before dictating his memo, Roosevelt called White, who agreed to give it a try.

What is clear from the August 2nd cabinet meeting is that Roosevelt, in dealing with Luce and the other Century Club members, had been trying to make sure that he would have public and congressional support for the destroyer deal. Roosevelt loved to organize public pressure to get him to do what he already wanted to do. Alsop describes what happened when he wrote a column denouncing FDR for not acting faster on the destroyers. "Steve Early [Roosevelt's press secretary] called from the White House to congratulate me on a 'useful and sensible' contribution. It was useful and sensible, of course to the extent that it was one of the morsels of propaganda for Roosevelt to take the course he wished to travel."

The August 5 issue of *Time* showed that Luce had heard FDR's message about applying pressure—its lead article made the case for the urgent need to give England the destroyers. The other members of the Century Group also got Roosevelt's point. Their purpose became, writes Miller, "to make it politically possible for him to act."

It was Roosevelt who suggested what may have turned out to be a crucial step in persuading the nation to support the deal. He urged Herbert Agar to ask General John Pershing to deliver a radio address making the case for turning the destroyers over to Britain. Pershing was a great national hero and enjoyed enormous prestige as an elder statesman, having been the commander of American forces in France during World War I. The Century Group, working through various intermediaries, arranged for the general to make the speech. Agar and Walter Lippmann wrote it, and Alsop secured the radio time. Pershing told the nation:

I'm telling you before it is too late that the British Navy needs destroyers to convoy merchant ships and submarines and to repel invasion . . . the most critical time is the next few weeks and months. If there is anything we can do to save the British fleet during that time we shall be failing in our duty to America if we do not do it.

Time ran a photograph of Pershing on the front page of its "Nation" section with the caption "He would not fail in duty." The *New York Times* headline was "Pershing would let Britain have 50 old U.S. Destroyers to guard our own liberty." It is a comment on the sense of urgency about the destroyer deal that gripped its proponents, including many journalists, that the *Times* became almost as propagandistic as the Luce magazines. Their sense of urgency became more desperate each day in August as the dramatic increase in German air attacks made invasion seem imminent and the British need for destroyers immediate.

As for the draft, although Roosevelt had seemed to clearly imply that he favored it in his acceptance speech at the Democratic National Convention, some contemporary observers were not satisfied, so at the same time that Pershing made his destroyer speech, FDR said "I am in favor of a [draft] bill and I consider it essential to our national defense."

Also that week, the *New Republic* came out in favor of the draft and the destroyer deal. Its support of the draft was particularly important because liberal voices were needed to counter the anti-conscription views of many leftists.

The leftists, of course, included the Communist Party, which, during the 1939–1941 era of the Nazi-Soviet pact, was slavish in its effort to appease Hitler and sabotage the Allied cause and American preparedness. Their soulmate in Congress was Vito Marcantonio of New York's American Labor Party.

Many other more respectable liberals also opposed the draft, including the socialist Norman Thomas, pacifist Oswald Garrison Villard, clergymen like the Protestant Harry Emerson Fosdick, and the Catholic Monsignor Michael J. Ready. Among the influential liberal Senate opponents, Burton K. Wheeler of Montana, George W. Norris of Nebraska, and Robert M. LaFollette of Wisconsin. North Dakota's Gerald Nye, another opponent, had played a seminal role in creating the isolationist movement with the Senate hearings in 1934 that exposed the bankers and ammunition makers as the profiteers from the terrible slaughter of World War I.

Furthermore, opposition to the draft wasn't confined to the isolationists. For example, William Allen White, one of the leaders of the aid to Britain movement, was against conscription.

The left, however, was only a minority among the draft's opponents. Conservative isolationists, like Robert Taft, Arthur Vandenberg, and Hamilton Fish, were much larger in number and equally dedicated to the cause. So, even though a Gallup poll taken in early August showed 67 percent of the people favored conscription, the August 12th issue of *Time* found that "the majority seemed about to be defeated." The Burke-Wadsworth bill was, *Time* wrote, "stalled, hacked to the point of emasculation. Minority pressure was for the moment at least triumphant."

The secret, of course, was that the minority felt strongly. Fueled by the passionate concerns of mothers who didn't want their sons sent to die in a foreign land, the minority's case had an emotional force that worried even the draft's most ardent proponents. Roosevelt had already risked antagonizing the mothers and wives of the 60,000 National Guardsmen he had asked Congress for the authority to call up. I remember riding my bike to Charleston's Broad Street station to watch tearful families saying goodbye to the West Virginia contingent.

On the destroyer deal, the situation was equally grim. Wendell Willkie's help was desperately needed. What would be the result of Roosevelt's call to William Allen White asking for help in persuading Willkie to come out in favor of the deal? Archibald MacLeish, the Librarian of Congress, had also approached Willkie's top adviser, Russell Davenport, with a similar plea, as had both Lewis Douglas and Joseph Alsop. Herbert Hoover and Arthur Krock, the anti-Roosevelt *New York Times* columnist who liked to advise important figures, talked Willkie out of making a clear statement of endorsement. (Francis Pickens Miller wrote, "Sinister are the meanderings of Arthur Krock's mind. He has done us dirt.") Instead of offering an endorsement Willkie said that only the president was in the position to command all the information to make the deal, and that Willkie could not assume responsibility for something he was insufficiently informed to appraise.

Significantly, however, Willkie refrained from making any negative public comment. As William Allen White told Roosevelt, "It's not as bad as it seems. I have talked with both of you on this subject and I know there is not two bits difference between the two of you." But then White kept the suspense alive by adding, "I can't guarantee either of you to the other." That it wasn't "as bad as it seems" became clear from Willkie's speech in Elwood accepting the Republican nomination.

Willkie had left Colorado Springs on August 16 aboard United Airlines' "Willkie Special." Greeted by a large enthusiastic crowd at the Indianapolis airport, he traveled by motorcade through the downtown and then forty-five miles to Rushville, where he was greeted by his mother-in-law Cora Wilk—who, like her daughter, seemed to have temporarily at least forgiven Willkie his affair with Irita Van Doren. She fed him "his favorite meal," fried chicken and apple pie, after which he and Edith spent the night at the home of Mary Steeth, the old friend who managed his farms.

The next day was hot. By mid-morning the temperature was ninety degrees and rising. By the afternoon it reached an official 102, but Marcia Davenport claimed that she saw a thermometer reading 112.

A special train brought Willkie from Rushville to Elwood where he arrived at 12:30 and was greeted by a huge crowd. About 150,000 people overwhelmed the small town, arriving in innumerable private automobiles, 1200 buses, and sixty-three special trains of the Pennsylvania and Nickel Plate railroads. Two hundred and fifty bands marched through downtown Elwood. During this parade John D. Collins, a *Life* photographer, took the memorable photograph of Willkie standing in the back of a convertible with his arms upraised, his car surrounded by the cheering throng, and the sun filtering through a fog of dust stirred by thousands of feet.

The parade stopped briefly at the high school. Willkie, who wore a coat and tie despite the temperature, almost fainted from the heat. He recovered enough to give a brief speech to old friends who had gathered there, and then went on to Callaway Park, where his acceptance speech would be delivered. By five that morning, 3,000 people had arrived at the site. By 9 AM, two thirds of the 30,000 seats were taken. By noon, the crowd had doubled, and it had doubled again by the time Willkie began speaking around 2:30 PM. Despite the temperature, the crowd had been enthusiastic, cheering frequently during Charlie Halleck's speech introducing Joe Martin and Martin's presentation of the nominee.

The crowd was ready for an old-fashioned, give-'em-Hell political stem-winder; but Willkie was clearly uncomfortable. The hot sun was shining directly on him, sweat was dripping from his forehead, and his speech had been written not for a crowd but for the ages, best suited to quiet perusal in the library. Willkie's delivery was awkward and ineffective. "The speech didn't go worth a damn," said Charlie Halleck, and his opinion was widely shared. *Time* reported that "there were long stretches when the crowd could find little to cheer about."

For Roosevelt, however, the speech contained some good news. For one thing, Willkie referred to himself as "a liberal democrat," a characterization not likely to quicken the hearts of Republican regulars. The party's old guard would have been delighted if Willkie's speech had then made clear that, although he had been sunk in the sin of liberalism, he now saw the light of sound Republican conservatism. Instead, however, the rest of the speech made clear that, as Norman Thomas put it, Willkie "agreed with Mr. Roosevelt's entire program of social reform."

More significantly, for Roosevelt's foreign policy Willkie proclaimed his "wholehearted support to the president in whatever activities he might take" to give "the opponents of force the material resources of this nation."

Just before these words, in a section of the speech drafted by Godfrey Parsons, the *Herald Tribune* editorial writer who was a member of the Century Group, Willkie had said:

> We must admit that the loss of the British fleet would greatly weaken our defense. That is because the British fleet has for years controlled the Atlantic, leaving us free to concentrate on the Pacific. If the British fleet were lost or captured, the Atlantic might be dominated by Germany, a power hostile to our way of life, controlling in

that event most of the ships and shipbuilding facilities of Europe. This would be a calamity for us.

Willkie was coming enticingly close to endorsing the destroyer deal. But Arthur Krock and the GOP regulars had just enough influence to keep him from going all the way.

After the Elwood speech, Douglas and White redoubled their efforts to persuade Willkie to come out clearly in support of the deal or at least to provide FDR with private assurance that he would not attack it. But Willkie's slowness to come around made it all the more unlikely that Congress would approve the transfer of the destroyers to Britain in time to do any good, and the prospects for congressional approval were already dim. Senator David Walsh's Irish Anglophobia proved strong enough to resist Roosevelt's importunings during a three-day cruise on the presidential yacht. Claude Pepper, a senator who was highly sympathetic to the idea of giving the destroyers to England, told Secretary Stimson that Congress would definitely not go for it. Without congressional approval, the Walsh amendment and the legal case Attorney General Jackson had made against the torpedo boat sale seemed insurmountable obstacles.

The Century Group's Dean Acheson came to the rescue. On August 11th, there appeared in the *New York Times*—where Acheson had a friend on the editorial staff—a letter signed by him and three other lawyers arguing that the destroyers could be transferred to Britain under existing law and that no congressional action would be required. Attorney General Jackson had advance notice of the Acheson letter and had had time to digest it when Roosevelt asked him if he could come up with something along similar lines.

But Roosevelt wanted to go beyond Acheson's argument, to contend that a trade for destroyers would be in America's defense interest. One reason why this was essential was because Roosevelt needed Admiral Harold Stark's support. Joe Alsop, who had been deputized by the Century Group to get Stark on board, thought he had been successful—until the ubiquitously unfriendly Arthur Krock got hold of Stark and persuaded him to drag his feet. Stark did have a real problem. He had gone on record telling Congress that the destroyers were needed for our own defense, and now the Walsh amendment meant that Stark could not approve the transfer unless he reversed his position and declared that the ships were not needed.

Roosevelt knew that he would not be wise to force the deal down the admiral's throat. The loss of the destroyers had to be outweighed by the gain of something of greater value to the national defense. The bases were the answer. FDR needed Jackson to make a persuasive case linking the bases and the destroyers, and that is just what Jackson did in a memo to the secretary of the navy, Frank Knox.

> The Chief of Naval Operations may and should certify . . . that such destroyers are not essential to the defense of the United States if in his judgment the exchange of such destroyers for strategic naval and air bases would strengthen rather than impair the total defense of the United States.

The question now was whether the British would agree to the trade. Hull and Welles had been negotiating the base issue through the British Ambassador Lord Lothian. They found that Churchill was more than willing to give the bases and that he desperately wanted the destroyers. But Churchill wanted to give the bases as an act of generosity and not as part of a vulgar tit-for-tat trade.

This difference in the British and American character proved almost insurmountable. Churchill wanted the exchange to be a spontaneous gift between gentlemen; Roosevelt needed to be the Yankee trader who makes the best deal possible so that Uncle Sam wouldn't be Uncle Sucker. One of Will Rogers's most famous roles was as just such a trader, David Harum.

Here, another lawyer came to the rescue. Green Hackworth, the State Department Solicitor General, suggested that the bases in Newfoundland and Bermuda be designated as gifts and the others as a trade for the destroyers. This proved sufficient to satisfy Churchill's pride and the deal was finally struck.

The final worry was Wendell Willkie. White, Douglas, and other committee and Century members had labored mightily to convince him, but powerful forces were working against them—not only Arthur Krock but Hoover and all those other Republican isolationists whose votes he would need in November. Even a Willkie loyalist like Sam Pryor, the man who had packed the galleries in Philadelphia, opposed the destroyer deal. What would Willkie do? Would he finally decide to support the deal or would he attack it?

On August 30th, Herbert Agar, Archibald MacLeish, and a few other Century and Committee friends gathered at the Hay Adams House across Lafayette Park from the White House. They had made their last approach to Willkie and now they waited together to hear the candidate's verdict. Two phone messages came in, one from Russell Davenport and the other from Lewis Douglas. Both said that Willkie would go along; he would not attack the deal. Roosevelt was told of the good news immediately. Now the coast was clear.

On September 3rd, Roosevelt was in West Virginia on a war plant inspection tour. After visiting the Naval Ordinance Plant in South Charleston, his car proceeded to Charleston to maximize the number of people who would see the president—these war plant tours were a way to disguise campaigning, as they always offered time for thorough exposure to local voters. As his car was driven past cheering crowds along the newly constructed Kanawha Boulevard—built, by the way, with New Deal money—he was flanked by the outgoing and incoming governors, the conservative Homer Holt, and the ardent New Dealer Matthew M. Neely, who symbolized the split in the Democratic Party that was evident at the July convention. When Roosevelt's car turned into Hale Street, I was part of a tightly packed crowd that caught a glimpse of the upturned chin, the magic smile, and the wave of his hand. The car proceeded to cross the Kanawha River Bridge to the C&O Railroad Station, where the president boarded his special train.

As the train chugged uphill through the New River Gorge about an hour after leaving Charleston, reporters were summoned to the president's car in the rear.

"In a sitting room just inside the observation platform, he waited there," reported *Time,* "smiling over his secret. His big head, white at the temples, cocked back and forth as he greeted correspondents, directing them to their places in the little room. It comfortably accommodated seven, but twenty-odd journalists were jostling each other as the train rolled along." Reporters who couldn't find seats crouched on the floor or attempted to listen from the corridor as Roosevelt announced the historic exchange of destroyers for bases. He called it "probably the most important thing that has come for American defense since the Louisiana Purchase." Roosevelt knew he had to emphasize the "bargain" aspect of the trade, so he devoted much of the press conference to Jefferson's steal from Napoleon, implying that he was now standing in the shoes of the man from Monticello.

When the train stopped at Hinton to take on water for its steam engine, reporters rushed to file their stories with the Western Union operator in the station. The media reaction was largely favorable—and this was no accident. Alsop had undertaken "to organize commitments of all the leading columnists to support Roosevelt when the destroyer deal was announced. I got commitments from all the major columnists save one." Luce made a similar effort to organize a favorable press. He certainly succeeded with his publication *Life,* which ran this headline over its story: "Destroyers for Bases; U.S. Trades 50 Old War Ships for Control of the North Atlantic." The New York *Herald Tribune* called the deal "Wholly admirable." The *Baltimore Sun* called it a "Bargain in which the United States gets far and away the better of the deal." The *Atlanta Constitution* said "It was one of the greatest defense strokes made in behalf of the protection of this country." The New Orleans *Times Picayune,* buying FDR's pitch, called it "Second only in importance to Jefferson's Louisiana Purchase." Even the isolationist *Chicago Tribune* was trapped into approval because it had long argued that the United States should acquire the British bases for the defense of the Western Hemisphere.

But the *St. Louis Post Dispatch* called it an "act of war," and said that Roosevelt had become "America's First Dictator." The Nazi press claimed that the deal was "a flagrant breach of neutrality," which must have been the party line, since the identical words were used by both the *Hamburger Fremdenblatt* and the *Deutshe Allgemeine Zeitung*. The *Telegrafo* of Rome said that the news proved Roosevelt's Jewish descent. According to the Italian paper, "the name Roosevelt was originally Rosenfeld of Jewish-Dutch origin."

Willkie, true to his commitment, said that the "public will undoubtedly approve" of the deal. But he criticized Roosevelt for not having consulted Congress, as did Walter Lippmann, who had been an original supporter of the trade (recall that he coauthored General Pershing's speech).

The Willkie-Lippmann concerns were far from frivolous. FDR himself, according to his secretary, Grace Tully, feared that the deal could result in his impeachment. Later historians have cited it as the moment the imperial presidency began, with subsequent presidents increasingly convinced that they could get away with practically anything in the name of national security.

My own conviction is that Roosevelt did what had to be done at that moment in history. Willkie's running mate, Charles McNary, had told Roosevelt that he could not support the deal if it came to a vote in the Senate, but that he would not criticize it if Roosevelt did it on his own. Legislative bodies are notorious for their inability to take on more than one controversial issue at a time, and the draft was already on the congressional plate. For FDR to seek a simultaneous vote in favor of the destroyer deal would have presented a significant risk of losing both it and the draft.

The first three destroyers left Boston on September 4th on their way to England and eight more departed on the next day. On September 16th Hitler decided to postpone invading England, a delay that was to prove permanent. The destroyers were far from being the only or even the major factor in the decision—remember the brave pilots of the RAF—but they did make, in Churchill's words, "a profound impression throughout Europe." The *New York Times* reported that the British were "jubilant."

In selling the draft, FDR was to display his public relations skill once more. He avoided words like "draft" and "conscription," favoring the term "muster," reminiscent of patriots gathering on the village green at Lexington and Concord. Wendell Willkie gave the draft an enormous boost when, in his speech accepting the Republican nomination on August 17, he said that "some form of selective service is the only democratic way."

Still the opponents fought on, led by Robert Taft, Arthur Vandenberg, and Hiram Johnson among the Republicans, Democrat Burton Wheeler in the Senate, and Republican Hamilton Fish in the House. The opposition proposed one amendment after another, the last by Fish, delaying the draft by sixty days. This was the most dangerous, because it would have kept the draft alive as a political issue until election day. It passed the House in a 185–155 vote September 5th. On September 6th, Roosevelt spoke out against the amendment. Even more important was a statement Willkie made on September 10th, which *The New York Times* headlined "Willkie Opposes Delaying of Draft—Despite Pressure, He Rebuffs Isolationists."

Willkie was able to persuade enough Republicans, including his campaign chairman, House minority leader Joe Martin—who had earlier advised Willkie not to take a stand on the issue, saying "People don't want their son[s] in uniform"—to change their minds and vote for the bill, minus the delaying amendment. When the bill finally passed on September 14, Senator Hiram Johnson said that Willkie had "broken the back" of the opposition to the draft.

Willkie's support for the draft never wavered, but his comments about the destroyer deal became more caustic as the election neared. He even characterized it as "the most arbitrary and dictatorial action ever taken by the president in the history of the United States." But he never called for the deal to be repudiated and, most important of all, the acquiescence he signaled through Davenport and Douglas before the deal was announced was crucial to giving Roosevelt the courage to make it.

CHAPTER THIRTEEN

★

"SAIL ON O SHIP OF STATE!"

Their staunch support of a military draft, not only in peace-time but in an election year, must entitle Willkie and Roosevelt to a special place in the honor roll of American leaders who rose above politics at crucial moments in the nation's history. Unfortunately, both men began to retreat from the heights as the campaign progressed into October and November.

On September 12 Willkie left Rushville, where he had stayed since his acceptance speech. Willkie's five farms outside the town had provided ideal settings for photographs designed to sell America on his rural roots. "It's getting so," Mary Steeth remarked, "every time a cameraman shows up the hogs run right over and strike a pose." But now Willkie's train was on its way to officially launch his campaign in Coffeyville, Kansas, where he had taught years before at the local high school.

"The Willkie Special" was twelve cars long, later to grow to fourteen, then to sixteen. Its cars were dark green in color, as were most trains of the era, the few exceptions including the maroon of the Pennsylvania and Norfolk & Western, the yellow Streamliners of the Union Pacific, and the silver Zephyrs of the Burlington. There were sleeping cars with bedrooms and compartments for the press and staff, with two dining cars that were, recalled Maria Davenport, "hitched and unhitched with murderous shoutings at dawn and late at night." One lounge car was used to entertain local politicians who would board the train for brief trips within their states. Another had been stripped of furniture and "jammed to the roof" with typewriters, filing cabinets, reference books, and mimeograph machines, and was crowded with typists and researchers.

At the rear of the train was the "Pioneer," a mahogany-paneled private car. Davenport remembered "its posh, heavily carpeted living room, a kitchen, compartments for maids and secretaries, and bedrooms for the candidate, his wife, Edith, and his brother Edward, the six-foot former Navy football star who had taken a leave from his Chicago firm to serve as companion and one-man security force."

In the car closest to Willkie were the top staffers, including Russell Davenport, who remained the candidate's closest adviser. Davenport and his wife Marcia had two adjoining compartments, one where they slept and one that served as Russell's office. "The facilities included a shower-bath, which never had any water in it," wrote Marcia.

> Everything relating to physical order and cleanliness, including laundry, was a nightmare. Some of the wildest tales of the Willkie train are stories of lost laundry which never caught up with the men who had left their shirts in a town which seemed to have slunk off the map when anybody tried to connect with it again.

Willkie, his staff, and seventy-five reporters were to spend seven weeks on the train, traveling 18,789 miles through thirty-one states, making 560 stops for speeches that quickly left Willkie's voice hoarse and in need of constant treatment by a specialist. The train was "a migrating hotel, camp, headquarters, traveling carnival, and smoke-filled politicians' hangout in one," wrote the *Herald Tribune*'s Joseph Barnes, who was one of the inmates. "Newspapermen called it 'the squirrel cage.'"

Another name they had for it was "organized chaos." Marcia Davenport called her husband Russell "a prodigy of disorder" and Willkie himself was no slouch in that regard. The chaos was exacerbated by the continuing warfare between the professional politicians and Willkie's amateurs.

The professionals—John Hollister, who had supported Taft at the convention, was an example—tended to be isolationist, as were most of the GOP's regulars. The hand of the professionals was strengthened as a Roper poll published in mid-September that showed Willkie falling further behind Roosevelt was followed a week later by another poll by Gallup that confirmed the trend. The isolationists argued that Willkie's "me too" policy of supporting aid to Britain and the draft did not sufficiently differentiate him from Roosevelt, and also failed to take advantage of what they were convinced would be a growing fear of war that would only increase as the nation's sons came closer to being drafted. Thus, although the main theme of the campaign continued to be anti–third term, a cause shared by both the amateurs and the professionals, Willkie gradually began to fan the fear of war.

One factor in the growing influence of the isolationists may have been Irita Van Doren's absence from the train. The need to preserve appearance meant that Edith Willkie had to travel with her husband. "Politics makes strange bedfellows," Mrs. Willkie joked. Willkie would telephone or telegraph Van Doren almost every day, but their contacts were too brief to permit her to have the voice in his life that she had become accustomed to and that had encouraged Willkie's internationalism and his rapid rise from nowhere to the Republican nomination.

It became even more important to keep Van Doren out of sight when Roosevelt threatened to reveal the affair if the Willkie campaign made public some imprudent letters Henry Wallace had written to his one-time guru, the White Russian mystic Nicholas Roerich. An Oval Office recording system briefly in service in 1940 caught Roosevelt telling his aide, Lowell Mellett, "[W]e can't have any of our principal speakers refer to [the affair] but the people down the line can get it out . . . actually she's a nice gal but there is the fact."

FDR's campaign had its own brush with a sex scandal when, on the presidential train to Speaker William Bankhead's funeral in September, Undersecretary of State Sumner Welles propositioned a Pullman porter who was male and black, to boot. The potential for unfortunate headline was limitless but the Democrats managed to conceal the event until well after the election.

An embarrassment for Roosevelt that did become public was his son Elliott's captaincy in the air force. Although it was not unusual for a man of Elliott's age—he was in his thirties—and experience in business to be given such a rank, a favorable light was not cast on the matter by the fact that through the draft hundreds of thousands of men were soon to be given the rank of private. Buttons appeared proclaiming, "I Want To Be a Captain, Too."

Still, on October 6 a new Gallup poll showed a bigger lead for Roosevelt—now twelve percentage points. As Willkie grew desperate, he increasingly attended to the advice of isolationists like Joe Martin and publishers Robert McCormick and Roy Howard, who urged him to step up his appeal to parents and potential draftees, making a firm pledge not to re-send American servicemen "over there," and Willkie responded with these words: "If you elect me president they will not be sent . . . if you re-elect the third term candidate, I believe they will be sent."

He even went so far as to accuse the administration of having made secret agreement to enter the war. Needless to say, this delighted the Lindberghs but was dismaying to Willkie's internationalist supporters. Columnist Dorothy Thompson, who had been backing Willkie, switched to Roosevelt. Walter Lippmann, who had been leaning toward Willkie, announced that he would be neutral.

But if Lippmann and Thompson were unhappy, Republican voters were responding to Willkie's new approach. The Gallup poll showed that Willkie had cut FDR's lead in half. As Willkie saw that the strategy was working, he became even more committed to it. The closer he came to the prize, the more he was willing to sacrifice his principles in order to seize it.

His behavior was reminiscent of two other decisive moments in Willkie's life. In Philadelphia, when he needed the support of Frank

McKay, the leader of the Michigan delegation, Willkie promised him control of Michigan federal judgeships. And, of course, there was the time when Gwyneth Harry had delivered her ultimatum "[B]ecome a fraternity man or lose me," and Willkie told his roommate that "if I don't join a fraternity I lose my girl and if I do, I lose my soul." Willkie chose the girl.

As the 1940 campaign drew to a close, Roosevelt was also choosing the girl. His promises not to send our boys overseas became just as strong as Willkie's, culminating in the famous declaration in Boston "I have said again and again and again your boys are not going to be sent into any foreign wars." Roosevelt explicitly rejected the advice of his speechwriter, Sam Rosenman, to add the words "except in case of attack."

When Rosenman reminded him that the Democratic platform used "except in case of attack," Roosevelt replied, "Of course we'll fight if we're attacked. If somebody attacks us then it isn't a foreign war, is it? Or do they want me to guarantee that our troops will be sent into battle only in the event of another civil war?" FDR had a point, but it wasn't exactly overwhelming. It seems clear that he wanted to make a definitive statement that was not emasculated by qualifying phrases.

Willkie had not been in politics long enough to develop those warning bells that guard against the spontaneous but ill-advised remark. Speaking to steelworkers in Pittsburgh, he promised that, if elected, he would appoint a union member as secretary of labor, and then added, "and it will not be a woman either." Needless to say, this jab at Frances Perkins did not enhance his prospects with female voters.

Still, Willkie won some important converts, including boxing champion Joe Louis, a great hero of black America, and John L. Lewis, the president of two major unions, the CIO and the United Mine Workers. But an important one got away. Joseph Kennedy, the ambassador to Britain who was reputed to have great influence on his fellow Catholics, had told Clare Luce, among others, that he was planning to come home just before the election and endorse Willkie.

But the minute that he landed on American soil, Roosevelt had him whisked to the White House for a private dinner. It must have been one of the more skillful stroking sessions in American political history, because instead of coming out for Willkie, Kennedy endorsed FDR in a speech broadcast throughout the country.

On Election Day, Roosevelt won by 5 million votes. But his margin was only half of what it had been over Landon, and Willkie got more votes than any previous Republican presidential candidate—22 million. Despite the compromises he made in the later stages of the campaign, Willkie's independence and personal warmth had stirred a very large number of Americans, whose commitment to him remained passionate.

.   .   .

With the election over, Roosevelt and Willkie became allies again and together forged another great triumph of statesmanship—Lend-Lease. Soon after the election, it had become clear that Britain was running out of the dollars needed to pay for military equipment it was acquiring from the United States. On November 22, Lord Lothian, the British ambassador, returned to the United States after a trip to England. Talking to reporters who greeted him at New York's LaGuardia Field, he abandoned the customary circumlocutions of the diplomat: "Well boys, Britain's broke. It's your money we need now."

When this comment appeared in the *New York Times* the next day, it was accompanied by a column by Howard Calender that said Britain's financial reserves would soon be exhausted. On November 26, the Associated Press's Drew Middleton reported, "Britain is reaching the end of her financial tether." The next issue of *Life* headlined, "Britain sends SOS to U.S." And *Time* declared, "When Britain runs out of cash for buying guns, aid to Britain will cease unless the U.S. comes up with a new kind of aid." That same week, the *New Republic* said, "[W]e must not permit Britain to go under . . . it is unthinkable that financial circumstances should be allowed to endanger the movement across the Atlantic of a huge and increasing quantity of war materials."

On December 2, Roosevelt departed for a cruise on the U.S.S. *Tuscaloosa* to inspect some of the newly acquired bases in the Caribbean. Before leaving, he instructed Treasury Secretary Henry Morgenthau to "use your imagination" to come up with an answer to Britain's financial problems.

On December 3, Morgenthau convened a meeting at which his aide Harry Dexter White threw cold water on the idea that Britain had suddenly become a poverty case. White, who after the war was discovered to have been a Soviet agent, appeared to be serving his masters in Moscow, who at the time were allies of Hitler and hostile to Britain. Fortunately, Herbert Feis, the State Department's economic adviser, argued against White's position and appeared to carry the day—which was important because the meeting was chock-full of heavy hitters including General George Marshall; White House aide James Forrestal; Stimson's "number two," Robert Patterson; and Undersecretary of State Sumner Wells.

On December 9, the White House received a detailed accounting from Churchill stating that the orders for war supplies already placed by the British would fully deplete their exchange reserves. Two days later, Lord Lothian, in a speech in Baltimore, again urged the United States to come to Britain's financial rescue.

Meanwhile, Wendell Willkie had extended the olive branch to FDR, concluding a late November speech in New York—given, by the way, to the National Inter-Fraternity Council, which must have delighted Gwyneth Harry—by pleading for national unity and raising his glass in a toast to "health and happiness of the president of the United States."

During that speech, Willkie returned to a theme that he had largely forsaken in the heat of the campaign, saying that "we must continue to help the fighting men of Britain to preserve that realm of freedom which is gradually shrinking, which if we continue to permit it to shrink, will shrink to the edge of our shores." During his post-election vacation at Sam Pryor's retreat on Jupiter Island in Hobe Sound, Florida, Willkie had decided, according to his biographer Steve Neal, that "military aid to Britain should become his next political cause."

Back in Washington, it turned out that Roosevelt had chosen not to rely on Morganthau's imagination after all. When he received Churchill's December 9 report while still aboard the *Tuscaloosa*, he had devoted himself to thinking about Britain's financial plight and nothing else for the next two days, according to Harry Hopkins, who was with him. Sometime during that period he came up with the Lend-Lease idea.

"I didn't know for quite a while what he was thinking, if anything," Hopkins later told Robert Sherwood. "But then I began to get the idea that he was refueling, the way he often does when he seems be resting and carefree. So I didn't ask him any questions. Then one evening he suddenly came out with it—the whole program. He didn't seem to have any clear idea of how it could be done legally. But there wasn't a doubt in his mind that he'd find a way to do it."

The day after he returned to Washington, December 16, FDR lunched with Morgenthau to explain his idea. He proposed to avoid lending money, which would be unpopular because of American cynicism about our loans to European countries that, with the single exception of Finland's, went unpaid after World War I, substituting instead the idea of lending military equipment to Britain. Morgenthau replied that, although "if I followed my own heart, I would say let's give it to them," he realized that it was important for Roosevelt to appear as the hard-nosed Yankee trader who wasn't giving away anything.

After lunch, Roosevelt met with reporters and explained the idea to them by saying that the United States would lend or lease the military equipment the British needed, with the understanding that the British would return the equipment or replace it after the war. There would be no debt in the form of dollars, only an obligation to return or replace.

The press conference was one of Roosevelt's masterpieces. It was not, however, devoid of mishap. At one moment, when asked who would have legal title to the leased equipment, FDR somewhat airily replied, "I don't know and I don't care." At another, when asked how Britain would pay for orders already in the pipeline, he replied that the British had "plenty of exchange" to finance the purchases, even though the whole idea of Lend-Lease was based on British poverty. Fortunately the media made little of the gaffes. On the whole, White House reporters, in contrast to their bosses, remained sympathetic to Roosevelt.

The idea of the lease had first occurred to Roosevelt during World War I, when he was an assistant secretary of the navy in the Woodrow Wilson administration. At that time, there was a law that kept the government from selling guns that would be needed to arm merchant ships. Roosevelt suggested that a lease would be a way to get around the prohibition. Wilson rejected the idea but, now that a Treasury lawyer had discovered a statute that specifically authorized the lease of army equipment for up to five years, FDR must have thought it was time to revive his World War I proposal. He knew he had a selling job to do with the public, so he went to work with Robert Sherwood and Sam Rosenman on a radio address scheduled for broadcast on more than 500 stations on the evening of December 29.

The speech was delivered in the Oval Room of the White House, where a small audience of invited guests had gathered, including Secretary of State Cordell Hull and Senate Majority Leader Alben Barkley. Also present was the actress Carole Lombard, a devoted fan of FDR's who would die in a plane crash while on a tour selling defense bonds just a year later, and her husband, the most celebrated leading man of the era, Clark Gable.

"The President came in five minutes before the broadcast on a small rubber-tired wheelchair" reported *Time*. (So much for the myth favored by Richard Nixon and recent historians that Americans didn't know about Roosevelt's paralysis.) At 9:30 PM, he began his speech: America must be "the great arsenal of democracy." As for appeasing Hitler, Roosevelt said "no man can tame a tiger into a kitten by stroking it." Helping Britain, he added, offered the "least risk" of getting into the war and the "greatest hope" of keeping out of it.

Of those who had read or heard the speech, the Gallup poll reported that 61 percent agreed with Roosevelt while only 24 percent opposed him. Incredibly, 59 percent of those polled had actually listened to the speech on the radio, and another 16 percent had read about it.

The speech's impact was heightened by the wide publicity given to an analogy FDR had used in his December 16 press conference: "Suppose my neighbor's home catches fire, and I have a length of garden hose. If he can take my garden hose and hook it up to his hydrant, now what do I do? I don't say to him 'neighbor, my garden hose costs me $15, so you must give me $15.' All I want is the garden hose after the fire is over." He added, "If the hose is damaged my neighbor can repair or replace it."

Once again, just as he had done on Christmas Eve of 1939, Roosevelt invoked the spirit of neighborliness. I remember how the garden hose comparison delighted my trial-lawyer father, whose work made him especially appreciative of down-to-earth explanations that appealed to the common sense of the average man. This one, however, was not entirely devoid of disingenuousness. After the war, Britain didn't give back the tanks we had given it under Lend-Lease, or repair or replace airplanes that had been damaged or destroyed. Still, those tanks and planes were used for our benefit against a common enemy. And that garden-hose metaphor—originally suggested to FDR by Harold Ickes—must rank as one of the more sublimely effective elucidations of public policy in American history.

Now that Roosevelt had sold the idea, a bill had to be prepared. The actual work was mostly done by Treasury Department lawyers Edward Foley and Oscar Cox, with help from New Deal brain truster Ben Cohen of the Department of the Interior and Supreme Court Justice Felix Frankfurter (a jurist of whom it may be confidently said that he was never guilty of excessive regard for the separation of powers). House Speaker Sam Rayburn urged that the final draft be prepared by Middleton Beaman, the legislative counsel of the House. Rayburn's reasoning was that, because the bill gave an unprecedented level of legislative power to the executive, it would be more "digestible" if it was presented as having originated in the Congress. Roosevelt agreed.

The bill was introduced on January 23. And it did, indeed, grant sweeping powers to the president. It authorized him to order any government official to manufacture or procure in any way any defense article, which was defined as practically anything, "not withstanding the provisions of any other law." It also enabled the president to order any defense article, "sold, exchanged, or transferred, leased, repaired or reconditioned for the use of any country he may name." Had there been an award for the use of the word "any" this bill would have won it hands down.

"Any country" was Hull's idea. An early draft had applied only to China, which Japan had invaded in 1937, Greece, which Mussolini had invaded in November, and Britain. Hull, however, knew of intelligence suggesting that Hitler might soon invade Russia so he deemed it prudent to make the identity of the beneficiaries open ended.

The reaction to the bill by the isolationists, who still included most Republicans, was hostile. The leader of the small group of Democrats opposed, Senator Burton Wheeler, comparing Lend-Lease to a New Deal policy aimed at avoiding agricultural surpluses, said that Roosevelt was going to "plow under every fourth American boy." The *New York Times* reported:

> Mr. Dewey and Mr. Taft in strong words denounced the president's message as seeking dictatorial power. Mr. Landon and Mr. Hoover also took the same course but in more moderate language. Mr. Vandenberg was suspicious of the whole thing.

Heated opposition came from the nation's two largest papers, the *Chicago Tribune* and the *New York Daily News*, and from the Hearst and Scripps-Howard chains, not to mention the Communist *Daily Worker*, which foolishly opposed a measure that would turn out to be as much Russia's salvation as Britain's.

Wendell Willkie spoke up for the bill, suggesting only that it provide for the unusual power granted the president to expire when the emergency was over. Willkie's support brought him some grief, including an intemperate denunciation from the usually mild Alf Landon, who said the Republicans would never have nominated Willkie if they had known his true feelings. The *Chicago Tribune* read Willkie out of the party.

But Willkie's stand won the praise of the *New York Times*, the New York *Herald Tribune*, and the *Christian Science Monitor* as well as of the Luce magazines. It also won Willkie an invitation to the White House to discuss a trip to London that he was planning. He arrived on January 19 at a not-yet-complete National airport at Gravelly Point where nary a taxi was to be had. So he bummed a ride with a photographer who had been sent to meet his plane. He was taken to the Carlton Hotel (now the St. Regis), where he was briefed by Cordell Hull. Then Willkie walked the two short blocks from the hotel to Lafayette Square and across the small park to the White House, where he met the man he had bitterly opposed less than three months earlier.

Roosevelt welcomed him warmly and the two men exchanged jokes. "Great bursts of laughter could be heard coming through the closed doors," said Jimmy Roosevelt, who was at the White House for the third-term inauguration.

Roosevelt urged Willkie to get together with Harry Hopkins, who was in London at the time, and with Averill Harriman, who was there to coordinate American military aid. "You'll like Averill," the president said. And then, without thinking that the next remark was not likely to delight Willkie, FDR said, "[H]e contributed to our campaign, you know." The president caught himself and was clearly embarrassed, but Willkie said, "Oh, that's alright, Harriman contributed to our campaign too. He gave me money for my pre-presidential campaign before I got the nomination. But, then he contributed to your election campaign."

The meeting was deemed important enough for the *New York Times* to make it the lead story on the next day's front page. Written by Turner Catledge, the article concluded: "[T]he former Republican candidate, himself an ardent advocate of the fullest possible material aid to Britain, found his fundamental views on the subject in close agreement with those of the President and Secretary Hull."

On January 20, Roosevelt was inaugurated for a third term. On January 22, Willkie left for London.

Willkie got the full treatment from the Brits. He saw the devastation around St. Paul's cathedral, visited bomb shelters in London,
and watched anti-aircraft batteries firing at Nazi planes along the
English Channel. He was given free access to the cabinet members of
his choice. Interestingly enough, he insisted on meeting with members of the Labor Party, including Ernest Bevin.

Willkie and Roosevelt both thought England would turn to the
left after the war. This sense may have been behind Roosevelt's
choice at this time of John Winant to replace Joseph Kennedy as ambassador to Britain. Although he was a Republican by party, Winant
was a New Dealer at heart.

Irita Van Doren's friend, the well-known British writer Rebecca
West, gave a dinner at London's Dorchester Hotel where Willkie, after
"saying how greatly he had been impressed by the Prime Minister and
what a great leader he was to have in times like these," recalled one of
the guests, "said he was not so sure, however, that Mr. Churchill
would be so valuable a leader when it came to the post-war period."

Willkie was especially impressed by a debate that he witnessed in
Parliament. While bombs were exploding outside, a Labor Party
member criticized the government for criticizing the *Daily Worker.* "It
was," Willkie said, "the most dramatic example of democracy at
work anyone could wish to see. Here Britain was fighting a war for
life yet a free House meets and denounces the administration."

Churchill entertained Willkie at both 10 Downing Street and at
Chequers, the prime minister's country residence. Churchill later
wrote that "every arrangement was made by us with the assistance
of the enemy to let him see all he desired of London at bay." Willkie
was suitably impressed: "I never saw such esprit." If Willkie was impressed by the British, so were they by him. One London paper concluded: "Willkie is the most interesting personality with the
exception of Mr. Roosevelt who has appeared on the American scene
since the other Roosevelt nearly 30 years ago."

The letter for Churchill that Roosevelt asked Willkie to deliver
contained this Longfellow poem:

Sail on o ship of state!

Sail on o union strong and great!
Humanity with all its fears,
With all the hopes of future years,
Is hanging breathless on thy fate.

Churchill gave his reply in a speech:

Here is the answer which I will give to President Roosevelt. Put your confidence in us, give us your faith and your blessing and under providence will all be well. We shall not fail or falter. We cannot tire. Neither the sudden shock of battle or the long drawn trials of vigilance and exertion will wear us down. Give us the tools and we will finish the job.

This was the exact answer that Roosevelt needed to hear. He was selling the American people on the idea that, by helping the British with Lend-Lease, the United States would be able to avoid getting into the war. Give *them* the tools, and *they* will finish the job. Churchill understood what Roosevelt needed, which is why he chose to give his answer not in a private letter, but in a public speech.

Meanwhile, the administration worked to get the bill through Congress. One problem was that the Senate Foreign Affairs Committee had been an isolationist stronghold, so considerable thought was given to putting the bill through the Military Affairs Committee, which was more internationalist in sympathy. But, since Sam Rayburn felt that House rules required him to refer the bill to the House Foreign Affairs Committee, Senator Barkley said the Senate would have to follow suit and send it to Foreign Affairs. The one reason to hope that this might prove the right course was that there were two vacancies on the committee. Roosevelt suggested to committee chairman Tom Connelly that he fill the vacancies with James Byrnes and Carter Glass, who just happened to be strong supporters of Lend-Lease. Connelly complied and the committee's balance of power shifted in favor of the bill.

Alben Barkley and John McCormack, the Senate and House majority leaders, were asked to introduce the bill. Barkley was happy to do so, but McCormack had a problem. Although he favored the bill, he represented a heavily Irish district in Boston where aid to Britain was not a popular cause. Lewis Deschler, the House parliamentarian, came to McCormack's rescue. He arranged to have the bill numbered H.R. 1776, which he was confident would make sure it would be known by that number rather than as the McCormack bill.

Deschler was right; 1776 caught the fancy of the press and became the way the bill was described, with John McCormack's sponsorship largely ignored. It did not, however, completely escape the attention of his constituents. Once, in Boston, an angry Irish woman asked him how he could possibly even think of helping Ireland's traditional oppressor. McCormack is said to have replied, "Madam, do you realize that the Vatican is surrounded on all sides by totalitarianism? This is not a bill to save the English, it is a bill to save Catholicism."

Opponents of the bill proposed several amendments. One provided a list of countries eligible for aid that omitted Russia. Another, obviously designed to prevent another destroyer deal, forbade transfer of any naval vessel. Administration forces managed to defeat both, but there was a growing sense among proponents that some amendment was necessary to deal with widespread anxiety about the broad powers given the president.

Rayburn urged Roosevelt to hold a meeting at the White House bringing together administration and congressional leaders to seek agreement on acceptable amendments. The bipartisan meeting included two Republicans, Senator Charles McNary and Congressman Joe Martin. Roosevelt declared that he would be "perfectly willing to accept any amendments that were desirable." Although the last three words deprived his concession of any meaning, they seemed to have been accepted as a sincere gesture of goodwill and the conferees agreed in principle to three amendments.

One amendment provided that the army and navy chiefs of staff would have to approve any transfer of existing military equipment. Another provided that the bill not be construed to authorize American navy vessels to convoy ships carrying military supplies abroad. This was actually meaningless because Roosevelt already had that authority, but it seemed to placate at least some of the bill's opponents. Also agreed to was a time limit for the president's authority under the bill. Finally, the administration agreed to accept an amendment that made clear congressional authority over appropriations, a matter already covered by the Constitution.

As H.R. 1776 proceeded through the houses of Congress it was shepherded by an administration team headed by Oscar Cox of the Treasury and John McCloy of the War Department. They crafted the necessary amendments and wrote memorandum after memorandum filled with facts and arguments for friendly congressmen to use in countering the bill's opponents. McCloy was later to become famous as the man that the late Richard Rovere called the Chairman of the Board of the Establishment in a memorable article in *Esquire* in the 1960s. Cox never became famous, but he deserved to. He was appointed general counsel for Lend-Lease and, in Sherwood's words, was "one of Hopkins' most brilliant aides." Cox was a member of a group of bright young Washingtonians, including Phillip Graham, Ed Pritchard, James Rowe, Ed Foley, Ben Cohen, and Joseph Rauh, who played essential behind-the-scenes roles during 1940–1941 in aiding Britain and getting the United States ready for war. Katharine Graham, Phillip Graham's widow and successor as publisher of the *Washington Post*, said that she felt Cox was preeminent in the group. Although she lost contact with him in later years, she made a point of attending his funeral when he died.

The amendments were important. Rayburn told Roosevelt that the bill would not pass without them. Opponents, led by the America First Committee, were well organized and vocal.

One argument used against Lend-Lease was that it would lead us into a war in which elderly statesmen would sacrifice the young:

They are usually old men, sterile biologically and sterile even of all dreams and memories of life, love, and youth, and would deny the right of youth to live. Their senile bodies, their cold, calculating brains frequently find compensation for their lost youth in hatred and false ambition for glory and gold.

That position, which would strike so many of us as persuasive during the war in Vietnam, was, in 1940, enunciated by the newsletter of the German-American Alliance, which seemed unaware of its applicability to Hitler and his cronies. Still, even though the Alliance may have been a bit biased, its argument is a reminder that the case against war could arouse strong emotion. Indeed, most isolationists were sincere in their hatred of war. The slaughter of World War I was too fresh in memory not to give pause to even the most devoted friends of Britain.

Of course, there were many Americans who were definitely not friends of Britain. Henry Ford was one example. He saw no difference between Britain and Germany: "There is no righteousness in either cause." Ford's solution: Give both sides "the tools to keep them fighting until they collapse."

Next to German-Americans, it was the Irish-Americans, as John McCormack knew, that constituted the group least friendly to Britain. That fact made Roosevelt worry about the possible impact of Joseph Kennedy's Lend-Lease testimony to the House Foreign Affairs Committee.

Kennedy had recently made some intemperate remarks to the *Boston Herald* that indicated that he had little hope for England and was disenchanted with administration policy. However, another White House stroking session saved the day. Kennedy testified against the bill, but his wholehearted endorsement of the concept of aid for Britain negated his opposition to H.R. 1776. The *New York Times* treated Kennedy's statement with the reverence usually accorded major presidential addresses. His payoffs to Arthur Krock—yes, Krock accepted generous gratuities from Kennedy—may have helped him get all that attention, but the net result was that Irish-Americans learned that one of their leaders favored helping the Brits.

The most prominent of the isolationist spokesmen was, of course, Charles Lindbergh. On January 23, Lindbergh testified before the House Foreign Affairs Committee. He told the committee that Germany controlled Europe and even with all the aid we could give, England would not be able to mount a successful invasion of the continent. He also thought that Germany could not successfully invade Britain. According to Harold Hinton of the *New York Times,* Lindbergh argued "that any negotiated peace to end the European War as soon as possible was preferable in the interest of the United States to prolonging the present conflict." In other words, Lindbergh was willing to leave Hitler much of Europe.

The diversity of the opposition to Lend-Lease was demonstrated the day before Lindbergh appeared, when Norman Thomas, the leader of the Socialist Party, also testified against the measure before the House Foreign Affairs Committee. Earlier the same day, Hanford McNider, Iowa's favorite son at the 1940 Republican Convention and a former national commander of the American Legion, told the committee that he was opposed. It was a rare moment in American history when the Socialist Party and the American Legion agreed on something.

Lord Lothian died in December. Lord Halifax, the new British ambassador, arrived in the United States on January 23 aboard the battleship *George V.* President Roosevelt traveled to Annapolis and took a launch into Chesapeake Bay to meet the ambassador. The gesture spoke volumes about the importance that Roosevelt gave to the British cause. Ordinarily a new ambassador comes to the president, not vice versa. The next day, Halifax, after meeting with Cordell Hull, spoke of the urgency of his country's need for help: "the quicker you can give it, the more helpful it is."

The biggest boost for Lend-Lease came from Wendell Willkie. Hull, worried about the bill's fate, cabled Willkie asking him to interrupt his trip to England and return immediately to testify before the Senate Foreign Relations Committee. Willkie left London on February 5. A roundabout route home was made necessary by Nazi aircraft and meant that Willkie did not arrive until February 9. Two days later, he made a dramatic appearance before the committee. A sign of the intense interest in his testimony was *Time's* report about the spectators gathered at the hearing: "there were 1,200 in a room built to hold 500."

Willkie's endorsement of Lend-Lease was wholehearted: "The powers asked for are extraordinary but in my judgment this is an extraordinary situation." He concluded that Lend-Lease was "the last, best chance" to keep America out of war. The committee reported the bill out favorably the next day and it soon passed both the Senate and the House. Cordell Hull's top aide, Carlton Savage, said of the struggle to pass Lend-Lease: "Wendell Willkie was the real hero."

Roosevelt biographer James McGregor Burns calls Willkie's a "powerful voice" for Lend-Lease, and Warren Kimball, author of *The Most Unsordid Act*, the most authoritative account of H.R. 1776, says Willkie gave it "an enormous boost." Doris Kearns Goodwin, in *No Ordinary Time*, writes that Willkie's was "the most important testimony in six weeks of hearings." At the time, Eleanor Roosevelt wrote in her column, "My Day," that she was "thankful beyond words" for Willkie's efforts. FDR himself said Willkie "is showing what patriotic Americans mean by rising above partisanship and rallying to the common cause." Irita Van Doren's feelings—and perhaps her role— may be deduced from the fact that Willkie's statement before the Foreign Relations Committee can be found among her papers in the Library of Congress.

As for the importance of Lend-Lease in history, Churchill called it "the third climacteric of World War II," after the fall of France and the Battle of Britain. (He saw the later ones as the Nazi invasion of Russia and the Japanese attack on Pearl Harbor.) When Hopkins told him of the passage of Lend-Lease, Churchill replied, "I thank God for your news."

On foreign policy and preparedness issues, Roosevelt and Willkie had become practically indistinguishable. Throughout the remainder of 1941, Willkie continued his vigorous advocacy of aid to Britain, even supporting Roosevelt's decision to use the U.S. Navy to convoy war supplies halfway across the Atlantic—a step that, by virtually inviting German submarines to attack U.S. escort vessels, took us a long way toward direct involvement in the war.

Willkie's help was important because the isolationists remained strong. Indeed their high-water mark was reached that August when they came within one vote of defeating the extension of the draft. If they had been victorious, the army would have been shrinking on

December 7, 1941, instead of being a growing force of 1.6 million, most of whom were drafted from all walks of American life.

The Japanese attack on Pearl Harbor and Hitler's declaration of war against us seemed, for a while at least, to put an end to isolationism. But, as the war progressed from a series of Allied defeats into turning point victories at Midway, El Alamein, and Stalingrad, the isolationists re-emerged to oppose American involvement in any postwar international organization.

Roosevelt, on the other hand, argued that the nations of the world were interdependent, requiring not only an international organization, but one that was clearly stronger than the League of Nations that had proved impotent against the threat of World War II. Willkie felt even more strongly. His views were made clear in a book he entitled *One World* that became the number-one best-seller in 1943. It was written at Irita Van Doren's apartment.

After the Republican Convention, where she had sat in a remote balcony seat, Van Doren had thought as she left the auditorium that she had lost Willkie forever, writes Richard Kluger, whose history of the *Herald Tribune* tells of the moment. But the relationship resumed after the election. As we have seen, there is evidence that she had a hand in Willkie's Lend-Lease statement to Congress, and *One World* was not only written in her apartment, it was edited by her; typed by her daughter; who lived across the hall, and published by her son-in-law's company.

Van Doren may not have been Willkie's only girlfriend in the post-election years. He is known to have had a relationship with the southern writer Josephine Pinckney. The movie actress Miriam Hopkins reported that he had made "a drunken pass" at her. Certainly his affair with liquor continued unabated. And during the trip that led to the writing of *One World*, Willkie met Madam Chiang Kai-Shek in Chunking. He returned early one morning after a long evening in her company, according to Gardner Cowles, who accompanied him on the trip, with a smile expressing the mixture of triumph and gratitude of a teenager after his first night with a member of the opposite sex. Indeed, when Roosevelt asked Madam Chiang what she thought about Willkie, she replied: "Well, Mr. President, he's an adolescent after all."

It is worth dwelling on Willkie's sex life for a moment. Public disclosure of his behavior could have wrecked his political career even before his notable contributions to history were made. The same could be said of Franklin Roosevelt's affair with Lucy Mercer. It seems unlikely that today's media would fail to investigate thoroughly the suspicion around Roosevelt's relationships with Missy Lehand, Margaret (Cousin Daisy) Suckly, Dorothy Schiff, and Princess Martha of Norway. It is more likely that the revelations that might have resulted would have weakened the president's position or cost him election or re-election.

The loss of either man could have had a disastrous effect on history. As to Roosevelt, this will be obvious to most people because scores of historians have celebrated his importance. Few, however, have made the case for Willkie's importance; so here it is.

As for the significance of his support for the draft, recall the judgment pronounced by one of its main opponents, Senator Hiram Johnson, that Willkie "broke the back" of the opposition of the draft. The role that Willkie played in Britain's survival has been described by Walter Lippmann:

> Second only to the Battle of Britain, the sudden rise and nomination of Willkie was the decisive event, perhaps providential, which made it possible to rally the free world when it was almost conquered. Under any other leadership but his the Republican party in 1940 would have turned its back on Great Britain, causing all who resisted Hitler to feel abandoned.

When *One World* appeared, its popularity did not extend to the isolationists, who remained concentrated in the Republican Party. Willkie's standing, while remaining strong with the general public, steadily declined among GOP leaders, a decline that was intensified by the growing realization that Willkie was a liberal on domestic issues, actually being to the left of FDR. (In 1943, he advocated even higher income taxes than those proposed by FDR.) And this time there was no giving in to the Frank McKays or Gwyneth Harrys. Willkie refused to compromise with the party's conservatives and isolationists.

The result was that, when he again sought the Republican nomination in 1944, Willkie was so soundly whipped in his first primary in Wisconsin that he withdrew from the race. By the middle of that year, he and Roosevelt were feeling each other out about starting a third party together.

But it all ended with Willkie's death on October 7, 1944. He had appeared to be in good health until near the end, but the cigarettes and alcohol had taken their toll, and he suffered a series of heart attacks in September and October, the last of which finally felled him.

Now Wendell Willkie would never be president; but it is arguable that his impact on this country and the world was greater than that of most men who actually held the office. At a crucial moment in history, he stood for the right things at the right time. His nomination as the Republican presidential candidate meant that Roosevelt could get away in an election year with doing what had to be done to keep Britain from falling to Hitler and to prepare this country for the great war it would soon have to fight. Before he died, Willkie said to a friend, "If I could write my own epitaph and I could choose between 'Here lies an unimportant president' or 'Here lies one who contributed to saving freedom at a moment of great peril,' I would prefer the latter."

The evidence is overwhelming that Taft or Vandenberg, had either been the Republican candidate, would have fought Roosevelt every step of the way. It is overwhelming because it is on the record—in their public statements against the destroyer deal, the draft, and Lend-Lease and, in the case of the latter two, actual votes against each when it came up in the Senate.

Dewey's record is more equivocal, as indeed were most of his public statements on the issues. What is clear is that, while he was a candidate for the 1940 nomination, Dewey's statements tilted toward the isolationist view of hard-core Republicans. Once he had lost the presidential nomination and his next feasible political target was the governorship of New York—to which he was elected in 1942—he tilted toward the internationalist views of the state's voters and of its great newspapers, The *New York Times* and the *Herald Tribune*. Dewey privately sent word to Willkie that he would not attack him if Willkie supported the destroyer deal. And, after first opposing Lend-Lease, he came out in favor of an amended version a few weeks before the bill passed. In 1944, however, when he again sought the Republican nomination, this time successfully, Dewey tilted enough in the isolationists' direction to lose the support of the Republican but internationalist *Herald Tribune*. So it seems probable that, while seeking national office, he would have remained isolationist during the crucial events of 1940.

As for Willkie's opinion of Dewey, following is an excerpt from a letter that the newspaper columnist and radio commentator Drew Pearson wrote to a listener who'd complained about a broadcast, made a few days after Willkie's death, in which Pearson had said that he believed Willkie would have come out against Dewey:

> Actually, I can tell you that Mr. Willkie went much further with me than I indicated over the air. Some of the things he said about Dewey were unprintable. He was, frankly, bitterly opposed to him and made no secret of it whatsoever. . . . He went over, in advance, the public announcement made by Russell Davenport, when Davenport incorporated the Committee of Independent Republicans for Roosevelt and thoroughly approved Davenport's plan.

Looking back on it, Willkie's nomination seems very nearly miraculous. Neither it nor the events it triggered could have happened without an alignment of the stars that would seem improbable to the most sanguine astrologer.

For one thing, the good side of the American character was in ascendancy. There has always been a struggle for the nation's soul— between, on the one side, the greedy, lying, snake oil salesmen represented by Mark Twain's King and the Duke; and, on the other side, those represented by the kind, commonsensical, down-to-earth Huck and Jim, and the decent, creative entrepreneur, Tom. During the time of this book, the good guys were winning.

American Christians responded to Roosevelt's call to neighborliness by supporting proposals like Social Security and Lend-Lease and by rejecting, as most German Christians shamefully failed to do, attempts to fan their anti-Semitism into the kind of hatred that would have made them isolationists, if not outright Nazis.

There was a lovely idealism abroad in the land. Related to the prevailing communitarianism, it was behind everything from that ovation those reporters gave Willkie the day before the nomination to the public's support for a draft. People believed that Mr. Smith really could go to Washington. That idealism got Willkie the nomination and, if it did not win him election, it still led to the triumph of his ideas.

All this meant that the American people were right, as sometimes they have not been, in rushing to give Willkie the support he needed to gain the Republican nomination just as they were later right in supporting the destroyer deal, the draft, and Lend-Lease.

The American Establishment was right, as it has so often not been, in supporting Willkie. Wall Street bankers and lawyers joined the *New York Times* and the *Herald Tribune* in exerting their influence at a time when that influence was still great.

The often wrong Henry Luce was sublimely right at a time when his publications were at the peak of their power.

War against Hitler was justified, as war so often is not.

The Republican Party nominated a Democrat who had not registered as a Republican until the year he was nominated.

State laws and party rules governing primaries and the selection of delegates and candidates were not nearly as stacked in favor of early anointing as they are today, meaning that delegates to the 1940 Republican convention would have the power to choose the best man as their candidate.

France surrendered the day before the Republican Convention started. This coincidence had a profound effect on many normally isolationist delegates. One of their arguments for keeping America out of the war had been that the mighty French army, thought by many to be the best in the world, was strong enough to stop Hitler without American involvement.

Finally, as a matter of practical politics, few coincidences could rival the death of pro-Taft Arrangements chairman Ralph Williams and his replacement by Willkie's man, Sam Pryor, less than a month before the Republican Convention began. This gave control of the convention tickets to Willkie's managers, who proceeded to pack the galleries with the throngs that chanted, "We want Willkie."

The more I think about it, the more convinced I am that Willkie's nomination could only have happened at the time that it did— maybe even only that week, because of the impact of the French surrender. I am reminded of a play by Thorton Wilder about how mankind survives. It's called *The Skin of Our Teeth*.

NOTES

The broad outlines of the story told in this book emerged from my memory of the events it describes. Although I was only thirteen or fourteen when most of them occurred, I followed politics like most other kids followed baseball. Because I *was* young then, however, I have made every effort to confirm, enrich, and (where necessary) revise what I remember through reading newspapers and magazines of the era and also from books and articles about it, and by talking to others who remember or—as has, alas, too often been necessary—to their sons and daughters with whom they may have discussed their experiences.

Although I believe that there is evidence for every statement of fact I have made, I do not propose to weary the reader, or myself, with citations of each source. I do however endeavor to cite authority for every quotation. When I know the facts are in dispute, or when a reasonable reader might suspect their authenticity, these notes seek to amplify and explain. For example, in the final chapter I contend that most Americans knew that FDR could not walk unaided. Because some recent historians have suggested otherwise, there is a note explaining and supporting my position. And sometimes I elaborate on a subject with facts or thoughts that did not fit the main narrative but that I think the reader may find interesting.

Chapter One: "World of Tomorrow"

3   Roy Jenkins, *Churchill, a Biography.*

Was Lindbergh anti-Semitic? Only a little bit argues A. Scott Berg, the Pulitzer-prize winning author of *Lindbergh.* FDR, on the other hand, called Lindbergh "a Nazi." The truth is probably somewhere in-between but leans in Roosevelt's direction. Even Berg concedes that both Lindbergh and his wife called Hitler "a great man." Berg, pp. 361 and 362. And consider this excerpt from Lindbergh's diary recalling a scene he witnessed in 1938 Europe: "The station platform is filled with Jews leaving for America. They were a poor-looking lot. . . .[They] gave me a strange feeling of pity and disgust. These people are bound to cause trouble if many of them go to America." See p. 386 of the *American Axis* by Max Wallace.

5   "Can It Happen Again?" *Newsweek*, July 22 (1968). This idea was explored in an issue of *Newsweek* that featured a cover photograph of a "We Want Willkie" sign being waved by a delegate to the 1940 Republican convention. The article addressed the fact that many Americans were unhappy with having to make a choice between Richard Nixon and Hubert Humphrey, and were hoping that another Willkie would emerge.

6   The quotes from and about Will Rogers are from Richard Ketchum, *Will Rogers: His Life and Times.* My favorite appears on p. 289: "I really believe that if it came to a vote whether to go to war with England, France, and Germany combined, or raising the tax rate on incomes over $100,000, [the Republicans] would vote [for] war."

The big bands played the music of the incredibly gifted composers who graced the era with songs of enduring popularity: George Gershwin ("I Got Rhythm," "Our Love Is Here to Stay"); Cole Porter ("Easy to Love," "I Get a Kick Out Of You"); Thomas "Fats" Waller ("Ain't Misbehavin," "I Can't Give You Anything But Love"); Irving Berlin ("Dancing Cheek to Cheek," "Isn't It a Lovely Day"); Harry Warren ("Stormy Weather," "Over the Rainbow"); Jerome Kern ("All the Things You Are," "The Way You Look Tonight"); and Richard Rodgers ("Bewitched, Bothered, and Bewildered," "My Funny Valentine"). I still hum those tunes, but I did gradually come to share my father's affection for country music, especially bluegrass.

7   "Social snobbery existed . . ." It seemed considerably more common among women than men. Because servants were so affordable—$10 a week for a full-time maid was the going rate in Charleston until 1939—middle-class women had leisure time (undreamed of today) for playing bridge, getting together for lunch, shopping, and going to the beauty parlor. Social organizations like garden clubs, the Junior League, the Colonial Dames, and the Daughters of the American Revolution, were important both as activities and as indicators of status.

"Franklin Roosevelt would even suggest a limit of $25,000 on net income . . ." James MacGregor Burns, *Roosevelt, the Soldier of Freedom*, pp. 257, 362.

"radio was the medium . . ." Here my memory was assisted by John T. Dunning, *On the Air: The Encyclopedia of Old-Time Radio*.

"Amos 'n Andy . . ." Here is what Henry Louis Gates Jr., the chairman of Harvard's School of African American Studies says about the show's popularity, in his book *Colored People: A Memoir*: "*Everybody* loved Amos and Andy, I don't care what people say today. For colored people, the day they took Amos and Andy off the air was one of the saddest days in Piedmont [Gates's hometown]." Pages 22–23.

8   Andy Hardy and Mickey Rooney. . . The Andy Hardy character was a scrubbed version of Huck Finn, as were many of the other roles that Rooney played. Indeed, when MGM made a movie featuring Huck, there was as little question as to whether Rooney would play the role as there was when Clark Gable was cast as Rhett Butler in *Gone With the Wind*.

Among the nation's handful of sophisticates, however, there was a more jaundiced view of Rooney. It was expressed in Richard Rodgers and Lorenz Hart's musical comedy *Pal Joey*, which appeared on Broadway in 1941 and in which there was this line in the lyrics of a song called "Zip": "Mickey Rooney makes me sickey."

9   Drew Pearson's column appeared in more than 1,000 daily and weekly newspapers at the peak of its popularity. As for Winchell, according to Ernest Cuneo's introduction to *Winchell Exclusive*, by Walter Winchell, "nine out of ten Americans heard or read Walter Winchell between his 9 P.M. Sunday night broadcast and his famed Monday morning column. His readers per day averaged 50 million. . . . his almost daily broadsides for President Roosevelt were a major factor in blasting FDR into a third term." Cuneo exaggerates, but not by much. Working out of room 1017 at the Reconstruction Finance Corporation, where he was an aide to the legendary New Deal fixer, Tommy "The Cork" Corcoran, he acted as intermediary between Winchell and the White House. Also see Neal Gabler, *Winchell: Gossip, Power and the Culture of Celebrity*.

10   "A two-page spread in *Life*. . . " George Gallup, quoted in James L. Baughman, *Henry R. Luce and the Rise of the American Media*. "In barbershops and two millions homes America thumbed through the glossy-paged picture magazine," Baughman explained. Alan Brinkley, a professor of history at Columbia who is working on a biography of Luce, says in an email that "each issue was usually read by several readers—in the case of *Life*, an average of four or five—very high for magazines." In my barbershop, it was a lot more than four or five; by the end of the week, *Life* was tattered to the point of falling apart.

"Tony Biddle has just gotten through from Paris . . ." James MacGregor Burns, *Roosevelt: The Lion and the Fox 1882–1940*, p. 394.

11   "Only Finland . . ." Martin Gilbert, *Winston S. Churchill*, Vol. 6, *Finest Hour, 1939–41*, p. 136.

"I supported every proposal to aid Finland . . ." Winston S. Churchill, *The Second World War*, Vol. 1, *The Gathering Storm*, p. 547.

12   "It was too impossible to warrant a comment . . ." Herbert Hoover, quoted in Oren Root, *Persons and Persuasions*, p. 16. Hoover's dismissal of the possibility of defeat of either France or Britain came in a speech to the Young Republican Club of New York in January 1940. It is cited as an example of the smug isolationism that drove him to found the Willkie Volunteer Movement that would overwhelm the Hooverites at the June Republican Convention.

"the first half of 1940 wages in West Virginia rose 25 percent above the same period in 1939 . . ." This would indicate that the Depression, which many historians depict as ending only when the United States entered World War II, was well on its way to ending in 1939–40. In fact the major increases in American defense spending did not kick in until the second half of 1940.

Plot summaries for *Margin For Error* and *There Shall Be No Night* are in Burns Mantle, *The Best Plays of 1939–40*. The full text of Sherwood's play is contained in John Mason Brown, *The Ordeal of a Playwright; Robert E. Sherwood and the Challenge of War*, ed. Norman Cousins.

"Bread was still ten cents a loaf . . ." The Web site www.nhm-ccd.edu/contracts/lre /kc/decade30.html says that bread was nine cents and milk 14 cents.

13   I may have stretched a bit to find social significance in my favorite song "Love Walked In" but, in 1939, the Saturday night radio show *The Hit Parade*, which presented the ten most popular

songs of the week featured "Over the Rainbow" for fifteen weeks and "Wishing" for fourteen. In 1940, "When You Wish Upon a Star," stayed in the top ten for thirteen weeks. *See* www.info.net. HITS.1939and1940.

"I've always thought Franklin's religion . . ." Eleanor Roosevelt, *This I Remember.*

14   Roosevelt's speech on Christmas Eve 1939 can be found in Franklin D. Roosevelt, *The Public Papers and Address of Franklin D. Roosevelt,* Vol. 8, *War—and Neutrality, 1939,* p. 609.

15   "On a straight division of the electorate . . ." John Culver and John Hyde, *American Dreamer: The Life and Times of Henry Wallace.*

The other possible contenders for the 1940 Democratic presidential nomination are described in Herbert S. Parmet & Marie B. Hecht, *Never Again, A President Runs for a Third Term—Roosevelt Versus Willkie, 1940,* and Warren Moscow, *Roosevelt and Willkie.*

The possibility that Paul McNutt may have been on the take came up in a 2004 conversation I had with Mary Bain, a former New Deal official. The copious amounts of whiskey consumed by Garner combined with his age (seventy-two) required him to maintain a urinal in the corner Capitol office. His successor, Henry Wallace, claimed "It stunk to high heaven," and had it removed.

"Jesus Christ came out Jesus Cwist . . ." Richard Ketchum, *The Borrowed Years, 1938–1941: America on the Way to War,* 264.

16   "Let's go to the Trans-Lux . . . " *The Complete Cartoons New Yorker,* ed. Robert Mankoff, p. 97. The exact caption is "Come along, we're going to the Trans-Lux to hiss Roosevelt."

"A weak Kerensky-type . . ." Burns, *The Lion and the Fox*, p. 417.

"cash and carry basis . . ." Burns, *The Lion and the Fox*, pp. 395–96.

17 "It's a terrible thing . . ." Samuel Rosenmam, *Working With Roosevelt*, p. 167.

Roper poll, in Ketchum, *The Borrowed Years, 1938–1941: America on the Way to War*, p. 324.

"[Dewey] threw his diaper into the ring . . ." Harold Ickes, quoted in Richard Norton Smith, *Thomas E. Dewey and His Times*, p. 296.

18 "particularly swell . . ." Tom Dewey, quoted in Norton Smith, p. 296.

19 "the Grand Canyon . . ." Lowell Thomas, quoted in Norton Smith, p. 296.

"control freak . . ." Norton Smith, p. 298.

"he was cold . . ." Ruth McCormick Simms, quoted in Norton Smith, p. 298.

Hitler as "a passing phenomenon" is from Dewey's own description of the views of his chief foreign policy adviser, John Foster Dulles. According to Dewey, Dulles believed that America should "stand aside and hopefully wait until a stalemate occurs and then exercise our weight to bring about a peace," which would presumably have left Hitler ruling Germany. Foster's brother Allen, who was pro-Allied, asked Foster "how he could consider himself a Christian and overlook what was happening inside Germany." Norton Smith, p. 303.

Smith's own observation that "Dewey drank deeply from the Dulles cup" but "heeded Foster more often," quoted in Norton Smith, p. 303.

20 "Why should I kill myself . . ." is the way Vandenberg's quote usually appears. In Gore Vidal's *The Golden Age*, however, it is rendered on p. 94 as "Imagine killing yourself to carry Vermont!"

Mitzi Sims' relationship to Vandenberg is described in Thomas Mahl, *Desperate Deception*, p. 145.

Many people who are otherwise knowledgeable about American history remember Vandenberg as the internationalist that he became in the aftermath of World War II. In the introduction to *The Private Papers of Senator Vandenberg*, the editor, Arthur H. Vandenberg Jr., writes that "Vandenberg was a symbol and a leader of isolationism—or as he preferred to say, 'insulationism'—in the United States up until four o'clock on Sunday afternoon December 7, 1941, when the phone in his study rang and he learned of Pearl Harbor" (which was well after most of the events described in this book had occurred).

As recently as March 4, 1941, Senator Vandenberg had written in his diary: "If America 'cracks up' you can put your finger on this precise moment as the time the crime was committed. It was at this moment that the Senate passed the so-called Lend-Lease bill." Vandenberg, Jr.

"the one I cared for most personally . . ." Turner Catledge, quoted in James T. Patterson, *Mr. Republican: A Biography of Robert A. Taft*, p. 224.

21 "It is the New Deal which may leave us weak . . ." Robert Taft, quoted in Patterson, pp. 217–18.

"[T]here was a good deal more danger" Robert Taft, quoted in

Patterson, p. 217. In this speech, Taft also said that America's participation in the war was "more likely to destroy American democracy than to destroy German dictatorship."

Even a German victory over England Taft viewed as "preferable" to American involvement. *See* Patterson, pp. 217–18. This remained his view until Pearl Harbor. "War," Taft told the Senate in February 1941, "is worse even than a German victory," Patterson, p. 243. Turner Catledge, travelling with Taft, was curious: Why had Taft resisted Landon's warning that "he was remaining too isolationist" when the public was moving the other way? Why wouldn't he change his views?

"I visited Taft in his Pullman car at a time when he was mulling over the issue. His glasses had slipped down halfway off his face and he kept repeating in a distant voice 'I'm just not going to do it.' He couldn't shift his views for political expedience."

"the fat was in the fire . . ." Martha Taft, quoted in Patterson, pp. 220–21.

Chapter Two: "A Stunning Combination of Intellect and Homely Warmth"

The main sources of biographical information on Willkie for this chapter are Steve Neal, *Dark Horse: A Biography of Wendell Willkie*; Ellsworth Barnard, *Wendell Willkie: Fighter for Freedom*, and Joseph Barnes, *Willkie: The Events He Was Part of, the Ideas He Fought for*. Each has its own special merit—Barnard is best on Willkie's time at Indiana University; Barnes on his experience in the public-utility business—but if I had to pick one as best overall, certainly the most vivid, it would be Neal's *Dark Horse*. Neal was a skilled interviewer and diligent in seeking out sources. Barnes had an elegant mind and had observed Willkie firsthand, both as a reporter and friend. Sometimes, however, the friendship seems to have led Barnes to be overly protective.

Other frequently cited books in Chapter Two are Marcia Davenport, *Too Strong For Fantasy*, and Jane Dick, *Volunteers and the Making of Presidents*.

"Willkie is a long shot candidate . . ." Arthur Krock, *New York Times*, February 22 (1939).

"a man wholly natural in manner . . ." Booth Tarkington, quoted in Joseph Barnes, *Willkie: The Events He Was Part of, the Ideas He Fought for*, p. 11.

24   "in Wendell Willkie the Republicans would have . . ." David Lawrence, Barnes, p. 157.

Time, July 1939.

"He is a big, shambling . . ." Marcia Davenport, *Too Strong for Fantasy*, pp. 261–62.

25   "of which incidentally I am a member . . ." Wendell Willkie, quoted in Steve Neal, *Dark Horse: A Biography of Wendell Willkie*, p. 46.

"only on the electric power question . . ." James Farley, quoted in Neal, p. 57.

"a constant atmosphere of reading and discussion . . ." Wendell Willkie, quoted in Neal, p. 12.

26   "Mother Trisch . . ." Barnes, p. 7.

27   "Another Willkie arrives. . ." *The Daily Student*, quoted in Ellsworth Barnard, *Wendell Willkie: Fighter for Freedom*, p. 31.

"the fact that [Willkie] did not belong to a fraternity . . ." Gwyneth Harry, quoted in Neal, p. 10.

"If I don't join . . ." Maurice Bluhm quoting Willkie in Barnard, p. 38.

28 "a telephone between his room . . ." Coffeyville (Kansas) High School Yearbook, 1914 quoted by the Associated Press in the Charleston Gazette, June 30, 1940.

"I believe my son will be a very good lawyer . . ." Herman Willkie, quoted in Neal, p. 13.

29 "he lacked all sense of time, tune, or rhythm . . ." Edith Willkie, Herald Tribune, June 29, 1940. See also Barnes, p. 31.

"never let me down . . ." Edith Willkie, quoted in *Herald Tribune*, June 28 (1940).

"I wouldn't marry a man who wasn't 'boss'. . . " Edith Willkie, quoted in *Gazette*, June 28 (1940). On the same day, however, the *Herald Tribune* quoted her as saying, "There is no boss in the Willkie family," but added that she "depended a great deal on her husband . . . he's a lot bigger than I am in every way." Edith Willkie, quoted in *Herald Tribune*, June 28 (1940).

"Sure you'll win . . ." Frank Daley, quoted in Barnes, p. 32.

31 "I think he's a comer . . ." D.C. Cobb, *Charleston Daily Mail*, July 4, 1940.

"I thought I was fixed for life . . ." Wendell Willkie, quoted in Neal, p. 24.

"My God, there isn't a soul here I know . . ." Wendell Willkie, quoted Barnes, p. 42.

"He loved girls . . ." Jane Dick, *Volunteers and the Making of Presidents*, p. 23. *See also* Neal, p. 38.

"He was very attractive to women . . ." Dick, p. 23.

32 "the Jesus Christ of the industry . . ." Barnes, p. 68.

33 "The kind of woman I like . . ." Harold Ickes, quoted in Neal, p. 29. See also Jane Dick, who describes Van Doren as "Tall, statuesque, and intellectual, not the kind of woman who usually appeals to a politician." Dick, p. 24.

"Her graciousness was innate . . ." Hiram Hayden, quoted in Neal, p. 50.

34 "Equally merry and serious . . ." Richard Kluger, *The Paper: The Life and Death of the New York Herald Tribune*, pp. 323–24.

"the uses of power . . ." Kluger, p. 325.

"traveled in liberal intellectual circles . . ." Kluger, p. 286.

"terribly attractive . . ." Kluger, p. 325.

"My dear Mrs. Van Doren . . ." Willkie letter to Irita Van Doren, from Irita Van Doren Papers, Collections of Manuscripts Division, Library of Congress.

"Your cousin Tom . . ." Willkie telegram to Irita Van Doren, January 1939, Irita Van Doren papers, Library of Congress.

35 "My dear dear Irita . . ." Willkie letter to Irita Van Doren, Irita Van Doren Papers, Library of Congress.

"You would never let me write anything . . ." Willkie, quoted in Irita Van Doren Papers, Library of Congress.

"acceptance of himself as a political leader . . ." Barnes, p. 156.

"In these times . . ." Marcia Davenport, quoted in Neal, p. 43.

"at the time I felt like she might be getting the short end of the stick . . ." Irita Van Doren's daughter, Barbara Klaw, quoted in Neal, p. 43.

36   "sprang from the grass roots all right . . ." Alice Roosevelt Longworth, quoted in Neal, p. 99.

36-37   Charlton MacVeagh may have been the first person to urge Willkie to run for president. His suggestion was made at Wall Street's Exchange Buffet in 1937, and was reported by Damon Runyon of International News Service on June 28 1940. It is possible that this may have ended MacVeagh's prominent role in the Willkie campaign because it is unlikely that Willkie and his associates would have been pleased to have it revealed that he was thinking of the presidency even that far back.

Another explanation for MacVeagh's departure from the campaign may be that he was close to John D. M. Hamilton and was upset by Willkie's failure to keep Hamilton as chairman of the Republican National Committee.

In any event, there was enough of a freeze in the Willkie-MacVeagh relationship after the convention that a letter from MacVeagh to Willkie, dated November 14, 1940, begins "Dear Mr. Willkie." It can be found among Willkie's papers in the Lilly Library of Indiana University.

"I've met the man . . ." Davenport, p. 259.

40   "I took [Edith Willkie] upstairs . . ." Davenport, p. 262.

"And there he sat . . ." Davenport, p. 262.

"preaching just plain common sense . . ." editorial, *Fortune*, April 1940.

41   "government, federal and state, must not only be responsible. . . "; "we should not relinquish . . ." Wendell Willkie, "We
the People," *Fortune*, April 1940.

"England and France constitute our first line of defense . . ."
Wendell Willkie, speech, Akron, Ohio, American Legion, May
1940.

Chapter Three: The Hurricane of Events

The main new source for this chapter is *Persons and Persuasions* by
Oren Root, the leader of Willkie's volunteer movement.

44   "it was a sublime act of faith . . ." Winston Churchill, *The Second
World War,* Vol. 2, *Their Finest Hour,* p. 143.

45   "almost hysterical . . ." Richard Ketchum, *The Borrowed Years,* pp.
316–17.

"The hand that held the dagger . . ." Franklin D. Roosevelt,
commencement speech, University of Virginia, June 10, 1940, *The
Public Papers and Addresses Franklin D. Roosevelt, 1940.*

46   "the groups consisted of men . . ." Oren Root, *Persons and Persuasions,* p. 20.

"We the undersigned people . . ." Root, pp. 22–24.

"I assumed one of my friends was pulling my leg . . ." Root, p. 25.

47   "Willkie had his own ideas . . ." Root, p. 27.

"The plan to which they had agreed . . ." Root, p. 27.
    The plan may have been hatched well before this or any

other book about Willkie suggests. While what follows is almost pure speculation, there are certain facts that indicate that the plot may have taken form as early as 1937. That was the year of MacVeagh's broaching of the possibility of a presidential race to Willkie.

Additionally, and as other histories fail to mention, the plotters knew each other by that time. MacVeagh and Pryor were already friends. Davenport served as godfather for Charlton MacVeagh Jr. who was born in 1936. In 1937, the first mention of Willkie as a presidential possibility appeared in *Fortune* where Davenport worked.

It also seems unlikely that all the publicity Willkie received and the public appearances that he made, including the *Town Meeting of the Air* in 1938, happened without a guiding hand behind them. It's also worth noting that main "business" of Pryor and MacVeagh was public relations. MacVeagh's monograph, in which Pryor plays a role as "Willard," says "There may [be] in Utopia NY a man with the character, the convictions and the ability but he may work in a relatively restricted circle. [Wendell Willkie in the utility industry]. . . . Publicity is about the only means by which he can expand his sphere of influence."

48　"asked me to meet him . . ." Root discussing Russell Davenport, Root, p. 28.

　　"[W]ell Oren, my boy . . ." Root, p. 31.

　　"[Y]ou will point out . . ." Russell Davenport letter to Raymond Clapper, quoted in Steve Neal, *Dark Horse: A Biography of Wendell Willkie*, p. 71.

49　"Some damn fool . . ." Willkie, quoted in Joseph Barnes, *Willkie: The Events He Was Part of, the Ideas He Fought for*, p. 168.

"If elected I would like . . ." Wendell Willkie, quoted in *New York Herald Tribune*, June 6 (1940).

50   "If I were you Charlie . . ." Joe Martin to Charles Halleck, quoted in Joseph Martin, *My First Fifty Years in Politics, Joe Martin; as told to Robert Donovan*, p. 152.

51   "Wendell, there's a story out that you're running . . ." Charles Halleck to Wendell Willkie, quoted in Herbert Parmet & Marie Hecht, *Never Again, A President Runs for a Third Term—Roosevelt Versus Willkie, 1940*, p. 113.

      "Now this is on the record . . ." Wendell Willkie, quoted in Parmet & Hecht, p. 113.

52   "a Republican with sex appeal . . ." David Halberstam describing Wendell Willkie, David Halberstam, *The Powers That Be*.

      "Davenport had ever been there . . ." Root, p. 34.

      "the most important fifty cents you have ever spent . . ." Willkie campaign advertisement, *Charleston Daily Mail.* June 19 (1940).

53   "Mr. Dewey's first ballot strength . . ." Damon Runyon, *Charleston Gazette*, June 20 (1940).

      "Seventy-five percent of the people of West Virginia . . ." D. Boone Dawson, quoted in the *Daily Mail,* June 25 (1940).

54   "Petain's first act . . ." United Press, June 18 (1940).

      "France signs Armistice with Germany. . . " *Gazette,* June 23 (1940).

      "France signs on Hitler's terms. . . " *Philadelphia Record*, June 23 (1940).

Chapter Four: "Just the Next President of the United States"

The best books on the convention—and on the politics of 1940—are Herbert S. Parmet & Marie B. Hecht, *Never Again, A President Runs for a Third Term—Roosevelt Versus Willkie, 1940*; and Warren Moscow, *Roosevelt and Willkie*. The former is more thorough, but Moscow speaks with the authority of an eyewitness, having attended both the Republican and Democratic conventions. Although my debt to both books is great, most of the quotes in this chapter are from newspapers, the *Philadelphia Evening Bulletin*, the *Philadelphia Record*, the *Philadelphia Inquirer*, the *New York Times*, and the *New York Herald Tribune*.

For background on how the candidates stood as the convention got underway, *see* Parmet & Hecht, pp. 125–32; Moscow, pp. 95–98; and also Steve Neal, *Dark Horse: A Biography of Wendell Willkie*, pp. 80–98; and Joseph Barnes, *Willkie: The Events He Was Part of, the Ideas He Fought for*, pp. 170–80.

In telling the story in chapters four through nine, I owe an immense debt to the daily journalists on whose reports I have relied. They include the *Philadelphia Inquirer*'s John O'Brien, William C. Murphy, Joseph H. Miller, Walter Ruch, and Richard Harkness; the *Philadelphia Evening Bulletin*'s Raymond C. Brecht and John Quinn; the *New York Times*' James Hagerty, Turner Catledge, Joseph Driscoll, Walter Huston, Charles W. Hurd, Meyer Berger, and Sidney Shalett; the *New York Herald Tribune*'s Joseph O'Reilly, Burt Andrews, Edward Bates, Ernest Crozier, Edwin McIntosh, and Emma Bugbee; and the *Philadelphia Record*'s Thomas P. O'Neill, Robert S. Allen, John M. McCullough, Robert Reiser, and Oren C. Evans.

An example of the extent of my debt is the description of the convention hall at the beginning of Chapter Four. Other than what I could see from the train, it is based entirely on reporting by the *Trib*'s Joseph O'Reilly and the *New York Times*' Sidney Shalett.

57   "a filthy, sweaty hell . . ." Marcia Davenport, *Too Strong for Fantasy*, p. 270.

58   "the rumor spread . . ." United Press, June 27 (1940).

60   "the biggest Republican magazine . . . " *Life*, June 27 (1940).

63   "the chance to see a major-league game was a major element in the appeal of a big city, especially in the eyes of the American male . . ." The closest equivalent to major-league baseball as a big-city attraction for female delegates and male delegates' wives were the great department stores, most especially John Wanamaker but also Strawbridge and Clothier. The latter offered television sets so that customers could keep an eye on the convention while shopping.

"each predicting victory . . . " *New York Herald Tribune*, June 23 (1940).

64   "normal" number of ballots and "three or four . . ." Taft to *Herald Tribune*, June 23 (1940).

"cavalcade of cars . . ." Warren Moscow, *Roosevelt and Willkie*, p. 68.

"[I]t's such a beautiful day . . ." Moscow, p. 68.

"They broke into a loud cheer . . ." Joseph McLaughlin, *Philadelphia Record*, June 23 (1940).

"with photographers scurrying along . . ." Ernest Crozier, *Herald Tribune*, June 23 (1940).

"What's all the excitement. . . " *Herald Tribune*, June 23 (1940).

65   "Headed right to the bar . . ." Damon Runyon, International News Service, June 22 (1940).

"He was so big . . ." Damon Runyon, International News Service, June 22 (1940).

"[E]ven the most enthusiastic..." Damon Runyon, International News Service, June 23 (1940).

66 "Pennsylvania delegates will be for me..." Arthur James, quoted in *Philadelphia Inquirer*, June 23 (1940).

"indicated he may stay..." *Butler Eagle* (Pa.), June 23 (1940).

"Hands off me Sir..." Frank Harris, quoted in *Record*, June 23 (1940).

"I don't like Joe Pew's brand of politics..." Willkie, quoted in *Philadelphia Evening Bulletin*, June 23 (1940).

67 "What's that?..." Here's how Arthur Krock put it in *Memoirs: Sixty Years on the Firing Line*, pp. 193–94: "I asked him if he had a floor leader. He didn't seem to know what I meant, and asked in turn if one was needed." *See also* for confirmation of Krock's account, Turner Catledge, *My Life and Times*, p. 121.

"MacVeagh's Bible..." Moscow, pp. 62–63. For discussion of MacVeagh's importance as Willkie's practical politician, see Jane Dick, *Volunteers and the Making of Presidents*, p. 22.

68 "Dewey and Taft deny deal..." *Herald Tribune*, June 23 (1940).

"[W]e can't get into this war..." Vandenberg, quoted in *Herald Tribune*, June 24 (1940).

69 "What Republicans?..." Vandenberg, quoted in *Herald Tribune*, June 24 (1940).

"a substantial number..." *Inquirer*, June 23 (1940).

70 "growing sentiment for Wendell Willkie..." *Herald Tribune*, June 23 (1940).

"upward of 75 votes . . ." Willkie quoted United Press, June 23 (1940).

Chapter Five: Monday, June 24, 1940

71   "meeting Roosevelt held late that morning . . ." Mark Skinner Watson, in *Chief of Staff: Prewar Plans and Preparations, United States Army in World War II* says the date of the meeting was June 22, not June 24. But Roosevelt—and not Marshall, Stark, or Welles—was in Hyde Park on June 22 and did not return to Washington until early on June 24. See *Times* June 24, June 25 (1940). See also Eleanor Roosevelt's *My Day* column, in the June 24 *Record*.

It seems that only one reporter, Paul W. Ramsay of the *Philadelphia Inquirer*, found out about the June 24 meeting—the *New York Times*, the *New York Herald Tribune*, and the other Philadelphia papers all failed to mention it—and even Ramsay did not learn about the subject of the meeting.

"We can't give anything more to Britain . . ." The most dramatic account of this meeting is provided in an interactive exhibit at the Franklin D. Roosevelt Library at Hyde Park. In the account, General Marshall says, "We have 200,000 men in uniform. Hitler has 5 million. We don't have enough equipment to *train* the men we do have . . . the three of us agree our own needs are too strong. So why give the British military supplies when our own army and navy need them so badly?"

One staff member at the FDR Library told me that he was not confident of this exhibit's fidelity to fact and I was unable to verify a quote from Ed Flynn in the exhibit. Otherwise, however Verne Newton, who was in charge of the FDR Library when the exhibit was created, vouches for its essential accuracy and most other sources support the exhibit's account. Watson, p. 111, cites Marshall's notes of the White House meeting as saying that the chiefs of staff believed that "to release to

Great Britain additional material will seriously weaken our present state of defense." Furthermore, in William L. Langer and S. Everett Gleason, *Challenge to Isolation, 1937–1940*, p. 568, Marshall is quoted as saying, "There was no doubt that we sold so generously to the Allied powers that our own stocks are below the safety point. . . . If Britain were defeated the army and the administration could never justify to the American people the risk they have taken." *See also* the War Planning Division memo of June 17 cited by Watson (p. 109) that recommended "no further commitments for furnishing materiel to the Allies."

72 "Those who were found to be party . . ." memo from Walter Bedell Smith (who later became Eisenhower's chief of staff in Europe), to General "Pa" Watson (a White House aide).

73 "a solemn hour of world tragedy . . ." Albert McCartney, quoted in Warren Moscow, *Roosevelt and Willkie*, p. 90.

"The atmosphere of this convention was different . . ." Moscow, p. 90.
   Drew Pearson put it this way: "This convention is one of the most independent in GOP history, also it is one of the most earnest."

"I've never seen anything like it . . ." *Philadelphia Record*, June 25 (1940).

"washed up . . ." Drew Pearson, *Record*, June 24 (1940).

"Willkie's good fortune . . ." Mark Sullivan, *New York Herald Tribune*, June 24. 1940.

"Willkie promised 14 Penna. votes. . . " *Philadelphia Evening Bulletin*, June 24 (1940).

"[M]any of them were wearing Willkie buttons . . ." describing New Jersey's delegation at a Willkie reception, *Herald Tribune*, June 25 (1940).

74   "returns from all sections of the country . . ." *Herald Tribune*, June 24 (1940).

The story about the betting odds favoring Willkie appeared in the *Herald Tribune*, June 25 (1940).

The story about utility stocks going up appeared in the *Record*, June 25 (1940).

"I have difficulty in finding where the Willkie talk is being translated . . ." Thomas Dewey, quoted in *Herald Tribune*, June 25 (1940).

"The Republican Party will win . . ." unnamed congressmen, quoted in *The New York Times*, June 25 (1940).

75   "Instead of keeping its eyes statesmanlike . . ." Governor Harold Stassen, keynote address (reprinted in its entirety), *Herald Tribune*, June 25 (1940); *Times*, June 25 (1940).

"New Deal incompetents . . ." Stassen keynote address.

"first real ovation. . . " *Herald Tribune*, June 25 (1940).

"we are too woefully weak . . ." Harold Stassen, keynote address.

76   "The gesture brought the delegates under every standard to their feet. . . " *Herald Tribune*, June 25 (1940).

"a crushing blow . . ." Damon Runyon, International News Service, June 26 (1940).

"We want Willkie!. . ." *Record*, June 25 (1940).

"Willkie's supporters made themselves heard—'We want Willkie,' they would chant from time to time. However they did not succeed in stirring up any vociferous Willkie demonstration—if that was their purpose."

Chapter Six: Tuesday, June 25, 1940

See Warren Moscow, *Roosevelt and Willkie*, pp. 93–8, Steve Neal, *Dark Horse: A Biography of Wendell Willkie*, pp. 100–03, and Herbert S. Parmet & Marie B. Hecht, *Never Again, A President Runs for a Third Term—Roosevelt Versus Willkie, 1940*, pp. 135–37.

77 "Keynoter hits third term. . ." *Philadelphia Record*, June 25 (1940).

"Nazi fliers strike widely in Britain. . ." *New York Times*, June 25 (1940).

"France signs Italian truce, fighting ends. . ." *New York Herald Tribune*, June 25 (1940).

"What is the record . . ." Walter Lippmann, *Herald Tribune*, June 25 (1940).

"Mr. Taft has admirable . . ." Walter Lippmann, *Herald Tribune*, June 25 (1940).

78 "Bells throughout Germany pealed. . ."; "We will sail against England. . ."; "Germany was ready. . ."; "will be like nothing the world has ever seen . . ." Associated Press, in *Record*, June 25 (1940).

"Hoover has been pointing out. . ." *Record*, June 25 (1940).

79　"It was obvious he had himself in mind. . ." *Record*, June 25 (1940).

"after the first ballot I wouldn't be surprised . . ." G.E. Carpenter, quoted by United Press in *Herald Tribune*, June 25 (1940).

"automobile traffic was stopped. . ." *Herald Tribune*, June 26 (1940).

"Herbert Hoover is not a candidate. . ." *Philadelphia Evening Bulletin*, June 25 (1940).

"[T]onight former president . . ." United Press, June 25 (1940).

"[M]arching clubs, bands . . ." John O'Reilly, *Herald Tribune*, June 26 (1940). (The *Trib*'s John O'Reilly was probably the best reporter at capturing the "color" of the convention.)

80　"Hotel lobbies . . ." John O'Reilly, *Herald Tribune*, June 26 (1940).

"Tempers were short . . ." And, added the *Philadelphia Inquirer*, "voices loud. Glass doors to the meeting room were locked and hung with opaque drapes . . . newsmen outside were shoved out of earshot . . ." June 26 (1940).

The timeline with the waiters coming in and out was provided by Associated Press, June 26 (1940).

81　"[D]elegates do not slip away . . ." Henry Allen, quoted in *Herald Tribune*, June 26 (1940).

"[T]here is no excitement . . ." Mrs. M.E. Noriss, quoted in *Herald Tribune*, June 26 (1940).

"[W]e're going to put Dewey over . . ." David Pomeroy, quoted in *Herald Tribune*, June 26 (1940).

"greatly impressed by Mr. Willkie . . ." Governor Merriam, quoted in *Herald Tribune* June 26 (1940).

"I led a fight . . ." Willkie, quoted in *Herald Tribune*, June 26 (1940).

82 "Every whale that spouts . . ." Hoover. The entire speech was reprinted in the *Times*, June 26 (1940).

83 "There was the dull rumble . . ." Gore Vidal, interviewed by author, June 2002.

"But to those in the hall . . ." Warren Moscow, *Roosevelt and Willkie*, p. 95.

"Hoover bids for nomination. . . " *Times*, June 26 (1940). Thomas O'Neill of the *Record* added "If the address was designed to start a stampede for a Hoover nomination, it was a complete flop."

84 "Tell Dewey . . ." and "I never heard . . ." Arthur H. Vandenberg, *The Private Papers of Senator Vandenberg*, ed. Arthur H. Vandenberg Jr.

85 "would have done as well . . ." Steve Neal, *Dark Horse: A Biography of Wendell Willkie*, p. 95.

Chapter Seven: Wednesday, June 26, 1940

See Warren Moscow, *Roosevelt and Willkie*, pp. 98–102, Steve Neal, *Dark Horse: A Biography of Wendell Willkie*, pp. 102–07, and Herbert S. Parmet & Marie B. Hecht, *Never Again, A President Runs for a Third Term—Roosevelt Versus Willkie, 1940*, pp. 140–45.

87 "[Landon] is opposed to Willkie . . ." Robert S. Allen, *Philadelphia Record*, June 26 (1940).

88 "If they don't nominate Mr. Willkie . . ." William Allen White, quoted in *New York Times*, June 27 (1940).

"Willkie boom gains strength . . ." *Philadelphia Inquirer*, June 27 (1940).

"There is no question . . ." *New York Herald Tribune*, June 27 (1940).

"There hasn't been one . . ." Wendell Willkie, quoted in *Herald Tribune*, June 27 (1940).

89 "Taft leading Willkie and Dewey . . ." *Philadelphia Evening Bulletin*, June 26 (1940).

"confidence soared [at Taft Headquarters] . . ." John C. O'Brien, *Bulletin*, June 26 (1940).

90 "Of what will it avail us . . ." Rabbi Michael Aransohn, quoted in *Herald Tribune*, June 27 (1940). (In contrast to Charles Lindbergh's opinion some Jews were isolationists.)

"America, preparedness, and peace . . ." Herbert Hyde, quoted in *Times*, June 27 (1940).

"to ensure against the overthrow . . ." Hyde, quoted in *Times*, June 27 (1940).

"step on no toe . . ." *Record*, June 27 (1940).

91 "so written that it will fit . . ." H.L. Mencken, quoted in *Time* July 1, 1940.

"was taken almost verbatim . . ." Hans Thomsen, quoted in Neal, p. 83.

"a well camouflaged blitz campaign . . ." Hans Thomsen, quoted in Steve Neal, *Dark Horse: A Biography of Wendell Willkie*, p. 83.

92 "so that they may work on the delegates . . ." Hans Thomsen, quoted in Steve Neal, *Dark Horse: A Biography of Wendell Willkie*, p. 84.

"among those who rendered services . . ." David Ignatius, *Washington Post*, September 17 (1968). Walter Lippmann, Walter Winchell, and Drew Pearson were among others named as helping the British.

"Senator from Mitzigan . . ." Walter Trohan, quoted in Thomas Mahl, *Desperate Deception*, p. 145.

93 "one steady deep-throated roar . . . " *Bulletin*, June 27 (1940).

"The delegates grinned . . ." Sidney Shallet, *Times*, June 27 (1940).

"be trusted to keep . . . "; "a life-long Republican . . ." John Lord O'Brian, quoted in *Times*, June 27 (1940).

94 "Ohio, mother of Presidents . . ." Grove Patterson, quoted in *Herald Tribune*, June 27 (1940).

"Finally, there was only one horn player . . . " *Herald Tribune*, June 27 (1940).

"[Dewey's demonstration was] weaker in volume . . . " *Bulletin*, June 27 (1940).

95 "You know that back home . . ." Senator James E. Watson, quoted in Neal, p. 89. A slightly different version appears in Joseph Barnes, *Willkie: The Events He Was Part of, the Ideas He Fought for*, p. 183.

"the most terrific demonstration . . . " *Bulletin*, June 27 (1940).

96   "None of the previous . . . " *Bulletin*, June 27 (1940).

"[W]e don't mind the boos . . ." Bruce Barton, quoted in *Herald Tribune*, June 27 (1940).

"away from the politicians . . ." Raymond Baldwin, quoted in *Herald Tribune*, June 27 (1940).

97   "Anyone wearing a Willkie button . . ." Damon Runyon, International News Service, June 27 (1940).

"a despicable worm . . ." Martha Taft referring to Sam Pryor, quoted in James T. Patterson, *Mr. Republican: A Biography of Robert A. Taft*, p. 228.

As to Colonel Creeger's complaint that Sam Pryor had packed the gallery, according to a story published in the June 27 issue of the *Times*, an investigation by the convention's assistant sergeant-at-arms, Samuel S. Lewis, concluded that "Thousands of tickets had been issued bearing the following legend: 'Republican National Convention, June, 1940. Special Admission, June 26, entrance 23.'"

Because they didn't have assigned seats, most of these "special admission" ticket-holders would have to stand. The *Record* reported that "hundreds of people seemed to be in the throng which jammed the mezzanine aisle between the first and second balcony." The *Herald Tribune* estimated that there were "about two thousand standees."

Perhaps the most impressive fact about the number of Willkie volunteers in Philadelphia was that they not only filled every vacant square foot of the convention hall that night, but they also staged an impressive parade through the city center during the same hours.

It should be added that Oren Root points out that many delegates who got their seats as friends of delegates for other candidates ended up cheering for Willkie. An example given in the text is William McCormick Blair Jr. who came to support Dewey and ended up rooting for Willkie.

Chapter Eight: Thursday, June 27, 1940

See Warren Moscow, *Roosevelt and Willkie*, pp. 102–07, Steve Neal, *Dark Horse: A Biography of Wendell Willkie*, pp. 107–18, and Herbert S. Parmet & Marie B. Hecht, *Never Again, A President Runs for a Third Term—Roosevelt Versus Willkie, 1940*, pp. 145–59; Ellsworth Barnard, *Willkie, Fighter for Freedom*, pp. 193–97, and Joseph Barnes, *Willkie: The Events He Was Part of, the Ideas He Fought for*, pp. 185–87.

98 "had their heads buried . . ." Walter Lippmann, *New York Herald Tribune*, June 27 (1940).

99 "the Willkie trend . . ." George Gallup, quoted in *The New York Times*, June 28 (1940).

"Willkie's Drive Is Stopped. . ." *Philadelphia Record*, June 27 (1940).

"a secret canvass . . ." Robert S. Allen, *Record*, June 27 (1940).

"This is a Republican convention . . ." Verne Marshall, quoted in *Herald Tribune*, June 28 (1940).

"We want a president . . ." Senator James S. Davis, quoted in *Herald Tribune*, June 28 (1940).

100 "milled around the hall. . ."; "delegates and alternates were so noisy. . ." *Herald Tribune*, June 28 (1940).

"Alabama casts 7 votes . . ." Alabama delegation chairman, quoted in *Times*, June 28 (1940).

101 "I said one thing to do. . . "; "the most annoying . . ." Gerald B. Lambert, *All Out of Step*, pp. 258–59.

104 "Willkie turned to me . . ." John Cowles, quoted in Joseph Barnes, *Willkie: The Events He Was Part of, the Ideas He Fought for*, p. 185.

"It looks like it's going to be Willkie . . ." Joseph Martin, *My First Fifty Years in Politics, Joe Martin; as told to Robert Donovan*, p. 156.

"The Willkieites made the rafters ring . . . " *Herald Tribune*, June 28 (1940).

"for a real Republican . . ." Washington delegation chairman, quoted in Steve Neal, *Dark Horse: A Biography of Wendell Willkie*, p. 114.

105 "had spent most of their days . . ." *Herald Tribune*, June 28 (1940).

106 "Some of my boys are worried . . ." McKay, quoted in Warren Moscow, *Roosevelt and Willkie*, p. 105.

"To hell with the judges . . ." Willkie, quoted Moscow, p. 106.

107 "McKay was a crook . . ." Gerald Ford to author, September 2001. For more on McKay, see James Cannon, *Time and Chance: Gerald Ford's Appointment with History*.

A candidate who has been neglected in this account is Frank Gannett, the newspaper publisher from Rochester, New York. He spent $500,000 in a fruitless quest for the nomination. Compare this to the $4,000 Willkie spent personally and the $23,000 that could be traced to his national campaign groups before the convention.

Gannett aroused no enthusiasm among the delegates. When he was nominated a group of alternates started to bring Gannett banners from the rear of the auditorium. No one joined in. The cheering was faint. It was all over in a couple of minutes. On the sixth ballot, he received only one vote.

Gannett's one contribution to the convention was the three elephants he paid for. They added color to the proceedings by marching around the downtown area during the week. They were, however, denied admission to the convention hall.

Chapter Nine: Friday, June 28, 1940

See Steve Neal, *Dark Horse: A Biography of Wendell Willkie,* pp. 117–21, Joseph Barnes, *Willkie: The Events He Was Part of, the Ideas He Fought for,* pp. 187–88, Ellsworth Barnard, *Willkie, Fighter for Freedom,* pp. 186–87, and Herbert S. Parmet & Marie B. Hecht, *Never Again, A President Runs for a Third Term—Roosevelt Versus Willkie, 1940,* p. 159–61.

109 "Factory whistles..." Associated Press, in the *New York Times,* June 28 (1940).

"Jubilant Hoosiers..." *New York Herald Tribune,* June 28 (1940).

110 "Hell no, I wouldn't run..." Charles McNary, quoted in Ellsworth Barnard, *Willkie, Fighter for Freedom,* p. 186.

"a tool of Wall Street..." "front man for Wall Street" is the term used in Steve Neal's *McNary of Oregon,* which contains the most thorough account of McNary's nomination, pp. 183–88.

"I remember the scene..." Joseph Alsop with Adam Platt, *I've Seen the Best of It,* pp. 106–07.

111 "The results last night..." C. Norman Stabler, *Herald Tribune,* June 28 (1940).

113 "I stand before you without..."; "so, you Republicans..." Wendell Willkie, speech quoted in *Times,* June 29 (1940).

"I have the general opinion . . ." Franklin D. Roosevelt, quoted in Barnard, p. 187.

Robert Sherwood quotes Roosevelt as calling Willkie's victory "a godsend for the country," Robert E. Sherwood, *Roosevelt and Hopkins: An Intimate History*, p. 174. Walter Winchell quotes Roosevelt as saying of Willkie "he's grassroots stuff. The people like him. His sincerity comes through. We are going to have a hell of a fight on our hands."

114 "my husband's banker . . ." quoted in Thomas Stokes column for the Scripps-Howard papers. "A lawyer delegate told of receiving a long-distance call from his hometown banker on Willkie's behalf, a banker who held the mortgage on his acres." Richard Norton Smith, *Thomas E. Dewey and His Times*, p. 311.

115 "A huge tidal wave of popular acclaim. . . " *Kansas City Star*, June 28 (1940).

"living rooms, crossroads, grocery stores. . . " *Los Angeles Times*, June 28 (1940).

"nomination of Mr. Willkie. . . " *Philadelphia Inquirer*, June 28 (1940).

"a genuine popular revolt . . ." Robert Bendiner and "A tremendous and historical revolt . . ." Edward T. Folliard, both quoted in *Life*, July 8 (1940).

Chapter Ten: "I Still Don't Want to Run"

The main sources for this chapter are John Culver and John Hyde's *American Dreamer* and *Jim Farley's Story: The Roosevelt Years* by James Farley. See also Herbert S. Parmet & Marie B. Hecht, *Never Again, A President Runs for a Third Term—Roosevelt Versus Willkie, 1940*, pp. 164–77.

120 "a deal might have been made . . ." The only evidence I could find of a deal between Willkie and Martin is that they met privately for an hour on the afternoon of Wednesday, June 25, just before Martin began to make his series of rulings in Willkie's favor, a striking coincidence but hardly a smoking gun.

"I've never known a man . . ." Joe Martin, quoted in Steve Neal, *Dark Horse: A Biography of Wendell Willkie*, p. 124.

"I like Mr. Willkie . . ." Charles McNary, quoted in Neal, p. 126.

124 "I want to beat him . . ." Wendell Willkie, quoted in *New York Times*, July 2 (1940).

126 "You know, I would hate to think . . ." Sara Roosevelt, quoted in James Farley, *Jim Farley's Story: The Roosevelt Years*, p. 247.

"Of course I'm pleased . . ." Eleanor Roosevelt, quoted in Farley), p. 247.

127 "This was heartbreaking for me . . ." Winston S. Churchill, *The Second World War*, Vol. 2, *Their Finest Hour*, p. 232. Churchill explains, "This was a hateful decision, the most unnatural and painful in which I have been concerned," p. 232.

"[Farley] looked like a thundercloud . . ." Franklin D. Roosevelt, quoted in Harold L. Ickes, *The Secret Diary of Harold L. Ickes*, Vol. 3, *The Lowering Clouds, 1939–1941*, p. 284.

128 "Jim, last July . . ." through "I would refuse to run . . ." Franklin D. Roosevelt to Jim Farley, quoted in James Farley, *Jim Farley's Story: The Roosevelt Years*, pp. 248–56.

The dialogue here may not be accurate in the word-for-word sense—indeed it sometimes sounds declamatory—but I have no doubt that it captures the essential truth of the two men's positions at that time.

130 "In that case you'll have to be vice president . . ." Sam Rosenman to Henry Wallace, quoted in John Culver & John Hyde, *American Dreamer: The Life and Times of Henry Wallace*, p. 210.

"the President might come as close to agreeing . . ." Harry Hopkins to Henry Wallace, quoted in Culver & Hyde, p. 210.

"the dedicated enthusiasm . . ." Culver & Hyde, p. 78.

"a searcher for methods . . ." Henry Wallace, quoted in Culver & Hyde, p. 82.

"One of the true galvanizers in scientific research . . ." John Culver & John Hyde, *American Dreamer: The Life and Times of Henry Wallace*, p. 190.

"genetically unequal rats . . ." Henry Wallace, quoted in Culver & Hyde, p. 190.

131 "the great liberal hope for 1940 . . ." John Franklin Carter, quoted in Culver & Hyde, p. 195.

Joseph Alsop in *A Centenary Remembrance* explains why Roosevelt preferred the food on his yacht to that available in the White House: "Eleanor Roosevelt had imported a nutritionist to be the Presidential Housekeeper and year after year this woman showed that nutritionists may know how to make food healthful but scorn to make it appetizing or even edible. . . . I suspected then and I still suspect that this extreme Puritanism about food . . . was only partly another manifestation of Eleanor Roosevelt's detestation of anything savoring of worldly ways. She was never against quiet revenges with a moral excuse. She equated plain living with high thinking, so it was moral to eat badly. And if her husband did not like eating badly, why there were passages in their joint past she hadn't liked either." *See* pp.

156–57. Henrietta Nesbitt was the housekeeper. Her defense can be found in *White House Diary* by Victoria Henrietta Nesbitt.

132 "One would never imagine . . ." Samuel I. Rosenman, *Working with Roosevelt*, p. 208.

Chapter Eleven: "The Convention Is Bleeding to Death"

The new newspapers quoted in this chapter are the *Chicago Tribune* and the *Chicago Daily News. See* Herbert S. Parmet & Marie B. Hecht, *Never Again, A President Runs for a Third Term—Roosevelt Versus Willkie, 1940*, pp. 181–95, and Warren Moscow, *Roosevelt and Willkie* pp. 108–27.

133 "I hurriedly dressed . . ." Samuel I. Rosenman, *Working with Roosevelt*, p. 210.

134 "a personal feeling. . . "; "I have never seen the President more stubborn. . . "; "On that basis . . ." Rosenman, p. 210.

134–35 "Is everything going all right . . ." through "take care of yourself . . ." Franklin D. Roosevelt to Jim Farley, conversation quoted in James Farley, *Jim Farley's Story: The Roosevelt Years*, pp. 271–72.

137 "Hatch Act or no Hatch Act . . ." Harold L. Ickes, *The Secret Diary of Harold L. Ickes*, Vol. 3, *The Lowering Clouds, 1939–1941*, p. 240.

138 "It was as simple as that . . ." Jim Farley, quoted in Farley, p. 273.

"I was aware of the pressure . . ." Jim Farley discussing Carter Glass, quoted in Farley, p. 273.

"Are you coming . . ." Jim Farley to Carter Glass, conversation quoted in Farley, p. 273.

139 "The situation is just as sour as can be . . ." Frances Perkins, quoted in Richard Ketchum, *The Borrowed Years, 1938–1941: America on the Way to War*, p. 465.

"The convention is bleeding to death . . ." Harold Ickes telegraph to Roosevelt, quoted in Ickes, p. 249.

"political spenders. . . " *Chicago Tribune* cartoon, July 16 (1940).

"Roosevelt's Peace Promises. . . " *Tribune* cartoon, July 15 (1940).

"Nazi troops mass on coast. . . " *Chicago Daily News*, July 16 (1940).

140 "That's incredible . . ." Frances Perkins, quoted in Farley, p. 278.

"Jim, I've been trying to reach you . . ." Franklin D. Roosevelt phone call to Jim Farley, quoted in Farley, p. 278.

141 "when Barkley mentioned the magical name of Roosevelt . . ." Arthur Henning, *Tribune*, July 17 (1940).

"the greatest instrument for good . . ." Alben Barkley, quoted in *New York Times*, July 17 (1940).

"I have a message for you from the President . . ." Alben Barkley, quoted in *Times*, July 17 (1940).

"Bedlam broke loose. . . " *Daily News*, July 17 (1940). The same day's *Tribune* said "the convention went wild."

142 "The stadium gates were manned . . ." Jonathan Mitchell, *New Republic*, July 29 (1940).

"The city organization called in the boys . . ." Sam Fuller, *Daily News*, July 17 (1940).

"several thousand rounded up late in the evening. . . " *Tribune*, July 17 (1940).

143 "unless we are attacked . . ." Rosenman, p. 212.

"the faint voice surged into a fighting roar . . ." describing Carter Glass, Farley, p. 285.

"a man who believes in the unwritten law of the Democratic Party . . ." Carter Glass describing Farley, *Times*, July 18 (1940).

144 "[M]y greatest thrill in politics . . ." Farley, p. 284.

"great and noble American . . ." Farley describing Carter Glass Farley, *Jim Farley's Story: The Roosevelt Years*, p. 291.

145 "showing a white slip of paper . . ." Jonathan Mitchell, *New Republic*, July 29 (1940).

"Now Jim, we have to give some consideration . . ." Franklin D. Roosevelt to Jim Farley, phone conversation quoted in Farley, pp. 293–95.

146 "By the way, you were great last night . . ." Roosevelt Farley, quoted Farley, pp. 293–95.

"Dear old Harold . . ." Roosevelt discussing Harold Ickes, quoted in Rosenman, p. 214.

"I don't want to come before the convention . . ." Eleanor Roosevelt to Jim Farley, Farley, p. 283.

147 "Willkie will get liberal financial . . ." Farley to Eleanor Roosevelt, quoted in Farley, p. 299.

"Franklin, I've been talking to Jim Farley and I agree with him . . ." Eleanor Roosevelt phone conversation with Franklin D. Roosevelt, quoted in Farley, p. 300.

Eleanor Roosevelt, however, remembered this conversation differently: "Jim Farley had said these things to me and I repeated very carefully what he said. But I never expressed a preference or an opinion on matters of this kind. And I am sure I didn't change my habits on this occasion." Eleanor Roosevelt, *This I Remember*, p. 216.

"Apparently you still have your sense of humor . . ." Franklin D. Roosevelt to Farley, p. 300.

"Henry's my second choice . . ." Governor Phillips to Governor Rivers, quoted in Farley, p. 302.

"Rebel yells grew in intensity. . . " *Times*, July 19 (1940).

148 "the greatest ovation of the convention. . . " *Time*, July 29 (1940).

"the best so far. . . " *Times*, July 19 (1940).

"In the first place . . ." Paul McNutt convention address, quoted in *Time*, July 29 (1940).

149 "I think nobody could appreciate more . . ." Eleanor Roosevelt convention address, quoted in Moscow, *Roosevelt and Willkie*, p. 124.

"This is no ordinary time . . ." Eleanor Roosevelt convention address, quoted in *Times*, July 19 (1940).

"Do you want a vice president . . ." Jim Byrnes, quoted in *Time*, July 29 (1940).

"An exceptionally quite place . . ." Rosenman, pp. 215–18.

150 "His face was grim. . . "; "Sam, take this inside . . ." Rosenman, pp. 215–18.

"Don't do it, Henry . . ." Jim Byrnes to Henry Wallace, quoted in *Tribune*, July 19 (1940).

"The President by this time . . ." Rosenman, pp. 219.

151 "He was wheeled . . ." Rosenman, p. 219.

"I found myself in conflict . . ." Franklin D. Roosevelt, quoted in *Times*, July 19 (1940).

"Then it was over. . . " *Times*, July 19 (1940).

"Angrily, sourly, in grave disunion. . . " *Time*, July 29 (1940).

"Many an observer. . . " *Life*, July 29 (1940).

152 "Fearful, panicky . . ." Jonathan Mitchell, *New Republic*, July 29 (1940).

"What could have been a convention of enthusiasm . . ." Ickes, p. 265.

"something has gone out of American life . . ." Raymond Clapper, *Charleston Gazette*, July 22 (1940).

"Give up Gibraltar. . . " *Daily News*, July 19 (1940).

"Peace now with England. . . " *Daily News*, July 20 (1940).

Chapter 12: The Deal and the Muster

The main new books relied on for this chapter are *Fifty Ships that Saved the World: The Foundations of the Anglo-American Alliance* by Philip Goodhart, *The Hawks of World War II* by Mark Chadwin, *The Battle Against Isolation* by Walter Johnson, and the *Challenge to Isolation, 1937–1940*, by William L. Langer and S. Everett Gleason.

155 "War Sentiment Found Declining..." *New York Times*, July 7 (1940).

"With a round face..." description of William Allen White, John Mason Brown, *The Ordeal of the Playwright; Robert E. Sherwood and the Challenge of War*, ed. Norman Cousins, p. 24.

"Dear Bill, I have had a few quiet weeks..." Roosevelt to William Allen White, quoted in Brown, p. 30.

157 "It's a great piece of work..." Roosevelt, quoted in Brown, p. 80.

"[Francis Pickens Miller had] fallen in love with England..." Phillip Goodhart, *Fifty Ships that Saved the World: The Foundations of the Anglo-American Alliance*, p. 113.

160 "simply result in causing confusion..." Joseph Kennedy, quoted in Richard Dunlop, *Donovan: America's Master Spy*, p. 206.

"Someone's nose seems out of joint..." Roosevelt, quoted Dunlop, p. 206.

"Could the RAF hold off..." Donovan, quoted in Dunlop, p. 210.

"The young RAF flyers..." Carl Spaatz, quoted in Dunlop, p. 210.

161 "do a little better . . ." Lee, quoted in Raymond E. Lee, *The London Journals of Raymond Lee 1940–1941* James Leutze ed., pp. 27–28.

"To Donovan it now appeared . . ." Dunlop, pp. 214–15.

"Mr. President, with great respect . . ." Winston Churchill to Franklin D. Roosevelt, Winston S. Churchill, *The Second World War,* Vol. 2 *Their Finest Hour,* p. 402.

"Harry, I can't come out in favor of such a deal . . ." Franklin D. Roosevelt to Henry R. Luce, quoted in Robert Shogan, *Hard Bargain: How FDR Twisted Churchill's Arm, Evaded the Law, and Changed the Role of the American Presidency,* p. 153.

"There was a long discussion . . ." Franklin D. Roosevelt memo, quoted Goodhart, p. 154.

162 "one of the most serious and important debates . . ." Henry Stimson, quoted in Goodhart, p. 155.

163 "good for the country . . ." Jim Farley, quoted in Shogan, p. 166.

"Steve Early . . . called from the White House . . ." Joseph Alsop, *FDR 1882–1945: A Centenary Remembrance,* p. 203.

"to make it politically possible . . ." Frances Pickens Miller, *The Man From the Valley,* p. 98.

"I'm telling you before it's too late . . ." General Pershing, quoted in *Times,* August 5 (1940).

164 "He would not fail in duty. . . " *Time,* August 12 (1940).

"Pershing would let Britain have 50 old U.S. Destroyers. . . " *Times,* August 5 (1940).

"I am in favor of a [draft]. . ." Franklin D. Roosevelt, quoted in *Times*, August 3 (1940).

165 "The majority seemed about to be defeated. . ." *Time*, August 12 (1940).

"Sinister are the meanderings of Arthur Krock's mind . . ." Miller, quoted in Mark Chadwin, *The Hawks of World War II*, p. 95.

"It's not as bad as it seems . . ." William Allen White to Franklin D. Roosevelt, quoted in Herbert S. Parmet & Marie B. Hecht, *Never Again, A President Runs for a Third Term—Roosevelt Versus Willkie, 1940*, p. 211.

166 "I can't guarantee either of you to the other . . ." William Allen White to Franklin D. Roosevelt, quoted in Parmet & Hecht, p. 211.

167 "the speech didn't go worth a damn . . ." Halleck quoted in Steve Neal, *Dark Horse: A Biography of Wendell Willkie*, p. 136.

"There were long stretches. . ." *Time*, August 26 (1940).

"[Wendell Willkie] agreed with Mr. Roosevelt's entire program . . ." Norman Thomas, *Times*, August 18 (1940).

"wholehearted support for the President . . ." and "we must admit . . ." Wendell Willkie, quoted in *Times*, August 18 (1940).

169 "The Chief of Naval Operations may and should certify . . ." Shogan, p. 221. *See also* Attorney General Jackson memo, quoted in Robert Jackson, *That Man: An Insider's Portrait of Franklin D. Roosevelt*, p. 97.

170 "In a sitting room just inside . . ." *Time*, September 16 (1940).

171 "probably the most important thing that has come for American defense . . ." Franklin D. Roosevelt, quoted in *Time*, September 16 (1940).

"to organize commitments . . ." Joseph Alsop, *I've Seen the Best of It*, p. 146.

"Destroyers for Bases; U.S. Trades 50 Old War Ships for Control of the North Atlantic . . ." *Life*, September 16 (1940).

"Wholly admirable. . ." *Herald Tribune*, September 4 (1940).

"Bargain in which . . ." *Baltimore Sun*, September 4 (1940).

"It was one of the greatest defense strokes. . ." *Atlanta Constitution*, September 4 (1940).

"Second only in importance. . ." *New Orleans Times-Picayune* September 4 (1940).

"act of war. . ." *St. Louis Post Dispatch*, September 4 (1940).

"a flagrant breach of neutrality. . ." *Times*, September 5 (1940).

172 "the name Roosevelt was originally Rosenfeld. . ." *Times*, September 5 (1940).

"the British were jubilant. . ." *Times*, September 4 (1940).

"public will undoubtedly approve . . ." Willkie, quoted in *Times*, September 4 (1940).

"a profound impression throughout Europe . . ." Churchill, p. 251.

"muster . . ." Franklin D. Roosevelt, quoted in Robert E. Sherwood, *Roosevelt and Hopkins: An Intimate History*, p. 190.

173 "some form of selective service . . ." Wendell Willkie, quoted in *Times*, August 18 (1940).

"Willkie Opposes Delaying of Draft. . ." *Times*, September 11 (1940).

"people don't want their son[s] in uniform . . ." Joe Martin, quoted in Neal, p. 139.

"broken the back . . ." Senator Hiram Johnson, quoted in Neal, p. 139.

"the most arbitrary and dictatorial action taken by the president . . ." Wendell Willkie, quoted in Doris Kearns Goodwin, *No Ordinary Time: Franklin and Eleanor Roosevelt: The Home Front in World War II*, p. 148.

Chapter 13: "Sail on O Ship of State"

The main new source for this chapter is Warren Kimball, *The Most Unsordid Act: Lend Lease, 1939–1941*. Lend-Lease warrants an entire volume in the 23-volume set *Documentary History of the Franklin D. Roosevelt Presidency*, edited by George McJimsey. For Willkie's life after the election see Steve Neal, *Dark Horse: A Biography of Wendell Willkie* (pp. 181–324) and Joseph Barnes, *Willkie: The Events He Was Part of, the Ideas He Fought for*, pp. 239–389.

For the fall campaign itself see Herbert S. Parmet & Marie B. Hecht, *Never Again, A President Runs for a Third Term—Roosevelt Versus Willkie, 1940*, pp. 222–73. For Willkie's part see Neal, pp. 142–75. And for insight into the thinking in the Roosevelt camp, see Robert Sherwood, *Roosevelt and Hopkins*, pp. 187–201.

I was surprised to find that the best reporting on the fall campaign appeared in *Time* in its issues from September 13 through November 11, 1940. Its National Affairs editor, T.S. Matthews, was largely successful in resisting Luce's effort to continue the pro-Willkie tilt that had characterized the magazine's work before the convention. *Life*, however, faithfully followed Luce's wishes through most of the campaign.

174   "every time a cameraman shows up, the hogs run right over and strike a pose..." Mary Steeth, quoted in Joseph Barnes, *Willkie: The Events He Was Part of, the Ideas He Fought for*, p. 196.

175   "hitched and unhitched with murderous shoutings..." Marcia Davenport, *Too Strong for Fantasy*, p. 277.

    "Its posh, heavily carpeted living room..." Davenport, p. 275.

    "the facilities included a shower-bath..."; "everything related to physical order and cleanliness..." Davenport, p. 277.

    "a migrating hotel..." Barnes, p. 197.

    "organized chaos..."; "prodigy of disorder..." Davenport, p. 274.
    Paul Smith in *Personal File* described the train as a "shambles." Turner Catledge said of the candidate, "Willkie was a most disorganized man" and also that the train resembled "a bawdy house where the Madam was away and the girls were running the joint." Turner Catledge, *My Life and The Times*.

176   "Politics makes strange bedfellows..." Edith Willkie, quoted in Neal, p. 144.

    "[W]e can't have any of our principal speakers refer..." Franklin D. Roosevelt to Lowell Mellett, quoted in John Culver & John Hyde, *American Dreamer: The Life and Times of Henry Wallace*, p. 254.

177   "If you elect me president they will not be sent..." Willkie, quoted Neal, p. 159.

178 "I have said again and again your boys are not going to be sent . . ." Franklin D. Roosevelt campaign address, quoted in Robert E. Sherwood, *Roosevelt and Hopkins: An Intimate History*, p. 191

"Of course we'll fight if we're attacked . . ." Franklin D. Roosevelt to Samuel I. Rosenman, quoted in Sherwood, p. 191.

"and it will not be a woman either . . ." Willkie, quoted in Barnes, p. 220.

179 "Well boys, Britain's broke . . ." Lord Lothian, quoted in Ted Morgan, *FDR: A Biography*, p. 579.

"Britain sends SOS to US . . . " *Life*, December 2 (1940).

"When Britain runs out of cash . . . " *Time*, December 2 (1940).

180 "We must not permit Britain to go under. . . " *New Republic* December 2 (1940).

"use your imaginations . . ." Franklin D. Roosevelt to Henry Morgenthau, quoted in John Morton Blum, *From the Morgenthau Diaries: Years of Urgency, 1938–41*, p. 202.

"health and happiness of the president . . ." Willkie, quoted in Neal, p. 180.

"We must continue to help the fighting men . . ." Wendell Willkie, quoted in Neal, p. 179.

181 "military aid to Britain . . ." Wendell Willkie, quoted in Neal, p. 186.

"I didn't know for quite a while . . ." Hopkins to Robert E. Sherwood, quoted in Sherwood, p. 224.

"if I followed my own heart . . ." Henry Morgenthau, quoted in Warren Kimball, *The Most Unsordid Act: Lend Lease, 1939–1941*, p. 120.

"I don't know and I don't care . . ." Franklin D. Roosevelt press conference, December 17, 1940. *Public Papers and Addresses of Franklin D. Roosevelt*, Vol. 9, *1940, War—and Aid to Democracies.*

182   "The President came in five minutes before the broadcast on a small rubber-tired wheelchair . . ." *Time*, January 6 (1941).

Most recent historians seem to think that because Roosevelt's staff, with the assistance of the press, avoided having him photographed in a wheelchair, the public did not know that he could not walk unaided. To believe that, you have to believe that the public failed to notice, throughout his long presidency, that FDR was never photographed walking—or even standing—unaided, usually on the arm of an aide or holding on to a rostrum or a railing.

Thousands of people also witnessed his laborious and painful attempts to walk, including former Senator Dale Bumpers, who describes his experience as a boy in Arkansas in *The Best Lawyer in a One-Lawyer Town*. A previous issue of *Time*—August 6, 1940—had described how a special ramp was carried on the presidential train, taken out of the baggage car, and attached to the president's car so that he could board or leave the train. The article described how the citizens of Hyde Park had watched him use the ramp.

People knew that FDR could not walk unaided. "*Everyone* knew" says Betty Beale, the veteran society columnist for the *Washington Post* and the *Washington Star* and who began reporting in 1937. Roosevelt drove a Ford that news reports told us was specially equipped with *hand* controls.

Furthermore, in the 1930s, polio was known as infantile paralysis; and because it was a major problem—this was before the breakthroughs of Salk and Sabin—most people knew one or more victims of the disease. There was no mystery—paralysis meant paralysis.

Additionally, FDR's birthday was an occasion for holding dances throughout the country which were sponsored by the polio charity, the March of Dimes, which used slogans such as, "Dance so they can walk."

In 1937, my father took me to the White House to a reception for presidential electors, of whom he was one. As we approached the head of the receiving line, we saw Mrs. Roosevelt and Jim Farley but not the president. When we asked about him, we were told that he had been there but had been taken away in his wheelchair. This was not a small exclusive party; it was attended by more than 500 presidential electors plus their spouses, and many children.

Jon Meacham, in *Franklin and Winston: An Intimate Portrait of an Epic Friendship*, quotes an article that Churchill wrote in 1934 and included in his book *Great Contemporaries* published in 1937: "His lower limbs refused their offices. Crutches or assistance were needed for the smallest movement from place to place. To 99 men out of a hundred, such an affliction would have terminated all forms of public activity except those of the mind. He refused to accept this sentence."

Churchill was writing for public consumption. Roosevelt was not his friend at the time. He had no special source of information that was not available to the public; and yet, even in faraway England, Churchill knew about the paralysis and wrote about it not as news but—just as *Time* mentioned the wheelchair in 1940—on the assumption that others knew as well.

"the great arsenal of democracy. . . "; "no man can tame a tiger. . . "; "greatest hope . . ." Franklin D. Roosevelt speech, December 29, 1940, reprinted in Franklin D. Roosevelt, *Public Papers and Addresses of Franklin D. Roosevelt*, Vol. 9, *1940, War—and Aid to Democracies*, pp. 633–44.

183   "Suppose my neighbor's house catches fire . . ." Franklin D. Roosevelt press conference, December 17, 1940, reprinted in

Franklin D. Roosevelt, *Public Papers and Addresses of Franklin D. Roosevelt,* Vol. 9, *1940, War—and Aid to Democracies,* pp. 604–15.

184 "not withstanding the provisions of any other law. . ."; "sold, exchanged, transferred . . ." H.R. 1776, 77th Congress, 1941.

"plow under every fourth American . . ." Senator Burton Wheeler, quoted in *Time,* February 10 (1941).

"Mr. Dewey and Mr. Taft. . . " *New York Times,* January 5 (1941). *See also* Kimball, p. 156.

185 "Great bursts of laughter could be heard . . ." Jimmy Roosevelt, quoted in Neal, p. 191.

"You'll like Averill . . ." Franklin D. Roosevelt, quoted in Neal, p. 191.

"Oh, that's all right . . ." Wendell Willkie, quoted in Neal, p. 191.

186 "[T]he former Republican candidate. . . " *Times,* January 20 (1941).

"saying how greatly he had been impressed by the Prime Minister . . ." Neal, p. 197.

"the most dramatic example of democracy at work . . ." Willkie, quoted in Neal, p. 195.

"every arrangement was made . . ." Winston S. Churchill, *The Grand Alliance,* p. 25.

"I never saw such esprit . . ." Wendell Willkie, quoted in Neal, p. 194.

187 "Willkie is the most interesting personality. . ." *Times of London*, quoted in *Time*, February 3 (1941).

"Sail on O Ship of State . . ." Henry W. Longfellow, quoted in Franklin D. Roosevelt letter to Churchill, Meacham, p. 95.

"Here is the answer . . ." Churchill, quoted in Neal, p. 196.

188 "Madam, do you realize . . ." John McCormack to an angry Irish woman, quoted in Kimball, p. 153.

"perfectly willing to accept . . ." Franklin D. Roosevelt, quoted in Kimball, p. 199.

189 "one of Hopkins most brilliant aides. . ." Sherwood, p. 228.

191 "that any negotiated peace to end the European War as soon as possible was preferable . . ." Charles Lindbergh, quoted in Harold Hinton, *Times*, January 24 (1941).

"The quicker you can give it . . ." Lord Halifax, quoted in *Times*, January 25 (1941).

192 "There were 1200 in a room. . ." *Time*, February 17 (1941). Ellsworth Barnard, *Willkie, Fighter for Freedom*, p. 285, says that there were 1800 present. Barnes, calls it "the largest crowd in history . . ." p. 252.

"The powers asked for are extraordinary . . ." Wendell Willkie, quoted in *Times*, February 12 (1941).

"Wendell Willkie was the real hero . . ." Carlton Savage, quoted in Neal, p. 206.

"powerful voice for Lend-Lease . . ." James McGregor Burns, *Roosevelt: The Soldier of Freedom*, p. 48.

"a tremendous boost . . ." Kimball, p. 156.

"The most important testimony . . ." Doris Kearns Goodwin, *No Ordinary Time: Franklin and Eleanor Roosevelt: The Home Front in World War II*, p. 213.

"thankful beyond words . . ." Eleanor Roosevelt, quoted in Kearns Goodwin, p. 214.

"is showing what patriotic Americans . . ." Franklin D. Roosevelt, quoted in Neal, p. 214. Once when Harry Hopkins criticized Willkie in Roosevelt's presence, Sherwood says that Roosevelt rebuked him, saying that without Willkie we wouldn't have Lend Lease or the Draft.

"the third climacteric of World War II . . ." Winston S. Churchill, quoted in Sherwood, p. 264.

"I thank God for your news . . ." Winston S. Churchill, quoted in Sherwood, p. 265.

193 "drunken pass . . ." Miriam Hopkins, quoted in Michael Janeway, *Fall of the House of Roosevelt*, pp. 105–06.

194 "Well Mr. President, he's an adolescent . . ." Madam Chiang, quoted in Frances Perkins, *The Roosevelt I Knew*, p. 74. Perkins adds that after Mme. Chiang had made this remark, Roosevelt asks, "What do you think I am?" "Ah, Mr. President, you are sophisticated." As Roosevelt told the story Perkins says "There was a gleam of pleasure in his eyes. His obvious pleasure belied its point."

"broke the back . . ." This quote from Senator Hiram Johnson of California was supported by Senator Edwin Johnson of Colorado as early as August 13 when he told the Associated Press that Willkie held the fate of the draft bill in "the hollow of his hands."

"Second only to the Battle of Britain . . ." Walter Lippmann, quoted in Neal, p. viii.

196 "Actually I can tell you that Mr. Willkie went much further . . ." Drew Pearson, letter to Mrs. C H Wright, dated October 16, 1944, Pearson Papers, Library of Congress.

198 It is intriguing to think that Thornton Wilder might have been contemplating the events discussed in this book as he was writing *The Skin of Our Teeth*. The play opened in New York on November 18, 1942.

BIBLIOGRAPHY

Books

Acheson, Dean. *Morning and Noon*. Boston: Houghton Mifflin, 1965.

Acheson, Dean. *Present at the Creation*. New York: Norton, 1969.

Agar, Herbert. *The Darkest Year*. New York: Doubleday, 1973.

Alsop, Joseph. *American White Paper*. New York: Simon & Schuster, 1940.

Alsop, Joseph. *FDR, 1882–1945: A Centenary Remembrance*. New York: The Viking Press, 1982.

Alsop, Joseph, with Adam Platt. *I've Seen the Best of It—Memoir*. New York: Norton, 1992.

Barnard, Ellsworth. *Willkie, Fighter for Freedom*. Marquette MI: Northern Michigan University Press, 1966.

Barnes, Joseph. *Willkie: The Events He Was Part of, the Ideas He Fought for*. New York: Simon and Schuster, 1952.

Baughman, James L. *Henry Luce and the Rise of the American News Media*. Boston: G. K. Hall, 1987.

Beard, Charles. *American Foreign Policy in the Making*. New Haven, CT: Yale, 1946.

Berg, A. Scott. *Lindberg*. New York: G. P. Putnam's Sons, 1998.

Beschloss, Michael R. *Kennedy and Roosevelt: The Uneasy Alliance*. New York: Norton, 1980.

Bliss, Edward, Jr., ed. *In Search of Light: The Broadcasts of Edward R. Murrow, 1938–1961*. New York: Alfred A. Knopf, 1967.

Blum, John Morton. *Roosevelt and Morgenthau*. Boston: Houghton, Mifflin, 1972.

Blum, John Morton, ed. *The Price of Vision; the Diary of Henry A. Wallace 1942–1946*. Boston: Houghton Mifflin Co., 1973.

Blum, John Morton. *From the Morganthau Diaries*. Vol. 2, *Years of Urgency, 1938–1941*. Boston: Houghton Mifflin, 1985.

Brinkley, David. *Washington Goes to War*. New York: Knopf, 1988.

Brown, John Mason. *The Ordeal of a Playwright; Robert E. Sherwood and the Challenge of War*. Edited by Norman Cousins. New York: Harper and Row Publishers, 1940.

Brown, John Mason. *The Worlds of Robert E. Sherwood; Mirror to His Times, 1896–1939*. New York: Harper and Row Publishers, 1940.

Bullitt, William C. *For the President, Personal and Secret: Correspondence Between Franklin D. Roosevelt and William C. Bullitt*. Edited by Orville H. Bullitt. Boston: Houghton Mifflin, 1972.

Bumpers, Dale. *The Best Lawyer in a One-Lawyer Town*. New York: Harcourt Brace Jovanovich, 1970.

Burns, James MacGregor. *The Lion and the Fox*. New York: Harcourt Brace and Co., 1956.

Burns, James MacGregor. *Roosevelt: The Soldier of Freedom*. New York: Harcourt Brace Jovanovich, 1970.

Butler, J.R.M. *Lord Lothian*. New York: Putman, 1972.

Byrnes, James F. *Speaking Frankly*. New York: Harper, 1947.

Cannon, James. *Time and Chance: Gerald Ford's Appointment with History*. New York: HarperCollins, 1994.

Casey, Steven. *Cautious Crusade: Franklin D. Roosevelt, American Public Opinion, and the War Against Nazi Germany*. New York: Oxford University Press, 2001.

Catledge, Turner. *My Life and The Times*. New York: Harper and Row, 1971.

Chadwin, Mark. *The Hawks of World War II*. Chapel Hill, NC: University of North Carolina, 1968.

Childs, Marquis. *I Write from Washington*. New York: Harper, 1942.

Churchill, Winston S. *The Second World War*. Vol. 1, *The Gathering Storm*. Boston: Houghton Mifflin, 1948. Vol. 2, *Their Finest Hour*. Boston: Houghton Mifflin, 1949. *The Grand Alliance*. Vol. 3, Boston: Houghton Mifflin, 1950.

Clapper, Raymond. *Watching the World*. New York: McGraw-Hill, 1944.

Cole, Wayne. *America First: The Battle Against Intervention, 1940–1941*. Madison, WI: University of Wisconsin Press, 1953.

Cole, Wayne. *Roosevelt and the Isolationists, 1932–1945*. Lincoln, NE: University of Nebraska Press, 1983.

Collier, Richard. *1940: The World in Flames*. New York: Penguin, 1979.

Culver, John, and John Hyde. *American Dreamer: The Life and Times of Henry Wallace*. New York: W.W. Norton and Company, 2000.

Dallek, Robert. *The Roosevelt Diplomacy and World War II*. New York: Holt, Rinehart and Winston, 1970.

Dallek, Robert. *Franklin D. Roosevelt and American Foreign Policy, 1932–1945*. New York: Oxford University Press, 1979.

Davenport, Marcia. *Too Strong for Fantasy*. Pittsburgh: University of Pittsburgh Press, 1992.

Davis, Forrest, and Ernest Lindley. *How War Came: An American White Paper: From the Fall of France to Pearl Harbor*. New York: Simon and Schuster, 1942.

Davis, Kenneth S. *FDR: The Beckoning of Destiny, 1882–1928*. New York: Putnam, 1971.

Davis, Kenneth S. *FDR, Into the Storm. 1937–1940*. New York: Random House, 1993.

Dick, Jane. *Volunteers and the Making of Presidents*. New York: Dodd, Mead and Co., 1980.

Doenecke, Justis. *In Danger Undaunted*. Palo Alto, CA: Hoover Press, 1990.

Doyle, William. *Inside the Oval Office: The White House Tapes from FDR to Clinton*. New York: Kodansha International, 1999.

Dunlop, Richard. *Donovan, America's Master Spy*. New York: Rand McNally, 1982.

Dunning, John. *On the Air: The Encyclopedia of Old-Time Radio*. New York: Oxford University Press, 1998.

Elson, Robert T. *Time, Inc.* New York: Atheneum, 1968.

Farley, James. *Jim Farley's Story: The Roosevelt Years*. New York: McGraw-Hill, 1948.

Fleming, Thomas. *The New Dealer's War: FDR and the War Within World War II*. New York: Basic Books, 2001.

Flynn, Edward. *You're the Boss*. New York: Collier Books, 1962.

Freidel, Frank. *Franklin D. Roosevelt: A Rendezvous with Destiny*. Boston: Little, Brown, 1990.

Freidel, Frank. *Franklin D. Roosevelt: The Ordeal*. Boston: Little, Brown, 1954.

Gabler, Neal. *Winchell: Gossip, Power and the Culture of Celebrity.* New York: Vintage Books, 1995.

Galbraith, John Kenneth. *Name-Dropping: From FDR On.* Boston: Houghton Mifflin, 1999.

Gallagher, Hugh. *FDR's Splendid Deception.* New York: Dodd Mead, 1985.

Gallup, George. *The Gallup Polls: Public Opinion, 1935–1971.* Vol. 1, *1937–1948.* New York: Random House, 1972.

Gates, Henry Louis, Jr. *Colored People: A Memoir.* New York: Vintage Books, 1994.

Gilbert, Martin. *Winston S. Churchill.* Vol. 6, *Finest Hour, 1939–1941.* Boston: Houghton Mifflin: 1983.

Goodhart, Phillip. *Fifty Ships that Saved the World: The Foundations of the Anglo-American Alliance.* Garden City, NY: Doubleday, 1945.

Goodwin, Doris Kearns. *No Ordinary Time: Franklin and Eleanor Roosevelt: The Home Front in World War II.* New York: Simon and Schuster, 1994.

Gould, Jean. *A Good Fight: The Story of F.D.R.'s Conquest of Polio.* New York: Dodd, Mead, 1960.

Graham, Katharine. *Katharine Graham's Washington.* New York: Alfred A. Knopf, 2002.

Gray, Ed. *General of the Army: George C. Marshall, Soldier and Statesman.* New York: Norton, 1990.

Greenfield, Kent R., Robert R. Palmer, and Bell I. Wiley. *United States Army in World War II: The Organization of Ground Combat Troops.* Washington, DC: Historical Division of the Army, 1947.

Gunther, John. *Roosevelt in Retrospect.* New York: Harper, 1950.

Halberstam, David. *The Powers That Be.* New York: Knopf, 1975.

Hassett, William D. *Off the Record with F.D.R.* New York: Harper, 1950.

Herzstein, Robert E. *Henry R. Luce.* New York: Scribner's, 1994.

Hoff-Wilson, Joan, and Marjorie Lightman, eds. *Without Precedent: The Life and Career of Eleanor Roosevelt.* Bloomington, IN: Indiana University Press, 1984.

Hull, Cordell. *The Memoirs of Cordell Hull.* Vol. 2. New York: Macmillan, 1948.

Ickes, Harold L. *The Secret Diary of Harold L. Ickes*. Vol. 3, *The Lowering Clouds, 1939–1941*. New York: Simon and Schuster, 1955.

Jackson, Robert H. *That Man: An Insider's Portrait of Franklin D. Roosevelt*. Oxford University Press, 2003.

Janeway, Michael. *The Fall of the House of Roosevelt*. New York: Columbia University Press, 2004.

Jenkins, Roy. *Churchill, a Biography*. New York: Farrar, Straus and Giroux, 2001.

Johnson, David Alan. *The Battle of Britain and the American Factor, July–October, 1940*. Conshohocken, PA: Combined Press, 1998.

Johnson, Walter. *William Allen White's America*. New York: Henry Holt, 1947.

Johnson, Walter. *The Battle Against Isolation*. Chicago, IL: University of Chicago Press, 1984.

Jones, Jesse H., with Edward Angly. *Fifty Billion Dollars: My Thirteen Years with the RFC*. New York: Macmillan, 1951.

Kabaservice, Geoffrey. *The Guardians*. New York: Henry Holt, 2004.

Ketchum, Richard. *Will Rogers: His Life and Times*. New York: American Heritage, 1973.

Ketchum, Richard. *The Borrowed Years, 1938–1941: America on the Way to War*. New York: Random House, 1989.

Kimball, Warren. *The Most Unsordid Act: Lend Lease, 1939–1941*. Baltimore: Johns Hopkins University Press, 1969.

Kimball, Warren, ed. *Churchill & Roosevelt: The Complete Correspondence*. 3 vols. Princeton, NJ: Princeton University Press, 1948.

Kluger, Richard. *The Paper: The Life and Death of the New York Herald Tribune*. New York: Alfred A. Knopf, 1986.

Krock, Arthur. *Memoirs: Sixty Years on the Firing Line*. New York: Funk & Wagnalls, 1968.

Langer, William L., and Everett Gleason. *The Challenge to Isolation*. New York: Harper, 1952.

Langer, William L., and Everett S. Gleason. *Undeclared War: 1939–1940*. New York: Harper, 1952.

Lash, Joseph P. *Eleanor Roosevelt: A Friend's Memoir*. Garden City, NY: Doubleday, 1964.

Lash, Joseph P. *Roosevelt and Churchill, 1931–1941: The Partnership that Saved the West*. New York: Norton, 1976.

Lee, Raymond E. *The London Journal of General Raymond E. Lee 1940–1941*. Edited by James Leutze. Boston: Little, Brown, 1971.

Leuchtenburg, William E. *Franklin D. Roosevelt and the New Deal*. New York: Harper, 1963.

Leuchtenburg, William E. *The FDR Years: On Roosevelt and His Legacy*. New York: Columbia University Press, 1995.

Liebling, A.J. *Just Enough Liebling*. New York: North Point Press, 2004.

Lindberg, Charles A. *Wartime Journals*. New York: Harcourt, 1970.

Lukacs, John. *The Duel: 10 May–31 July 1940: The Eighty-Day Struggle Between Churchill and Hitler*. New York: Ticknor & Fields, 1991.

Lukacs, John. *Five Days in London May 1940*. New Haven, CT: Yale University Press, 1999.

Lukacs, John. *Churchill: Visionary, Statesman, Historian*. New Haven, CT: Yale University Press, 2002.

Macdonald, Dwight. *Henry Wallace*. New York: Viking, 1947.

Mahl, Thomas. *Desperate Deception*. London: Brassey's, 1998.

Manchester, William. *The Glory and the Dream: A Narrative History of America, 1932–1972*. Boston: Little, Brown, 1974.

Mankoff, Robert, ed. *The Complete Cartoons of the* New Yorker. New York: Black Dog & Leventhal Publishers, 2004.

Mantle, Burns. *The Best Plays of 1939–40*. New York: Dodd Mead, 1940.

Marshall, George Catlett. *The Papers of George Catlett Marshall*. Vol. 2, *"We Can't Delay," July 1, 1939–Dec. 6, 1941*. Edited by Larry Bland. Baltimore: Johns Hopkins University Press, 1981.

Martin, George. *Madame Secretary: Frances Perkins*. Boston: Houghton Mifflin, 1976.

Martin, Joseph. *My First Fifty Years in Politics, Joe Martin; as told to Robert Donovan*. New York: McGraw-Hill Book Company, 1960.

Matloff, Maurice. *Strategic Planning for Coalition Warfare, 1943–45*. Washington, DC: Office of the Chief of Military History, 1959.

McJimsey, George. *Harry Hopkins: Ally of the Poor and Defender of Democracy*. Cambridge MA: Harvard University Press, 1987.

McJimsey, George, ed. *Documentary History of the Franklin D. Roosevelt Pres-*

idency. 23 vols. Bethesda, MD: University Publications of America, 2001.

Meacham, Jon. *Franklin and Winston: An Intimate Portrait of an Epic Friendship.* New York: Random House, 2003.

Merry, Robert W. *Taking on the World: Joseph and Stewart Alsop— Guardians of the American Century.* New York: The Viking Press, 1995.

Miller, Francis P. *Man From the Valley.* Chapel Hill, NC: University of North Carolina Press, 1971.

Moran, Charles McMoran Wilson, Baron. *Churchill; The Struggle for Survival, 1940–1965, Taken from the Diaries of Lord Moran.* Boston: Houghton Mifflin, 1966.

Morgan, Ted. *FDR: A Biography.* New York: Simon and Schuster, 1985.

Morison, Samuel Eliot. *History of U.S. Naval Operations in World War II.* Vol. 1, *The Battle of the Atlantic. September 1939–May 1940.* Boston: Little, Brown, 1947.

Moscow, Warren. *Roosevelt and Willkie.* Englewood Cliffs, NJ: Prentice Hall, 1968.

Mosley, Leonard. *Lindbergh.* Garden City, NY: Doubleday, 1976.

Mosley, Leonard. *Marshall, Hero for Our Times.* New York: Hearst Books, 1982.

Neal, Steve. *Dark Horse: A Biography of Wendell Willkie.* Garden City, NY: Doubleday, 1984.

Neal, Steve. *Charles McNary of Oregon a Political Biography.* Portland, OR: Western Imprints The Press of the Oregon Historical Society, 1985.

Nesbitt, Victoria Henrietta. *White House Diary.* Garden City, NY: Doubleday, 1948.

Neustadt, Richard E. *Presidential Power and the Modern Presidency: The Politics of Leadership from Roosevelt to Reagan.* New York: Free Press (Macmillan), 1990.

The New Yorker Book of War Pieces, London, 1939, to Hiroshima, 1945. New York: Schocken Books, 1947.

Panter-Downes, Molly. *London War Notes, 1939–1945.* New York: Farrar, Straus and Giroux, 1971.

Parish, Thomas. *Roosevelt and Marshall*. New York: Morrow, 1989.

Parmet, Herbert S., and Marie B. Hecht. *Never Again, A President Runs for a Third Term—Roosevelt Versus Willkie, 1940*. New York: Macmillan, 1968.

Patterson, James. *Mr. Republican: A Biography of Robert M. Taft*. New York: Houghton Mifflin, 1973.

Perkins, Frances. *The Roosevelt I Knew*. New York: Viking Press, 1946.

Perrett, Geoffrey. *Days of Sadness, Years of Triumph: The American People, 1939–1945*. New York: Coward, Cabell and Geoghegan, 1973.

Persico, Joseph E. *Roosevelt's Secret War: FDR and World War II Espionage*. New York: Random House, 2001.

Pilat, Oliver. *Drew Pearson: An Unauthorized Biography*. New York: Harper's Magazine Press, 1973.

Pogue, Forrest C. *George C. Marshall: Ordeal and Hope, 1939–1942*. Vol. 2. New York: Viking, 1966.

Rauch, Basil. *Roosevelt: From Munich to Pearl Harbor; a Study in the Creation of Foreign Policy*. New York: Creative Age, 1950.

Reynolds, David. *Lord Lothian and Anglo-American Relations*. Chapel Hill, NC: University of North Carolina Press, 1981.

Roosevelt, Eleanor. *This I Remember*. New York: Harper, 1949.

Roosevelt, Elliot, ed. *FDR: His Personal Letters*. New York: Duell, Sloan, and Pearce, 4 vols. 1947, 1948, 1950.

Roosevelt, Franklin D. *Complete Presidential Press Conferences*. 9 vols. New York: Da Capo 1972.

Roosevelt, Franklin D. *Public Papers and Addresses of Franklin D. Roosevelt*. Compiled and with a Foreword by Samuel I. Rosenman. 13 vols. Vol. 6, *The Constitution Prevails, 1937*. Vol. 7, *The Continuing Struggle for Liberalism, 1938*. Vol. 8, *War—and Neutrality, 1939*. Vol. 9, *War—and Aid to Democracies, 1940*. New York: Macmillan, 1941. Vol. 10, *The Call to Battle Stations, 1941*. Vol. 11, *Humanity on the Defensive, 1942*. Vol. 12, *The Tide Turns, 1943*. Vol. 13, *Victory and the Threshold of Peace, 1944–45*. New York: Harper, 1950.

Root, Oren. *Persons and Persuasions*. New York: Norton, 1974.

Rosenman, Samuel I. *Working with Roosevelt*. New York: Harper, 1952.

Roth, Phillip. *The Plot Against America*. Boston: Houghton Mifflin Co., 2004.

Schlesinger, Arthur M., Jr. *The Age of Roosevelt.* Vol. 3, *The Politics of Upheaval* Boston: Houghton Mifflin, 1960.

Schlesinger, Arthur M., Jr. *The Imperial Presidency.* Boston: Houghton Mifflin, 1973.

Schlesinger, Arthur M., Jr. *The Cycles of American History.* Boston: Houghton Mifflin, 1986.

Schlesinger, Arthur M., Jr. *A Life in the 20th Century Innocent Beginnings, 1917–1950.* New York: Houghton Mifflin Co., 2000.

Sherwood, Robert E. *Roosevelt and Hopkins: An Intimate History.* New York: Harper, 1948.

Shirer, William L. *The Rise and Fall of the Third Reich: A History of Nazi Germany.* New York: Simon and Schuster, 1959.

Shogan, Robert. *Hard Bargain: How FDR Twisted Churchill's Arm, Evaded the Law, and Changed the Role of the American Presidency.* New York: Charles Scribner's Sons, 1995.

Smith, Paul. *Personal File.* New York: Appleton-Century, 1964.

Smith, Richard Norton. *Thomas E. Dewey and His Times.* New York: Simon and Schuster, 1982.

Sparks, C. Nelson. *Wendell Willkie.* New York: I. Washburn, 1957.

Steel, Ronald. *Walter Lippmann and the American Century.* Boston: Little, Brown, 1980.

Stettinius, Edward R. *Lend-Lease: Weapons for Victory.* New York: Macmillan, 1944.

Stimson, Henry L., and McGeorge Bundy. *On Active Service in Peace and War.* New York: Harper and Brothers, 1947.

Stone, I. F. *The War Years, 1939–1945.* Boston: Little, Brown, 1988.

Thompson, Kenneth. *Lessons from Defeated Presidential Candidates.* Lanham, MD: University Press of America, 1994.

Tully, Grace. *F.D.R. Was My Boss.* New York: Charles Scribner's Sons, 1949.

Vandenberg, Arthur H. *The Private Papers of Senator Vandenberg.* Edited by Arthur H. Vandenberg, Jr. Boston: Houghton Mifflin, 1952.

Vidal, Gore. *The Golden Age.* New York: Doubleday, 2000.

Wallace, Max. *The American Axis.* New York: St. Martin's Press, 2003.

Ward, Geoffrey C. *Before the Trumpet: Young Franklin Roosevelt, 1882–1905.* New York: Harper, 1985.

Ward, Geoffrey C. *Closest Companion: The Unknown Story of the Intimate Friendship Between Franklin Roosevelt and Margaret Suckley*. New York: Harper and Row, 1985.

Ward, Geoffrey C. *A First-Class Temperament: The Emergence of Franklin Roosevelt*. New York: Harper, 1989.

Watson, Mark S. *Chief of Staff: Prewar Plans and Preparations*. Washington, DC: Historical Division, Department of the Army, 1950.

Welles, Sumner. *The Time For Decision*. New York: Harper, 1944.

Willkie, Wendell. *Occasional Addresses and Articles*. Stamford, CT: The Overbrook Press, 1940.

Willkie, Wendell. *This is Wendell Willkie: A Collection of Speeches and Writings on Present-Day Issues*. New York: Dodd, Mead, 1940.

Winchell, Walter. *Winchell Exclusive "Things That Happened to Me—and Me to Them."* Englewood Cliffs, NJ: Prentice-Hall, 1975.

Periodicals

The magazines consulted were the issues of *Time*, *Life*, and *The New Republic* from January 1, 1940 through March 31, 1941. Newspapers consulted were all issues of the *New York Times* and the *New York Herald Tribune* from January 1, 1940 through March 31, 1941. Also the *Charleston Gazette* (W. Va.) and the *Charleston Daily Mail* from April 1 through July 30, 1940; the *Chicago Daily News* and the *Chicago Tribune* from July 15 through July 20, 1940 and the *Philadelphia Evening Bulletin*, the *Philadelphia Record* and the *Philadelphia Inquirer* between June 20 and June 30, 1940.

Papers

Roosevelt's papers are at the Franklin D. Roosevelt Memorial Library and Museum at Hyde Park, New York; Wendell Willkie's at the Lilly Library of Indiana University at Bloomington, Indiana; Robert Taft's, Irita Van Doran's, and Drew Pearson's at the Library of Congress in Washington, D.C.

PHOTO CREDITS

Images appearing in the photo insert are courtesy of the Franklin D. Roosevelt Library with the exception of "For sheer force . . . "; Russell Davenport and Wendell Willkie . . . ; Wendell, Edith and son . . . ; courtesy of The Lilly Library, Indiana University, Bloomington, Indiana. The post-convention Willkie campaign team . . . ; "The plaza in front . . . "; Wendell and Edith make their way. . . ; courtesy of Bettmann/Corbis. Delegates struggle for the New York Standard . . . ; With the thermometer at 102 . . . ; courtesy of AP/Wide World Photos; Another fisherman . . . ; courtesy of Charles Bartlett.

ACKNOWLEDGMENTS

When I described the idea for this book to the late Steve Neal, the author of the most recent Willkie biography, he reacted with warm enthusiasm. He thought I was on the right track, and he was generous in pointing out where I could find support for my thesis. Coming from one who knew the subject as well as he did, this both encouraged me to move ahead, and gave me a roadmap on how to proceed. Equally encouraging was the early endorsement of the project by two, lamentably now also departed, legends of Washington journalism, Herbert Block and Chalmers Roberts, both of whom attended the 1940 Republican convention. I was also heartened by the fact that three eminent historians—John Morton Blum, Alan Brinkley, and Arthur Schlesinger Jr.—took the project seriously enough to offer their counsel. I am grateful to them all.

The research for this kind of book can be tedious, but there have been some delightful moments along the way. These include having dinner in Dublin, New Hampshire, with the son and son-in-law of the two earliest members of the Willkie campaign team, Charlton MacVeagh Jr. and Harvey Schwartz, whose late wife, Nell, was the daughter of Russell Davenport; listening to Gore Vidal recount his experiences at the 1940 convention over drinks at his villa in Ravello; discovering that the father of Charles Breiseth, the director of the Franklin Roosevelt Institute, was a Willkie delegate in 1940; hearing the bluntly honest Gerald Ford call Frank McKay a crook; and learning from Wendell Willkie II, Willkie's grandson, that his father and mother, Mr. and Mrs. Philip Willkie, had met Irita Van Doren—guess where—at a party given by Edith Willkie at her apartment several years after the death of her husband and Van Doren's lover. I was comforted to learn that Edith had apparently forgiven Irita and that the two women who had loved Willkie most had come together.

Of all the people who helped me with the book, Joe Dempsey stands out. My gratitude to him is immense. Patrick Wiley, my first intern at the Woodrow Wilson Center, where I was a public Scholar in 2002–2003, was also of great help. To the two other Wilson interns who helped, and whose names have, alas, escaped my aging memory, I offer my apologies and thanks. And of course I'm indebted to Lee Hamilton, the center's director, for my stay there—and for his insight into Indiana politics.

Both my wife Beth and my old friend Preston Brown provided continuing moral support and practical research assistance. Jonathan Alter, Russell Baker, Jason DeParle, James Fallows, Joshua Green, and Jon Meacham, were kind enough to read early drafts, and tough enough to challenge me to do better. Many others—through letters, emails, and conversations in person or on the phone—offered assistance that ranged from guiding me to a source or being one themselves. They include: David Acheson, R.W. Apple, Jr., Mary Bain, Charles Bartlett, Betty Beale, Arnold Beichman, James Billington, William McCormick Blair Jr., Bob Clark, Robert Dahl, Paulette Diallo, Jim and Molly Dickenson, Tom Eagleton, Stewart Feldman, Mark Feldstein, Thomas Fleming, Paul Glastris, Katharine Graham, Fred Greenstein, Soyoung Ho, Stephen Kaiser, Peter Kovler, Anthony Lewis, Stanley Meisler, Martin Morris, Gaylord Nelson, Verne Newton, Tom Pinckney, Sue Pressnell, Mrs. Oren Root, Robert Shogan, Ev Small, Sally Bedell Smith, Frank Stanton, James Symington, Strobe Talbott, Eleanor Pryor Thomas, Lucy Thrasher, Geoffrey Ward, Dwayne and Linda Watson, and John Zentay. I know that the frail memory that mislaid the names of those interns must have failed in the case of others who helped. To them, too, I offer my apologies and thanks.

And, of course, I am grateful to Peter Osnos for his support from start to finish; to Paul Golob, the book's first editor; to David Patterson, his successor, and the book's thoughtful shepherd for most of the journey; and to all the folks at PublicAffairs who helped make this book a reality.

INDEX

PUBLICAFFAIRS is a publishing house founded in 1997. It is a tribute to the standards, values, and flair of three persons who have served as mentors to countless reporters, writers, editors, and book people of all kinds, including me.

I. F. STONE, proprietor of *I. F. Stone's Weekly*, combined a commitment to the First Amendment with entrepreneurial zeal and reporting skill and became one of the great independent journalists in American history. At the age of eighty, Izzy published *The Trial of Socrates*, which was a national bestseller. He wrote the book after he taught himself ancient Greek.

BENJAMIN C. BRADLEE was for nearly thirty years the charismatic editorial leader of *The Washington Post*. It was Ben who gave the *Post* the range and courage to pursue such historic issues as Watergate. He supported his reporters with a tenacity that made them fearless, and it is no accident that so many became authors of influential, best-selling books.

ROBERT L. BERNSTEIN, the chief executive of Random House for more than a quarter century, guided one of the nation's premier publishing houses. Bob was personally responsible for many books of political dissent and argument that challenged tyranny around the globe. He is also the founder and was the longtime chair of Human Rights Watch, one of the most respected human rights organizations in the world.

.   .   .

For fifty years, the banner of Public Affairs Press was carried by its owner Morris B. Schnapper, who published Gandhi, Nasser, Toynbee, Truman, and about 1,500 other authors. In 1983 Schnapper was described by *The Washington Post* as "a redoubtable gadfly." His legacy will endure in the books to come.

Peter Osnos, *Publisher*